Inside the Japanese Company

In this ethnographical study of a major Japanese white-collar company, the author explores the attitudes of Japanese employees towards their work, their company, and to related issues.

Based on extensive original research inside a Japanese insurance company (C-Life), which subsequently went bankrupt, the book shows that attitudes towards life-time employment, company loyalty and the other characteristics of Japanese working life, which are often portrayed in stereotype form in the West are, in fact, more complicated than is at first apparent.

Fiona Graham was the first white woman to study at Keiō University, and the first to work in the Japanese life insurance industry. She subsequently gained her Masters Degree in Management Studies and Doctorate in Social Anthropology from the University of Oxford. Her experiences as a regular employee in a Japanese company at the time of the bubble, and later as a film-maker producing a documentary for NHK, form the basis for the fieldwork in this book.

Inside the Japanese Company

Fiona Graham

RoutledgeCurzon
Taylor & Francis Group

LONDON AND NEW YORK

First published 2003 by RoutledgeCurzon
11 New Fetter Lane, London EC4P 4EE

Simultaneously published in the USA and Canada
by RoutledgeCurzon
29 West 35th Street, New York, NY 10001

RoutledgeCurzon is an imprint of the Taylor & Francis Group

© 2003 Fiona Graham

Typeset in Times by GreenGate Publishing Services
Printed and bound in Great Britain by Antony Rowe Ltd, Chippenham,
Wiltshire

British Library Cataloguing in Publication Data
A catalogue record for this book is available from the British Library

Library of Congress Cataloguing in Publication Data
Graham, Fiona, 1961-
    Inside the Japanese company / Fiona Graham
        p. cm.
    Includes bibliographical references and index.
        1. Insurance, Life–Japan–Management.
        2. Industrial relations–Japan.3. National characteristics,
        Japanese. I. Title

    HG9165.G73 2003
    368.32′00952–dc21   2003040926
    ISBN 0-415-30670-1

Contents

1   Introduction

In early Japan literature, the stereotype of the Japanese company was a large, white-collar organisation with hundreds or even thousands of employees. It is only over the past decade that this picture has been balanced by studies of other types of Japanese companies and employees – blue-collar companies, small companies, female workers and so on. In fact, the backlash has been so great that the large white-collar company has now become somewhat neglected. This book seeks to redress the balance by providing an in-depth view of employee life inside a rather typical, large, white-collar traditional company. It looks at what everyday life is like for the very many Japanese employees who work in such companies, and investigates the dynamics of the social relations inside the company.

Before introducing C-Life, the company which is the subject of this book, it is necessary to describe briefly its economic context. My purpose is not to give an exhaustive account of the Japanese economy; this book is not intended as a detailed description of the company's economic situation or the nature of its business. Rather, my intention is to describe the everyday life and social relations of its employees, and what I present here is offered merely to set the context for the fieldwork which follows.

The economic background

In 1945 Japan was in ruins, with up to 80 per cent of some of its cities destroyed. No-one could have predicted the amazing turnaround that would be achieved by 1950. In five short years, Japan had achieved financial stability, rebuilt large parts of its cities and industries and recommenced trading. In fact, the country had been so successful that its income per capita was higher than the pre-war level, and its industrial output had actually doubled. In the following decades, Japan continued to defy economic analysis by expanding at an unprecedented pace for a non-Western nation.

But by 1986 and 1987 economic growth had slowed down as the yen rose. The central bank lowered the official discount rate from 5 per cent to 2.5 per cent to boost the economy. This sparked a massive economic boom: money was poured into the stock market and the property market. These investments were financed by using land and stocks as collateral for the credit, which meant that both land

and stock prices were pushed through the roof in a seemingly endless upward spiral: the 'bubble'.

The benchmark Nikkei index reached its highest point on 31 December 1989. And then it collapsed; the Tōkyō stock market crashed, and the 'bubble' burst, with devastating results. By the end of 1990 the Nikkei had dropped 50 per cent. It kept on falling over the next ten years, dropping into the 12,000s in 1999, a 70 per cent decline from its peak. As stock prices plummeted, the price of the land supporting the borrowed credit also tumbled. The banks were suddenly facing enormous bad loans, and became increasingly reluctant to lend further – especially on the basis of property. So there was no support for companies struggling in the aftermath of the stock market crash, and they began to go bankrupt at record rates.

The banks themselves began to fail. This in turn sent stock prices crashing even lower. Japanese companies are mostly tied together in a complicated system of cross share-holding, begun as an attempt to fend off corporate raiders. At the height of this system, more than 60 per cent of shares were held in cross share-holding arrangements and were never traded, thus aggravating fluctuations in an illiquid market. With the bursting of the bubble, many companies decided to start unwinding these cross share-holdings, exacerbating the negative spiral.

With the collapse of the bubble, it now became evident that Japanese companies were far from uniformly successful. In fact the financial industry was astonishingly backwards compared to the manufacturing sector. The Japanese were rather badly prepared for the ten-year economic downturn that followed the crash, a downturn that was exacerbated by the effects of deregulation and increased competition from foreign companies. Rather than reacting aggressively to the changed environment, many companies still seem at a loss to know what to do.

The slump has now lasted for over a decade. With the passing of the old economic climate, change has come to the corporate culture that once seemed immutable and monolithic. As companies flounder, their employees are forced to re-examine the old ideals of life-time employment and self-sacrificing loyalty.

The literature

The topic of Japanese management has been of more than academic interest to many people. As Fuse (1990: 24) aptly puts it: 'Faced with the startling economic progress of Japan, the world was first stunned into amazement; the amazement was eventually turned into admiration and envy, and finally in the 1970s the admiration was transmuted into open fear and covert hostility.'

During this period, economists were understandably eager to explain the reasons for the Japanese 'economic miracle', and if possible to replicate it. Different theories were devised to explain Japan's economic success. Some were purely economic, attempting to explain the success in terms of manufacturing systems or Japan's late development compared to the West; others tried to explain the success by use of cultural factors. Japan at the time stood out as the sole counter-example to Western economic theory, which basically contended that non-Western nations would develop into Western-style capitalist economies as they matured. Japan's success was unprecedented for a non-Western nation, and this raised, for the first time, the possibility that successful non-Western styles of capitalism would be possible in the modern world. Was this due to clever economics? Or was it something deeper, within Japan's national identity and culture?

Academics tried to identify the elements of Japanese culture that might be at the root of it all. Was it due to the way in which Japanese workers are trained, or to their unique decision-making systems? Was it because Japanese are inherently hard-working, or was it more to do with Japanese values, which have traditionally stressed loyalty, harmonious relations and diligence? Was the miracle a nationwide phenomenon, happening in all companies, or was it in fact only a small percentage of companies that were successful while the rest of the country rode on their coat-tails? And crucially, could the factors which brought about the miracle be imported into other countries?

Many theories went along the lines that the Japanese are 'different', which was why they had created an unprecedented new style of capitalism on a Japanese model. The so-called 'nihonjinron literature' – or theories of Japaneseness – were touted by a range of academics from anthropologists to psychologists to brain specialists. Although long debunked by the spectacular demise of the bubble economy, this literature is particularly interesting as an example of a native people making cultural interpretations of their own economy. This genre of literature has now largely disappeared, and the rational economic theory versus cultural debate is largely subsided. Yet the literature remains of interest because it describes the ideal that many Japanese held of themselves and of their country. This is why this genre of literature was overwhelmingly popular with a mass audience.

The collapse of the bubble, and the realisation that the Japanese were subject to the same economic laws as everyone else after all, provoked an immediate backlash to the 'theories of Japaneseness' literature. Books with titles like *Japan as-anything-but-number one* (Woronoff 1991), which had already begun to appear even during the 1970s and 1980s, multiplied. It was realised that the first genre had attempted to explain Japan's success in terms of Japanese traits, but mainly described an ideology, mistaking it for reality. So now, the new literature rejected this blind idealism in favour of rather negative descriptions of the 'reality'. Authors aimed to describe what they *saw* in the workplace rather than what people there *believed*. In other words, the idealistic portrayal of Japanese society in the nihonjinron literature was replaced by accounts covering common negative elements: gross inefficiencies of many companies, cruel training, ruthless competition, bullying, forced dismissal and so on.

Neither the old literature nor the new provided a balanced account of both the ideology and the practice. Anthropologies of large white-collar Japanese companies have been rather sparse in the following years, or they have looked at issues other than that of ideology and practice. This book aims to redress the balance. In it, I look at both the ideology and the practice of working life in a large company, and at how the employees trod their everyday working lives between the two extremes.

C-Life

C-Life was founded in 1904 by Ikunoshin Kadono as a mutual insurance company – the first in Japan with an Anglo-American structure. In 1999, the total value of life insurance in force was 54 trillion yen. The company had traditionally been the smallest of the so-called 'big eight' life insurers, but in 1999 it was struggling to maintain position as a major, having had a series of bad results as Japan's economic downturn in the 1990s worsened.

The central C-Life building is in an unusually suburban location for a major Japanese insurer. It is at NM station, two stations from Shibuya, in a thoroughly suburban area of Tōkyō. Go down the steps outside the station and you will find yourself on the busy thoroughfare Yamate Dōri. Walk to the right for a minute or two; turning right again one enters NM Ginza, a small shopping street gaily decorated with coloured lanterns and plastic flowers celebrating the season. This is the main artery of the suburb, and home to C-Life. Among the mainly residential area of two-storey shops, houses and small business, the huge C-Life building towers, dominating the surrounding landscape. The main buildings fill two sides of the block of land and the rest is sculpted Japanese garden, unusually large and beautiful for a corporate headquarters in Japan.

The 1999 annual report says of the company:

> C-Life has grown into one of the leading life insurers in Japan. This steady progress is rooted in our alertness to emerging trends, the skills of our financial professionals and the confidence of policy-holders.

However, C-Life was, at this stage, generally recognised by analysts to be the weakest of the life insurance majors. All eight of the industry leaders showed a decline in income from insurance premiums for the fiscal year ending March 1999. But C-Life fell the most, by 23 per cent. And over the same year, the company's investment income dropped 23.1 per cent, premiums were down 42.1 per cent, and total assets fell 13.3 per cent.

The fieldwork

My experiences during several extended periods of fieldwork at C-Life form the basis of this book. I was at the company in several different capacities, over a total period of 15 years. The first and most substantial period of fieldwork was the two years I spent employed at C-Life as a fresh graduate. I worked there as a regular employee in the International Department for a two-year period from 1985 to 1987. As a trainee I was assigned to help Mr Y, who was in charge of buying and selling international shares. My work involved analysing foreign companies, buying and selling, doing the paperwork for the transactions, keeping track of the daily share prices, and producing the profit and loss statements of our portfolios every week. Although the responsibility for my portfolios rested, of course, with my seniors, I did all of the day-to-day investments for a two billion yen stock portfolio. I also taught English to members of the International Department for one hour a day during lunch hour, and did occasional English-related work such as producing the English-language annual report.

At that time in Japan, it was very unusual for a Westerner to be employed as a regular employee, as it was normally only possible for graduates of the Japanese school system. The linguistic and cultural difficulties normally prevented foreigners from working with the same status as normal Japanese employees. However, I had already lived in Japan for a period of nearly ten years by the time I was hired by C-Life. I graduated from both high school and university in Japan in the same manner as a Japanese student, and lived for some years as part of a Japanese family. This experience offered me the opportunity to be integrated into Japanese life and society to an unusual degree.

C-Life originally decided to hire me because they thought that my unusual background would enable me to fit in with the totally Japanese world of the company, and with Japanese-style management. I was the first Western woman to graduate from Keiō, a university that provides 30 per cent of regular C-Life employees. Although I originally had no intention of being employed in a Japanese company, this opportunity was too good to resist.

A number of factors persuaded me to stay at the company. First, when I graduated, C-Life was one of the most prestigious and coveted employers. In Japan, all of the industries and companies in Japan are ranked by the media in order of preference for entry each year. As employment is generally long term in Japan, the criteria for being highly-ranked on these lists include future growth of the industry, its present state, personnel policies and numerous other factors. The life insurance industry was the top-ranked industry in Japan that year, and C-Life was the seventh company within the industry. At the time, joining such a high-ranking organisation was considered very important by most fresh graduates.

Moreover, the position I was offered was very unusual. By accepting the job at C-Life I became the first Westerner ever to work as a normal employee in the Japanese life insurance industry, the largest in the world.

At the same time, I recognised a unique opportunity to do fieldwork. Although the nihonjinron literature dominated at the time, I knew that the reality of working in a Japanese company was quite different from the rosy picture painted by the literature. I wanted to document a Japanese company as an insider would experience it.

My second period of fieldwork took place during a summer some five years after I left the company. I revisited my colleagues and wrote copious notes on the company structure and organisation in preparation for my master's thesis. I also distributed a comprehensive survey to those employees who had been members of the international section during the period under study in 1985–7. The responses I received shed considerable light on the employees' feelings about job satisfaction and motivation.

I carried out the third stint of fieldwork in late 1999 and 2000, whilst making two anthropological documentaries, one of which was to be shown on NHK. I was lucky to have access to the company at that time. Because of the precarious financial state that C-Life was in by this stage, not even the Japanese media had access to interviews with top officials. Yet I was able to film C-Life's employees with relative freedom.

During the months that I spent filming in the company, I interviewed all of the international division employees whom I had worked with and followed over the duration of my involvement with C-Life. I also interviewed a number of high-ranking officials, some retired members of the division, and members of the publicity department and the personnel department. The first documentary focused on the international department; the second focused on the members of my own year-group (my 'dōki'), including those who had since left the company. It is this period of fieldwork that is most represented in the present work, since I have made extensive use of the transcripts of the interviews that I carried out at this time – although of course my understanding of the issues raised in the interviews dates back to my period of employment in the company.

I have made extensive reference in my descriptions of C-Life to the work of the anthropologist Thomas Rohlen, who studied a Japanese bank for a year, as his work is one of the most complete anthropologies of a Japanese organisation. Rohlen's work is one of the few studies to focus on the head office of a service industry organisation in Japan, as opposed to the extensively described manufacturing or blue-collar organisations. However, my study differs from Rohlen's in important respects. First, it is based on fieldwork conducted at three different times over a 15-year period – a period, moreover, of great economic change, during which the company went from great prosperity to imminent bankruptcy. So my study describes the company in transition, whereas Rohlen's is more like a snapshot of one year in the life of his organisation. Second, as an actual employee of the company, I enjoyed a degree of access and participation unavailable to outsiders.

Note on the advantages and disadvantages of my position in the company

During my first period of fieldwork, I was a participant in C-Life in a way that would have been impossible for an anthropologist coming to study the company from outside. As a new employee in the company I was unable to gain an all-encompassing understanding of the organisation, and I did not try to do this. Instead, I got to know a narrower group of individuals very well who made up one section of the company – the international division. My goal was to explore and fully understand the everyday world of company employees.

Outsiders find it much more difficult to operate in the Japanese company with freedom, even if they are a former employee, as I found in my later follow-up studies. For the subsequent visits for the purposes of my doctoral research, I returned as an observer and an outsider. My status as a documentary producer and co-director of an NHK programme, and as an ex-Reuters financial journalist whose job included reporting on the Japanese economy, gave me a very different perspective on the company and reception. Nevertheless, although I was treated by the company with considerably more respect than when I worked there, I was still treated as an ex-employee. This meant that I was still more of an insider than an anthropologist studying the company would normally have been. It was noticeable that I was still introduced to strangers in terms of the position I would still have had in the company had I remained, instead of using the polite language accorded to outsiders. My colleagues of the same year intake still considered me 'dōki'.

Other anthropologists have found the issue of entry to be of crucial importance in a Japanese company environment. Rohlen's introductions – a chief of the training section and a former managing director – were inadequate to give him a *carte blanche* to study whatever he wished. He says of his visits to informants, 'I visited some in their offices, but in most cases I felt this was a bad policy, for it would disturb others working there and give an impression of exclusiveness that could damage both my own and my informants' positions' (Rohlen 1974: 257).

Rohlen listed additional obstacles to his fieldwork as follows:

1   His ability to collect information varied directly in proportion to closeness in age.
2   He was unable to collect much material from women.
3   He lacked influential connections at the top.
4   His view of the bank was coloured by the fact that he started his research at the training institute.
5   His interviewees were cautious because they knew that what Rohlen wrote about 'Uedagin' would be published.

In summary, these limitations can be said to be typical of case studies carried out by an outsider. By being an employee I managed to avoid most of them. The disadvantage to my insider position was the limited extent of my focus, which was narrowed more to an in-depth study of a division rather than a comprehensive description of the whole company. However, I found that the dual approach of being an insider first, and then an outsider, was extremely valuable.

Objectives

My main aim in this book is to provide a comprehensive and detailed ethnographical analysis of a major Japanese white-collar organisation. As I explain later in this chapter, the purpose is not simply to describe the form of the company from an objective standpoint, but to give a detailed account of what it is actually like to work there from the viewpoint of a normal employee. I consider the company in transition, a subject neglected by many researchers in the past. Most ethnographies of Japanese organisations have been a portrait taken at one point in time. Few anthropologists have revisited to provide a picture of the organisation in transition, and few have documented the change in employees' perceptions and beliefs about their working situation over time and the process of that change. So my study has rather a different focus from that of other ethnographies of Japanese companies.

I should stress that my aim in this book is not simply to replicate work done by previous researchers. Thus, I do not go into great depth regarding the organisational structure of C-Life, since this would be to retread the work of others, such as Rohlen (1974). In Chapters 3 and 4, I merely describe those aspects of it which are relevant to my concerns. Nor do I describe the formal structure of C-Life – a mutual company – as this is not relevant to my main focus, the lives of the individual workers inside the company. Similarly, I do not dwell on the 'company ideology' in the form of the company songs and daily routines. Other authors, from Rohlen (1974) to Matsunaga (2000), have extensively described the official songs and speeches of the companies they studied, and it is clear that most large Japanese white-collar companies have very similar company ideology. Those of C-Life were certainly very similar to those in the literature. I have therefore focused on what is not covered in other literature: very extensive individual voices showing a range of individuality.

Structure of the book

The book is divided into three sections. The first provides the literature review for the subjects covered. In Chapter 2, I devote a chapter to the existing Japan literature, providing the background to the study of C-Life in particular. I look at the 'nihonjinron' literature and the backlash against it.

The second part of the book presents the fieldwork I carried out at C-Life. It is divided into four chapters, each of which considers the company from a different angle. The material is arranged in this way to provide an ever-deepening discussion of the company; the major themes are gradually introduced and explored in more depth as the chapters progress. As Rohlen says (1974: 260):

> For the anthropological observer, the organisational landscape is indeed difficult to describe in general and inclusive terms. The surface of routine appears so arid and flat, and yet as the perspective is rotated with the study of each additional element, the terrain becomes more and more uneven, shadows appear, and one comes to sense dynamic forces, that, one assumes, lie below the surface.

I tried to look at C-Life from a number of perspectives and describe some of these 'dynamic forces'. First I examine the company structure, then I consider the stages in the career of a typical employee. Building on this material, I then turn to personal relations within the company, paying particular attention to the way different groups categorise and relate to each other. Each chapter both introduces new themes and re-examines those of previous chapters from a slightly different angle.

The third part of the book builds on what has already been presented. In Chapter 7, I address the issue of individualism in Japan, engaging with both the existing literature on the subject and the evidence presented in the preceding fieldwork chapters. I argue that, in Japan as anywhere else, there is always an autonomous individual, with an individual viewpoint, not wholly determined by social structure. I also address the sometimes confusing issue of 'honne' and 'tatemae', in the context of the relations between the individual and the group.

Note on Japanese words

Throughout this book I have used standard romanisation of Japanese words, with macrons to indicate long vowels (apart from place names). Many of the Japanese terms I use vary in meaning according to context. For this reason, I have not made a glossary of Japanese terms, but have explained them where they occur in the text.

In particular, Japanese has a variety of terms to describe different kinds of ideology and practice, what is apparently the case (tatemae) and the underlying reality (honne), soto (outsiders) and uchi (insiders), or ura (back realm) and omote (front realm). Another pair of words with similar connotations are ninjō (human feelings: belonging to the back realm) and giri (official duty: belonging to the front realm). In the direct quotations, I have put the particular Japanese word used in brackets after the English translation. Throughout this book, I have, for the sake of convenience, generally used honne (reality or real feelings; practice) and tatemae (appearance or formal statement; ideology) to express this dichotomy, even where a range of different words might have been used in Japanese to express it more finely.

I have also used, for the sake of convenience, the terms 'Japanese' and 'Western' throughout the book. This is not at all to suggest that there is a single entity, the 'West', with a single 'Western' thought. However, in the context of C-Life, and indeed Japan, Japanese concepts and ideas are popularly explained by juxtaposing them against a fictitious entity, the 'West', which is a purposely rather vague term used to denote Anglo-Saxon-derived, British, American. For the purposes of contrasting Japanese values against something sharply different, this works in practice in Japan, and it is in such a popular, non-academic sense that I use it in this book.

In the translations of the interviews, I have aimed at as literal a translation as possible, providing some of the original Japanese expressions in brackets where helpful.

2   Literature review

The purpose of this chapter is to lay the groundwork for the body of the book, by introducing its themes and looking at some of the existing literature that deals with them. I look at the 'nihonjinron' literature, or 'theories of Japaneseness', that I discussed briefly in the previous chapter. I consider why this literature was so popular, before looking at some of its deficiencies and at what has replaced it. In particular, I focus on how ideology and practice have been treated in the literature, noting how, where the nihonjinron authors tended to mistake ideology for practice, more recent authors have focused on practice to the extent of ignoring ideology altogether. I argue that a more balanced approach is needed.

Early ethnographies

Some of the first ethnographies on Japan include those by Embree (1939), and Benedict (1946). Embree's fieldwork in a small village stresses co-operation in economic and social matters. Benedict, who was influenced by the 'Culture and Personality School' of anthropology, focused heavily on Japanese 'values', especially the concepts of on, giri, and ninjō.

Both Embree and Benedict were later strongly criticised for over-emphasising the element of harmony in Japanese culture, at the expense of any discussion of competition or conflict.

Nihonjinron

The 'nihonjinron' (literally, theories of the Japanese people) literature sought to explain Japan's success by reference to cultural factors. 'Japaneseness' was now identified not only in the village, but in factories, large companies and bureaucracies (Morris-Suzuki 1998). Scholars tried to find the essence of 'Japaneseness' in institutions that are common to all cultures, because it would be easier to isolate the peculiar characteristics of the Japanese versions.

Nihonjinron is built on the claims that Japan is 'unique', and that Japanese management is also 'unique'. The Japanese are unique, we are told, in their consensus approach to human relations and decision making, and in the harmony and co-operation between members of the group, minimising conflict. Ethnographies of traditional culture were distilled for Japanese 'values', and these were applied to modern organisations to explain the unique characteristics of Japanese management.

The early management literature was particularly interested in how companies motivated their employees to work hard. Reischauer (1977) argued that managers and workers gain pride through being members of a company, where company songs are sung with enthusiasm and company pins are proudly displayed. Ouchi in *Theory Z* (1981) argued that especially close relationships between employees encourage honest action in the group, since abused relationships cannot be left behind. Vogel (1979) examined the group-directed quest for knowledge, arguing that devoted leaders worry about the future of their organisations. Gibney (1998) described Japan as a true meritocracy where one can move up if one obeys the rules and go a long way through sheer competence. Christopher (1983) wrote that wealth in Japan is evenly spread, so there is no strong sense of class consciousness, and no group of ultra-rich. Curtis (1969) described grass-roots level political campaigning with a heavy emphasis on co-operation and little mention of conflict.

Nihonjinron literature proved enormously popular, in Japan and overseas. It was eagerly devoured by management studies academics and managers looking for an explanation for Japan's phenomenal post-war success. But most importantly, ordinary employees read it too. Many people in Japan were enormously impressed that Vogel – an American – could write a book with a title like *Japan as Number One* (1979); and as we shall see, this book, which was a best-seller in Japan, is cited frequently by my correspondents in the fieldwork chapters of the present work.

Anti-nihonjinron literature

There were dissenting voices among this nihonjinron literature even before the bubble collapsed, but it was only after the bubble that the nihonjinron approach became generally discredited and dismissed. The bubble was thought to 'prove' that the Japanese economy behaves like any other capitalist economy in a developed nation, and discussions of Japanese culture in connection to management were largely put aside.

Prominent critics of nihonjinron include Mouer and Sugimoto (1986), Yoshino (1992), Dale (1986), Clark (1979), Emmott (1989), Fukutake (1981), McCormack (1996), Nakane (1970), Prestowitz (1988), Rohlen (1974), Sethi *et al.* (1984), van Wolferen (1989), Wolf (1983), and Woronoff (1980, 1986). The holistic or consensus model that is represented in the nihonjinron literature was rejected as an unrealistic description of Japan as an integrated and balanced whole (Mouer and Sugimoto 1986). Nihonjinron was seen as emphasising only the positive elements that led to keeping the harmonious balance of the organisation: social harmony, consensus, groupism, and group solidarity. The result was a wholly unbalanced portrayal of Japan, an ideal, not the reality.

The critics charged the nihonjinron authors with focusing on the group to such an extent that they ignored the individual. They had portrayed the individual as a shallow character with no individuality, and ignored the possibility of conflict and discord. Focusing solely on the group meant that disagreement between different members of the group was marginalised or ignored. Issues of power, such as who holds power, how they get it, and how they use it to influence others, were not addressed.

On a wider level, the nihonjinron literature has been charged with blindness to the diversity that characterises Japanese society. This applies both to diversity within companies and between them. On the one hand, the groupist emphasis meant that differences between members of the group were minimised, and, on the other, only certain kinds of groups were studied. The literature concentrated on large, traditional Japanese companies, and assumed that the results from this research could be applied across the board to Japanese companies in general (Kondō 1990).

Indeed, nihonjinron theorists have been regarded as rather naïve in general. They were criticised for having an ideological agenda, or for being hoodwinked by their informants' ideological agenda. They failed to appreciate two things: first, ideology does not necessarily accurately reflect what actually goes on; and, second, individuals may manipulate ideology to their own ends – which may affect what they tell anthropologists. The nihonjinron accounts were therefore criticised for relying too heavily on anecdotal evidence.

Even putting aside these problems, the nihonjinron literature failed to show that Japanese culture was responsible for Japanese economic success, despite its claims to do so. Simply listing characteristics of Japanese management did not establish a connection between those characteristics and success. Some American companies do share some of these characteristics with Japanese companies, but not necessarily with the same success rates. Moreover, there are unsuccessful companies as well as successful ones in Japan and they all share the same cultural heritage. In the years immediately after World War Two, for example, Japanese companies were thought to lag behind American companies for some of the very same reasons that the nihonjinron literature later identified as the keys to their success (Abegglen 1958; Takamiya 1970)! In fact, management practices cited in the nihonjinron literature as beneficial to the company may in fact disguise underlying inadequacies. For example, although practices such as the life-time employment system and the seniority-based pay scale may increase the security of employees, it also locks them into one company, making them unable to leave without significant financial losses.

So the nihonjinron literature was frequently guilty of a shallow analysis, confusing ideology and practice. More serious, however, were the underlying methodological problems, a number of which were detected at an early stage by Cole (1979). There is not one single entity that we can call 'Japanese management' that always has the same characteristics. Japanese management varies according to the type of company, the size of the company, according to whether one includes only élite male workers or includes all categories of workers, whether the company is white-collar or blue-collar, whether it is one of the highly successful companies in the manufacturing industry or not, and whether it is a multinational entity or a domestic enterprise.

New literature

There was, then, a considerable backlash against the nihonjinron literature. After this died down, what has taken its place? The new literature diverges in several directions. There has, first, been a widening of the context of study in connection with organisations. Academics have taken an interest in different types of organisations, not just the stereotypical large Japanese company, and also in different types of employees, not just the stereotypical salary-man inside the life-time employment system. Rather than the bounded view of one company as the object of study, we are beginning to see a focus on the individual and meaning.

Widening the context – other kinds of organisations

In the pre-bubble years, studies of organisations that were outside the large company and life-time employment category of worker model were rare (although Kamata (1982) who followed temporary workers in a car assembly factory was one notable exception). In recent years, however, there has been an increasing number of studies set in contexts outside that of the large Japanese company (Plath 1983; Shirai 1983; Okimoto and Rohlen 1988; Yamamura and Yasuba 1987). More recently, studies of medium-sized companies and smaller (Miwa 1996; Sugimoto 1997; Whittaker 1997) have shown that the ideology of life-time employment in the large Japanese company is very different from the practice in other types of companies. Chalmers (1989) showed that small companies are more dynamic than their stable, large counterparts, and have played an important role in Japan's economic progress.

Other studies have narrowed the focus onto the employees, rather than the company. Where older studies have mostly taken one organisation as a bounded enterprise and followed all employees within the organisation, newer studies have taken a certain type of worker inside the organisation or laid the focus on a certain type of activity. Turner (1995), for example, takes an in-depth look at workers in a union in a medium-sized company.

Additionally, there has been a widening of interest in the economic world beyond these companies. Creighton (1992) has looked at the world of retail, Moeran at advertising (Moeran 1996, 1998) and magazines (Moeran 1995), and Clammer (1997) at consumption. Allison's (1994) study of hostess clubs – although not directly on companies at all – has added to a total view of the salary-man in the context of his after-work activities, a crucial part of Japanese salary-man life (also see Moeran 1986; Kelly 1991).

Widening the context – other kinds of workers

Again, there were few studies in the pre-bubble period that looked at non-regular employees. Notable examples of that period that did so include Steven (1983) and Patrick and Rohlen's (1987) look at family businesses in Japan. However, the pre-bubble stereotype of the Japanese worker remained a man employed in the 'life-time employment system' in a large company. Recently, there has been wider recognition – as we have seen above – that this model, at best, only ever applied to a significant minority of employees. Thus, there has been a new interest in workers other than the stereotype. Moeran (1984, 1986, 1990) has looked at craftspeople and found them to be quite different in work ethic from the stereotype of the company worker. Chalmers (1989) has looked at peripheral workers and those outside the regular workforce.

The focusing of attention away from stereotypes has inevitably invited greater interest in female workers in Japan (e.g. Saso 1990; Cook and Hayashi 1980; McLendon 1983; Pharr 1984; Kondō 1990; Brinton 1993; Lam 1992b; and Hunter 1993). Most pre-bubble studies expected the employees to be male, a fact that has been both observed and rectified by Lo (1990) and Roberts (1994). Roberts' look at female factory workers in a smaller company shows a dramatically different picture from that of the male worker employed in a large company. Her study also highlights the discrepancies between ideology and practice inside this organisation, which, while employing women workers exclusively in routine factory positions, promoted the ideology that women should expect to be primarily in the home. Others have focused on the lower status of Japanese women workers (Brinton 1989; 1993, Osawa 1993), or on the way in which the Japanese life-time employment system actively discriminates against working women (Lam 1992a). This interest in working women was associated with the introduction of the Equal Opportunity Law in 1986, which meant that – in theory – discrimination in the workplace was no longer possible.

More broadly, a number of studies have examined women's lives in general (Lebra 1984; Iwao 1993; Saso 1990; Smith 1987), and although these are not directly on working women, they serve to highlight the ideology that the home is the place for women, while the working world is for men. Although most of the studies of women in the workforce look at them in terms of the weak position they hold in the working world, some studies look at their strengths. Anne Allison (1994) looks at the weak position that men occupy in some contexts – namely, in financial matters, where the wife in Japan often holds the purse strings and the man is given pocket money. Iwao (1993) has also focused on the different social roles that men and women are expected to play, and on the fact that women are clearly dominant in some areas, namely the home, education of children, and finances. Women in the workforce can assume power indirectly – despite their typically weak position – by behaving in a motherly way towards younger male employees (Kondō 1990) or by taking surreptitious revenge on male workers of whose behaviour they disapprove (Ogasawara 1998). These findings confirm those of Rohlen, who demonstrated that women are humoured in the large company because they quit easily. Clark (1979) also showed that women have more leeway to rebel against orders that they are not keen on obeying and that they are able to go further than men can in, for example, refusing transfers.

Widening the focus

The literature has increasingly focused on a wider range of issues within the company than the stereotypical 'harmony' model of the pre-bubble period (Cole 1971; Kamata 1982; Roberts 1994). Rather than showing a simple portrait of the organisation as a whole, this literature delves deeper to follow specific issues inside companies. It shows that, despite the ideology of the company being a haven of harmonious working relations, the reality is quite different (Mouer and Sugimoto 1981, 1986; Pharr 1984; Turner 1995; Eisenstadt 1990; Krauss *et al.* 1984). Some of these works used small case studies to show the way that human relations and conflict resolution work in practice. Susan Pharr (in Krauss *et al.* 1984), for example, describes in detail the outcome of a rebellion of office secretaries against the requirement that they pour tea for the male workers in the office. Employment termination was rarely discussed in the pre-bubble era, with the exception of Cole's (1971) discussion of how companies get rid of unwanted workers. But in recent years – and because of the recession and increased restructuring – this issue has become more important (Beck and Beck 1994; Roberts 1994).

Another topic of renewed interest is that of class. In the nihonjinron literature the issue of class was mostly dismissed. Nihonjinron writers simply argued that class in the Western sense does not exist in Japan, or that almost all Japanese are middle class so it is not an important issue in organisations. In fact, most Japanese do describe themselves as middle class in Prime Minister's Office surveys (see Kosaka 1994). But to take this at face value is to confuse ideology with practice. The claim that Japan is a classless society has been exposed as a myth and an ideology of the large company (Steven 1983; Kosaka 1994). Ishida (1993) has looked at class in the context of social mobility. As my own study confirms, a surprising number of job transfers occurs even in large company environments. Ishida found that the Japanese class structure is characterised by clear polarisation of companies by firm size. There is a huge intermediate stratum, whose members are highly homogenous in their lifestyles and attitudes; but it is clear that, given that employers occupy the most advantageous position in the distribution of status attributes, and the manual working classes are at the bottom of the hierarchy, class does exist.

New approaches

The recession in Japan has renewed focus on the organisation and employee in the context of the environment. New literature has grounded its ideas of Japanese management in an economic context. Following the backlash against nihonjinron, when writers focused on the role that Japanese management played in creating and exacerbating the recession, current discussion of Japanese management is often couched in terms of whether Japanese management practices will survive the recession (Inoue 1997; Kaneko 1997; Yahata 1997). Debate is centred around how those living in the recession are affected by their environment, and on what effect economic reality will have on society. Sako (1997) argues that the sense of community in the Japanese company will now diminish, because the company can no longer offer security to its employees. The very definition of 'company' has changed dramatically, with 'company' now referring to employment in subsidiaries as well as in the parent company. The implication of this is that companies can expect employees to have much less loyalty to the company.

Now that most authors have relinquished the idea that the company should be followed as a bounded entity, the way has been opened up for a shift to focusing on the employee's career as a whole, rather than on the view of the employee inside a company. Alvesson (1993) maintains that no trait or belief will cover the whole organisation and every individual within. Therefore, it is recommended that we study different aspects inside organisations rather than the organisation itself. In the past, large Japanese companies were quite limited by the inability of employees to transfer even if they desired to do so (Graham 1992). Most C-Life insurance salesmen, for example, could not go to other companies when I asked them about it in 1992 – they were limited to the company they were already in. But in fact, employees in large Japanese companies are much more similar to their counterparts in other companies in outlook, work content, relation to company and virtually every aspect than they are to employees of different status inside the same company. It therefore makes more sense to analyse employees according to their similarities of work content rather than because they are in the same company. Thus we should look at career as one aspect in the course of the employees' lives, including outside work and also movement between companies (Roberson 1998).

Meaning

An approach that has particular relevance for this book is that which looks at the ways in which the Japanese represent their world (Bachnik and Quinn 1994). This approach looks primarily at the individual – rather than at the company as a whole – and at what meaning the company, career and work have for the individual. This follows the same thread as the interpretative approach in anthropology that argues that the individual constructs meaning for himself out of the events that make up his life; but in the Japan studies literature this is still quite a new approach.

Japanologists have looked at this issue through their investigations of workplace as the focus of identity. Tobin (1992) suggests that Japanese locate their identities in their productive professional roles as employee, or craftsperson or housewife. Kondō (1990) looks at the company not in order to discover objective 'truth' about companies but as an arena of negotiation. The idea is to look at the variety of individual interpretations and viewpoints that co-exist in different individuals in the company. The recession has had a dramatic impact on the meaning of work for individuals, a topic which is the primary focus of this book. It is no longer sensible to look at a company as a bounded entity, especially now that the boundaries are changing so much. Because the meaning of work, the company, and the career is different for each individual involved, we must look at these different meanings from an individual perspective. This is especially so since even if a company remains the same, the situations of the individuals within it are undergoing rapid change as the recession continues. The whole idea of a concept with an absolute meaning is in the process of being abandoned in anthropology – see the discussion of community in Matsunaga (2000), for example. Cohen (1985) suggests we look at the community in a flexible manner, recognising that the individuals involved are renegotiating it continually.

In a slightly different context, we can see how the very same concept changes its meaning for individuals over time. In a fascinating example of this, Tabata 1998 (in Matsunaga 2000) points out that the notion of company as community in Japan is often negative. The term 'kaisha ningen' ('company man'), which used to be positive, has shifted so far that it is now almost a derogatory term. Thus, the collapse of the bubble has meant significant shifts in ideology and interpretation of that ideology. Large Japanese companies are no longer seen as always successful – or even as symbols of Japaneseness – unless in a negative sense. Later in this book, I will examine how ideology lags behind practice, slowly changing to reflect it.

The research of Mathews (1996) into the 'meaning of life' – or ikigai – for Japanese is particularly interesting, and has deep implications. He looks at the factors to which the Japanese attribute the meaning of life and concludes that, to the extent that the cultural model of Japanese 'socio-centrism' describes today's Japan, 'commitment to group' will be the dominant form of ikigai. That is, while Japan is ideologically a group-oriented society where the primary affiliations of the individual are to groups, most individuals will see the 'meaning of life' as being commitment to the group. Because individual selves have been enculturated to be socio-centric, they articulate their ikigai as 'commitment to group'. Mathews uses the concept of social 'channelling' to describe how individuals choose socio-culturally accepted concepts – out of an infinite range of possibilities – in order to make their lives explicable, logical and meaningful.

Ideology and practice in the Japan literature

We saw that one of the flaws of nihonjinron literature was that it failed to recognise that ideology may not match practice. Matsunaga (2000) warns of the dangers of the anthropologist subscribing to ideological views of their informants, but notes that the ideology – as ideology – still serves an important role. On returning after ten years to the company that she studied, she found that her memories of the place sharply contrasted with those of her informants, whose memories had been enhanced by time, and by nostalgia for the past:

> … the ideal of the corporate community remained important, at least in some contexts, albeit vague in terms of precisely whom it encompassed. The importance of teamwork and co-operation among employees was frequently emphasised by Nagasakiya management, and older employees in particular often evoked nostalgic images of community in their accounts of a past Nagasakiya. It was striking that these accounts tended to be located in the past and contrasted with current attitudes, particularly among young employees.

(176)

There is an extensive literature on ideology and practice in relation to Japan, particularly from the angle of how the individual relates to society (Bachnik and Quinn 1994; Doi 1973, 1985; Kondō 1990; Bachnik 1992).

The acceptance of a dual order of ideology and practice helps us to understand what lies at the bottom of the debate (Rohlen 1989; Mathews 1996) over how to explain Japanese behaviour. Can order in Japanese society be best explained by a 'cultural' or bottom-up model wherein employees are socialised into a certain type of behaviour, or by a top-down authoritarian one wherein employees obey an order that is imposed from above? In other words, is order in a company like C-Life actually imposed from above or does it emerge naturally from internalised socio-cultural moulding? Lebra (1976), Smith (1983) and Kondō (1990) adhere to the former point of view. Mouer and Sugimoto (1981, 1986), on the other hand, argue that Japan is not intrinsically group-oriented as a cultural phenomenon, but constitutes a society controlled from above where, in the absence of other choices, the individual must conform.

New nihonjinron

While books with a largely economic focus constituted the majority of those touching on Japanese management following the collapse of the bubble, a few writers continued to argue for the role of culture in explaining differences in management systems. These can be said to constitute, in fact, a new type of nihonjinron. Sakakibara's *Beyond Capitalism* (1993) argues that Japan's market economy is formed according to different principles from Western economies. Shintaro Ishihara, the author of the popular *The Japan that Can Say No* (1991), argues that Japanese society is founded on uniquely Asian cultural principles. Like the nihonjinron of the previous era, these books have proved popular with some Japanese, who still seem to want to believe in the 'special' nature of Japanese management, or in an ideology of Japan as culturally unique. This literature is actually extremely interesting as proof of the meaning and continuing relevance that Japanese find in the ideology of Japan's uniqueness. I agree with Joel Kahn (1995), who argues that such waves of interest in cultural values and identity are typical of societies in transition. It is not surprising, he says, to find such values emerging at the same time as trends toward internationalisation and globalisation. He points out that the same thing occurred in Japan in the 1920s and 1930s.

The Japan literature: the future

Recent literature has taken a much more rounded view of life in Japanese companies than the pre-bubble literature. But there are still gaps in our knowledge and the approaches taken are sometimes rather limited, in my view. Much of the literature, for example, only deals with a single company, and often covers too many categories within that company. Does it really make sense to look at male permanent employees, women part-timers, women permanents, and door-men all within the same ethnography? We have seen above that there is already recognition amongst scholars that most Japanese workers have more in common with their counterparts in other companies than with most of their colleagues in their own company, but the implications of this have not always been followed through. Similarly, there is a need to put the company in the context of the economic environment but while there have been calls to do this, not many ethnographies have done so.

Recent literature has certainly widened the subject of Japanese company research, but to gain understanding it must also be deepened. Most authors writing on the large company are still citing Rohlen, as there has been little work done on male 'life-time' employees in large white-collar companies since the collapse of the bubble and the explosion of interest in other kinds of companies and employees. However, the traditional companies are at the forefront of company crisis in the economic downturn. In the present work, my subject is clearly limited to 'life-time' white-collar, primarily male, employees. I do, on the other hand, do something different from previous white-collar studies, in attempting to deepen our knowledge of, and individualise, the worker in the large Japanese company. I study different aspects of life in the company in depth, extensively citing the voices of the employees themselves, to provide a deeper account of what it is like to work at the company. This contrasts with some recent work, which provides a good overview of the subject but suffers somewhat from superficiality on many of the topics covered.

A related limitation of recent work has been its tendency to focus on the viewpoint of the company rather than on that of the individual who works at the company. Roberson (1998: 11) comments: 'Not enough research has attempted to understand (or even just present) company employees and factory workers as people, to understand work and employment in interrelationship with the other contexts and dimensions of people's lives as wholes.' Few studies have slipped beyond a relatively surface level to deal in this way with the employee as an individual and his one-on-one personal and work relations with other individuals in the company. This is, perhaps, an inevitable consequence of taking a very broad approach. In this book, I have attempted to approach the subject from the opposite direction: to focus on the individuals at the company, using their comments and actions as a 'way in'. The broader picture of the company is therefore slowly developed from the individuals' accounts. This is a rather different approach from that of beginning with the company in general and regarding the workers as, essentially, little more than the component parts of the company.

In my view, authors frequently treat the company as an objective reality – an apparent assumption which is associated with their neglect of the individual in the company. As I will argue in a later chapter, my fieldwork showed that the economic situation of the individual and of Japan itself was crucial in determining his or her views of the company, work, and his co-workers.

A related issue is how fieldwork is done. In Japan the divide between insider and outsider is particularly high and impenetrable. Thus, the status of the researcher in relation to the object of his research becomes particularly important in influencing what he is able to find. Most of the Japanese ethnography has been done in the traditional way: a person observes a company for a time, having identified himself as an anthropologist. In my view, such a person is participating, but merely observing as long as the Japanese regard him as an outsider and treat him as such. However, there are some new approaches in the literature. Ogasawara is a notable example. She conducted her fieldwork by joining a bank as a participant – which involved participating in the financial rewards of the organisation – not identifying herself as an anthropologist. This enabled her to obtain particularly insightful data from her fieldwork although she had the problem of not being able to interview her subjects directly. She attempted to resolve this by coupling her main project with in-depth interviews with workers in a range of different companies, but comparable to the one for which she worked, that enabled her to ask questions about what she had observed in the fieldwork. If anthropology's premise is participant-observation then I argue that participation to this degree is crucial to the enterprise.

An interpretative approach is particularly important. We need to be able to portray the complexity and multiple views that abound in the company. Views of harmony and views of conflict both exist: we need to include them both, to show where individuals are similar and where they are different, and to put their views in the context of their times, their positions in the company, and the overall environment in which they live.

On the question of ideology and practice, to consider only whether the views of the company expressed in the nihonjinron literature were 'true' or not is to mistake the point entirely. The ideology of harmony is an important one in that it is still relevant to Japanese company men in their lives now. As ideology, it is important that we look at it as it is through – and in contrast to – such ideologies that company men make sense of their lives. As Matsunaga points out (2000: 9):

> In untangling the idea of company as community, then, context is crucial. We need to know much more about who says what about the company, when, and in what situation. And this needs to be done in tandem with an examination of the external economic constraints within which the company operates. What sorts of representations of the company arise in what sorts of contexts? How does the individual employee relate to the wider company? And how do representations of company life and identity shift over time?

The large company continues to be of immense importance. On a purely practical level, as Brinton (1993) has showed, a large majority of company employees – both men and women – work for a large company (defined as one with over a thousand employees) for their first jobs. This is so even if they subsequently move on. Large companies thus provide the basis for the stereotypical view of the salary-man, and this is the image of company life that most graduates have when they enter the company. So the ideology of the large company is very important. In my fieldwork we will see how this image of a salary-man, and this image of a company, shape the ideas of those who stay in the company and conform to its ideals. But most importantly, it is also this same image that shapes and forms the opposition and alternative views of work of those who move out. The tendency of anti-nihonjinron literature to minimise the importance of the large company in Japan therefore misses the importance of the ideology of the large company, which is instrumental in shaping the expectations towards work held by a majority of Japanese, at least initially. In this view, it is not the 'truthfulness' of the ideology that is important, although it is important to note how the ideology relates to practice and where it is different. We need to look at both together.

In looking at employees in a large company I am attempting to do several things that have not been commonly done in other literature: putting the employees' lives into context in terms of the economy, and looking at work in terms of the meaning it has for the individual employees. My study looks at a group of workers who were employed in an organization 14 years ago, covering both those who are still in the company and those who are not. Their voices illustrate the range of individuality among employees. I have followed these people over three points in time, during good and bad economic periods. This enables us to go beyond the view of the company as a bounded entity to look at employees in the context of the wider economic environment, and in terms of their careers and individual lives.

3 The company and structure

C-Life is very typical of the kind of white-collar Japanese company that is generally discussed in the literature. Like most major Japanese companies, it is composed of bu (departments) and ka (sections). The section is the most important social and work construction. For young employees, work is usually done within the section, and the contacts they have in other sections are usually mainly through their dōki (the generation of people entering the company in the same year as themselves). They will have one or two dōki in each section. Each young employee will have a direct sempai (superior), usually two or four years older, under whom they will learn their work in a disciple-like manner. They will acquire direct kōhai (juniors) themselves only after they have worked for about two years. There is thus a strong sense of hierarchy and rank within the company. However, the company is not static, but both responds to change in the outside environment, and constantly evolves inside itself as it harmonises its different internal sections to work co-operatively together. Different 'Japanese practices' inside C-Life combine to function together as a whole system. Conversely, that system often determines the nature of the practices that it comprises.

For example, Clark (1979) reports that as 'Marumaru' – the white-collar company that he studied – grew, they found it difficult to continue to promote people according to ability. The larger number of people meant that managers were no longer sure about how to assess their juniors. Clark says: '...could such benign "life-time employment" really be combined with meritocratic principles? Now that there were recruits who might have to spend much of their working lives together, would it really be possible to choose some, and leave the rest behind?' Thus, he shows that seniority promotion in Marumaru came about both as a function of the size of the organisation and out of the need to avoid conflict in a long-term employment environment.

In a similar way, many 'Japanese' practices in C-Life have come about as a result of the structure of the organisation. The company must therefore be seen as a complete social system, the structure of which has evolved partly through necessity. So, for example, the ideology of harmony regulates the competitive atmosphere of the company.

The 'ringi' system, whereby any potential decision is passed along a large number of people, all of whom add their opinions, is another example. This process is slow compared to systems where each decision is the responsibility of one person alone, but it does mean that any potential problems are likely to be ironed out before the decision is implemented, because so many people have considered it in advance. Decisions made under the ringi system are often quick to implement after they have made. The system also promotes the appearance of harmony and concord, since all decisions are made jointly and people are less likely to contest them after they have been made. The ringi system thus functions to solve potential conflict before it surfaces at a formal level, and to assign responsibility.

Another example is tsukiai, or drinking sessions after work hours with work colleagues. These are necessary to keep in touch with one's fellow workers in a large and constantly changing work environment, and to maintain harmony in a close social atmosphere. Drinking is necessary to regulate stress levels and to provide a stimulant to better communication. The close relations between Japanese workers have been said to promote success in companies. But, as we shall see here, tsukiai are not necessarily positive, and must be looked at within the context of the whole Japanese company.

After this brief survey, I now explore in a little more detail two of the departments within the company, the international division and the personnel department.

The international division

The section that I studied in particular in C-Life in my first bout of fieldwork was the international investment department, which I joined in 1985 and worked in for a two-year period. The department was less than 20 years old at the time. It had been created after 1971 when the laws were revised to allow increasingly large funds to be invested by Japanese companies in foreign securities. The department began to grow rapidly following the further revision of the Investment Asset Application regulations in 1984 allowing increases in the 'Special Trust Funds' that were used to invest in foreign securities. These legal changes resulted in sharp growth in overseas investment by Japanese life insurance companies. Such investment grew from 0.1 per cent of total assets in 1975 to 12 per cent in 1984. The international section was therefore one of the most dynamic entities in the company. In addition to foreign securities, the section controlled foreign bonds, foreign real estate and foreign loans. The offices in London and New York came under the jurisdiction of the international investment division, and it was staff from this division who were usually sent to serve in the foreign offices. The section was headed, in descending order of seniority, by the Buchō (department head), Fukubuchō (vice department head), and Kachō (section head). The section head did most of the practical work of the department, while the department head had a more supervisory role and functioned as a liaison with other department heads throughout the company.

There were 24 employees altogether in the international department at that time, with an additional two members in the London Office, and three in the New York office. The international section was housed in the main C-Life building: a large rectangular building with a passage down the middle of each floor. On either side of the passage were two enormous open-plan spaces. The floor in which the international section was situated also contained the finance, domestic loans, domestic securities and domestic real estate departments. Altogether about 150 people were working in the one area. The only subdivisions of the room were a small office for one of the directors at one end of the room and small rooms for conferences and for holding meetings with guests to the company. The other sections ran the entire length of the room. Thus, one's every action was visible to everyone else for every minute of the day. The desks were placed close together and there was no room for files, so the desks were piled sometimes two feet high with documents.

A large number of C-Life employees hoped to be sent abroad at some point. Before this could be achieved, it was necessary to get into in the international department. The section therefore had an élite atmosphere amongst company employees and was the most popular placement choice for new graduates entering the company. However, the department seemed a lot less glamorous to outsiders. One employee who transferred into C-Life in 1985 from a company that was experienced in international investment had the following to say:

> H: The new international department was really in a big mess [mechakucha]. It was a situation where they had absolutely nothing at all – there was a normal domestic section head where nobody could speak English and there was no international experience, and we entered into that situation as the foreign corps.

The primitive nature of the insurance companies, compared to foreign companies which did overseas investment work, was noted by the foreign securities companies operating in Tōkyō at the time. I was the only Westerner in the entire insurance industry in Japan until a young American joined Sumitomo Life. He commented at the time that there was not a single computer in sight in the international investment section there either.

An important factor behind this characteristic of the department was the haste with which it was set up. When overseas investment became possible in the early 1970s, many C-Life managers, in common with other Japanese companies, wanted to internationalise as quickly as possible. Huge new investment possibilities had been opened up, and there were many Japanese companies eager to expand quickly into this new field. However, the very newness of this field meant that management had no clear idea of how to go about enabling the company to exploit it efficiently. As the personnel department head at the time said later, 'We were just thinking, "Internationalisation! Internationalisation!"' They had not considered carefully exactly how to do this, or what the consequences would be. Much of their thinking proved in time to have contained contradictory elements. One major problem, for example, was the fact that, whilst management had a strong but vague desire to internationalise, they were deeply distrustful of letting in anyone from outside without putting them through the normal C-Life initiation and training.

By hiring me, the personnel department head thought they had found the perfect solution. Having graduated from a Japanese university, I was of the same age and inclination as the other fresh graduates. I was fluent in Japanese and Japanese in character, having spent my teenage years in Japan. I was even a graduate of Keiō, which is not unimportant in C-Life. The manager who hired me commented:

I: At the time fourteen years ago when we hired Fiona, we had to internationalise fast because we were investing overseas. In order to internationalise we needed to be able to speak English. To be able to make contracts in English we needed that kind of talent, and we scouted Fiona... The main reason was that we wanted to internationalise. So we wanted someone with a global view; someone with an interest in fund management. As for the role we expected of Fiona in the organisation, there was a lot of news that was available overseas but that was never translated into Japanese, and we needed to circulate that information around the different departments. There were also contracts that needed looking over. We needed foreign visitors looked after when they came. She fulfilled all those roles... We wanted to get on the wave and not be left behind. So C-Life was trying as hard as it could to internationalise and get the appropriate people into the company. It is pretty impossible for the entire company to internationalise, and especially for a life insurance company, so just for the asset investment department to internationalise was the immediate task. I think that Fiona worked very hard. I think that inside the company as well they were glad to have a new wind blowing in the company and it was very helpful inside the company to have her spread to the other employees the consciousness of the winds of internationalisation. Internationalisation at the time was really about investing our assets overseas, changing from domestic stock investments, which were mainly representative of what we do, along with loans. So the new investment by the international department in overseas assets equalled internationalisation at the time. For a life insurance agency, selling life insurance is the main business and that is basically a domestically orientated market. Investing overseas had only just begun, so the comparative weight of it inside the company was very low. But as the Japanese economy was growing stronger, investment came to Japan from overseas and Japan began to put more weight on overseas investments. And that gradually increased until about 20 per cent of our assets were invested overseas and after that real estate was added to that as well.

One of the motivations behind setting up a separate department for international-related work was the wariness felt by many managers about 'foreignness' in general, and foreigners in particular. I examine the views of company employees on this matter in Chapter 6, where we will see that 'foreignness' often had a negative ring to it for many people at C-Life. Because of this, it was felt best to try to keep it contained within one department – essentially to avoid 'contamination' of the rest of the company. A further aspect of this thinking concerned the fact that many new employees were brought into the international department from other companies. We shall see later that such people were also viewed with great suspicion by many people as potentially disloyal employees. It thus seemed sensible to try to contain these people within one department as much as possible.

> I: Because of the special characteristics of life insurance companies, we wanted just the international department to become internationalised. The rest of the company work was fine as a domestically orientated company. So we only needed internationalisation in that special department.

There was, then, considerable pressure to do something in response to global opportunities. But there was also a strong feeling amongst management that the company as a whole should not change. The personnel department at the time went to considerable trouble to think of ways to obtain international personnel and be seen – both by company employees and people outside the company – to be 'internationalising', but without allowing the foreign influence to taint the rest of the organisation. This backfired badly in several ways, as we will see, particularly when considering what happened to the mid-career transferees. Containing employees within one section alone inside the larger structure of a Japanese company proved to be impossible.

Because of the élite nature of the international department, and because it had a number of unusual employees – a foreigner, a department head from outside (from the Bank of Tōkyō) and a number of transferees poached mid-career from other financial institutions – other employees thought of the department as very exotic and different from the rest of the domestic-oriented company.

> H: The character of the international department inside C-Life was really different – the culture in that department was really different – it was like an outlying island. There are a lot of people with international experience inside the international department, so the atmosphere was really different. Looking from the point of view of other departments of the company it was a little bit eccentric or outside of normal reality (tonde iru).

There was an element of jealousy mingled with this, since so many people wanted to be posted abroad, as members of the international department frequently were. This was commonly regarded as rather like having a holiday.

In general, envy and jealousy between different people and sections in the company are rife. In the absence of large differences in salary and other personal circumstances among employees, and under the constant all-pervasive pressure of needing to keep up with those who entered the company in the same year as oneself, status and position became all-important to most employees. This is exacerbated by the relative lack of ability to choose one's own career direction. There were many cases of people who applied to enter the international division year after year for most of their careers, but who were never transferred there. The lack of clear standards in evaluation makes the situation worse, since employees are never sure exactly why they are not able to make their desired career moves. It was natural under those circumstances that transferees who had come into the coveted international department mid-career, and from other companies, were deeply resented.

Status in the company is reiterated constantly, by where a person sits, by the way they are addressed by others and by their experience in the company. A great deal of significance is attached to seating arrangements, which reflect people's status and relations with each other. Issues which might appear minor to a Westerner, such as how close one is sitting to the section head, take on a lot of meaning in the close atmosphere of the section. When I was explaining who was who in the hierarchy of C-Life to anyone Japanese, it was easiest to pull out a large piece of paper and draw a seating plan of how the international division was arranged at the time that I worked there.

All of the managers of section head level or above had their desks on one side of the room in a long row, with their backs to the window facing in to the room. All other personnel had their desks arranged in fours, so that no-one ever sat facing the back of another person (Rohlen also found the same inward-looking perspective in the bank that he studied). Apart from these general principles, each seating arrangement was only in effect for a short while. The desks of the entire section were changed around once every two months or so, something that took a great deal of time and energy to organise. This served to let different people sit next to each other, to let them get to know each other better, see each other working, alleviate stagnation and also, I believe, to shake up the order so that relationships didn't get too close or too much in conflict, and so that members couldn't feel they were in inferior or superior places. Much energy was invested in making sure that there was constant variety among who interacted with whom. The fact that this had to be done very carefully, so as to maintain the ranking system, and at the same time avoid annoying equally-ranked employees by putting some of them in superior positions, meant that it was an incredibly complicated business.

In this section, we have introduced some of the key themes we will be examining in more detail subsequently, particularly attitudes towards 'foreignness', uniformity, and the suspicion surrounding those who stand out. In examining the personnel department, we shall also introduce some themes which will become increasingly important in later chapters.

The personnel division

The personnel division in C-Life – as in most large Japanese companies – is an enormously powerful but mysterious entity. All authority to hire and move people belongs formally to the personnel department. The department makes its decisions ostensibly based on the recommendations of the various department heads and section heads, but the personnel department usually has the last word. This has several implications. Because the career of employees in C-Life is intended to be life-long, the personnel department provides, in some senses, an objective arena for evaluation that remains constant regardless of the career movements of the individual employee through the company. So the employee's file remains with the personnel department and the influence of individual bosses on the employee's record is in many ways, limited. The personnel department only judges the employee cumulatively, through successive internal job rotations and on the basis of the evaluation of the different bosses. So the view of the employee in the company's eyes is only slowly accumulated and can always be subsequently altered to some extent.

The disadvantage with this system from the point of view of the employee being moved around is that he may have little idea of how he is seen by his bosses or by the personnel department. Slowly, the employee gains an idea of how he is being evaluated, but this takes many years.

Employees in C-Life have an annual meeting with their bosses and with the personnel department. Before the meeting they submit a standard form evaluating their own performance through the year and summing up their goals and preferences for their next work assignment. However, these may or may not be taken up. They are most likely to be effective only if the employee has guessed what the personnel department has in mind for him, and has asked for a transfer that is within those limits. Here we note the importance of understanding the 'rules', and how an understanding of those rules is the key to success.

The way in which employees move through the company, from department to department, gradually increasing in status as they spend more time in the company, is examined in more depth later in the book. The brief explanation of the system given here will put this later examination in context.

There are several advantages of the system from the point of view of the employee being moved. No one boss can ever be too influential, so having a boss with whom one has poor relations will not necessarily wreck one's career. There is always room for change, so no position is permanent and thus permanently unbearable. The massive disadvantage, however, lies in the absence of any real control over one's career. In many cases, the employee may not be doing the kind of work that he desires to do. We will see in later chapters the effect this can have on employees' morale.

> H: If people are doing the kind of work that they like doing they won't question having to work hard or having to work after hours, and it won't be a hardship for them. But at the moment, they are the same as soldiers... and work has become an obligation, so they just happen to arrive at a certain section and they know that they will be somewhere else in two or three years, so they are continually insecure. For example, in the C-Life subsidiary, among the people that came there there were people who studied investments for three years but they might have to go on to do insurance sales. That kind of thing was actually happening. So nobody can be settled and comfortable in working, and that is the fact of the matter.

> Y: I haven't been able to do everything that I wanted to in the company. I wanted to do Japanese stocks ten years ago but I wasn't able to do it then. And now I have been in the company for 19 years and I have still not been able to do that. There just wasn't that kind of transfer for me. I asked for the transfer but I didn't get it. You

ask and sometimes you get it and sometimes you don't. That is up to the decision of the personnel department. You talk to your direct boss after you ask for a new assignment. Then your boss can transmit what was discussed on to the personnel department. And then the actual orders come down from the personnel department. Do we live in uncertainty because of that? Not really uncertainty, but you don't know what kind of work you will do at all, so when the order comes you know what you will be doing then whatever comes your way.

The above employee was permanently assigned to doing foreign-related work. Because he had graduated in English from a top university it is likely that he was seen from the very beginning by the personnel department as somebody who would work in foreign investment regardless of his personal interests; and once this idea was set into motion there was little he could do about it. In most cases, the preferences of the workers themselves are not taken into account very much at all. We will see in later chapters the effects that this situation has on employees' morale and ambition.

The union

In these circumstances, it is appropriate to examine another organisation within C-Life, the labour union. The union introduces some important aspects of typical employees' attitudes towards work and the company which will be explored in more depth in the chapters which follow.

The union inside C-Life is an enterprise union rather than an industry-wide union. This typical characteristic of Japanese unions in large companies means that the whole focus and meaning of the union is different from that of the industry unions found in the West.

A: As for the union? In America, you have unions that are made up of people from the same industry. For example, you would have a union of people doing life insurance sales. But in Japan, unions are connected to the companies and are organised like that. So there is a labour union in C-Life and another one in Nippon Life, and then on top of those two life insurance unions you have a union of everyone in the life insurance industry, called the Seiho Rōren. So it is the same structure as other industries. For steel, you have ShinNittetsu Union and NKK Union and above those company unions you have a union of everyone in the steel industry. And then above that you have something called Renrō: the All-Japan Labour Union.

Because the unions are enterprise-based it makes no sense for them to fight the company. The union is there essentially to complement the company management, not oppose it; it works with the company, not against it. This contrasts with the general attitude of labour unions in the West, and it means that the position of the union as a body representing the workers' interests is actually quite a weak presence.

A: And what they actually do is – well, a long time ago they used to work for pay raises – but now they try to protect the rewards given to workers. So that not only in individual companies but in Japanese society as a whole they try to make policies so that everyone can work all their lives. So it is not just C-Life that is like that. So because of that, it is not easy to just fire someone in Japan. And that is one result of the labour unions. The company and the union respect each other mutually. But because the union is an inside-the-company thing, if the company doesn't exist then the union can't exist either. So the union is thinking about what it can do to make things better for the company and they ask the company. And the company also asks the union and those are the kinds of negotiations that they have. So just a narrow focus on wage raises is not seen as very important now.

Critics of the Japanese system might say that the union system acts to protect the interests of present management rather than the interests of the workers.

A: Well, the union says, 'Because we want it to be a better company, please do this!' Or the union will say, 'Please give us more information.' For example, information to do with what is happening about the bad loans. Or to do with what is happening to next year's management plan. They ask the company directly if they can tell that to the union members. I think that the company and the union have a good relation in that sense; a very good relation. If they can possibly do it, they want to protect life-time employment.

So in C-Life, at least, the primary concern of the union is to protect the life-time employment system itself. The workers are more concerned with job security than with pay. In the case of C-Life, the union accepted several pay-cuts – including the most recent and very substantial company-wide cut of 6 per cent in late 1999 – because the negative aspects of the pay-cut were balanced by the positive fact that it allowed the company to protect the workforce from being laid off. When a huge restructuring plan was finally implemented, the union put up no real opposition at all as it was made quite clear that the company would cease to exist if this drastic step was not taken.

It seems, then, that what most concerns employees is security and the prospect of being employed for life in the same company. They are relatively unconcerned about immediate material rewards (although, of course, life-time employment has long-term financial benefits). This contrasts quite sharply with unions in the West, for whom current pay levels are much higher on their list of priorities.

Because of the close relations between the company and the union, and because both organisations are co-dependent and involve the same members who are employed for life in the company, being involved in the union, whilst not necessarily a strong career move, is at the same time not considered problematic to advancing in the company.

One of my respondents said the following:

A: Doing a stint in the labour union is not an 'advancement course'. If you want to go on the fast-track advancement course, it is probably a good idea not to be in the union. It is really hard to be in the union. It is really tough.

Some respondents, including high-ranking members of the personnel department, told me repeatedly that it was a prestigious position to be sent to serve in the company union, or in the industry-wide union that is an amalgam of each inner-company union of the companies in the industry. Working for the union involves management, representing the voice of employees, negotiating with top management, putting forward a position and defending it, and these are all seen as vital skills to advance inside the organisation itself. Employees who have successfully completed stints in the industry-wide union are expected to have fostered important ties with influential members of other life insurance companies, and with personnel at the bureaucratic bodies that deal with life insurance.

A: If you work for the union with optimism and a forward-looking attitude [maemuki ni] then you can make it useful towards the next step in your career. Because the labour union leaders are exactly the same as the company management. It is members of the same organisation that want to make both the labour union and the company better.

In my case, we had ten thousand members in the union and the top of the union was the top of those ten thousand members. So it is exactly the same principle as being the top management of a company. You have to have the kind of thinking that a top person has or you can't work as a union leader. So it is easy to develop that kind of leadership thinking in the labour union so you can go on and become a leader. Because it is the same thing as becoming a manager.

In some cases, members of the union of C-Life are sent out to work for the union of the industry body, and in this way may become involved in working for members of other companies that have applied for help from the union.

The main reason for individual company employees to seek the union's help is that they have been asked to retire, and they must look for employment in another company. The union, and thus indirectly the company, is often involved in helping such employees get entry into other companies. In such cases, the company or the union might ask smaller companies that are indebted to the employee's company to take the employee on in a management position. Or, in C-Life's case, they might ask other companies that have taken out group insurance policies with C-Life and thus have a business relationship with them, smaller companies that have business loans with the company, or have other ties of one kind or another. The most usual outcome in such a case is for the employee to be re-hired by a smaller – in many cases, much smaller – company.

A: I had the experience of working in Nissan Life, on temporary assignment from C-Life, as well. There were issues involved in finding re-employment for Nissan union members in other companies and I had to work really hard at that. But I could see all kinds of different things in that position and that is the case if you work for the union.

The relative lack of power of the Japanese large company unions is especially evident when companies go bankrupt. The following voice is one employee of C-Life who was actually working inside the industry union when Nissan Mutual Life Insurance Company went bankrupt – the first major life insurer to go under in the post-war period. Even the union had no idea that the company was going under and no say or part in negotiations at all.

> A: As far as the labour union was concerned, when Nissan Life went under, well, employment disappears basically. So when it went under, suddenly one day there was no more employment for many of the people. So three days before they were negotiating on their wages with the company. But there was no resolution. There was no conclusion again and again. Even on 25 April, there was still no conclusion. Despite the fact that the end of March is the end of the fiscal year. And then one day they looked at the papers and the company had gone under and everyone was shocked. The employees didn't know at all about what was going to happen. And I went at ten in the morning and there were the media corps who had all come into the company. And they all asked me who I was, if I was media but I said no. At that company, there were about 500 temporary [naikin] workers and three thousand normal employees.

Keiō University

Another group within the company is those who have graduated from Keiō University. Clearly, this is not a discrete, official structure like the international department or the union, but it is no less significant, since a third of the general workforce are Keiō graduates – including all of the presidents and most of the directors.

> H: C-Life is sometimes called 'Mita Life' because of the Keiō connection. The founder of C-Life was a Keiō graduate [Kadonoshin]. I think that he was a really talented person at the time. He was a really forward-looking person and he put that thinking into the company. I think he was at the same level as we are [referring to the international corps of C-Life]. But he brought all Keiō people around him so C-Life is called 'Mita Life' and there are almost no directors in C-Life that didn't come from Keiō. Over 90 per cent are Keiō people. Inside C-Life, there is a Keiō name list and a Keiō society. Basically, if you are not in that group then you can not become a director; those are the facts of it.

The personnel department was adamant that this connection with Keiō was not a conscious strategy of C-Life's. They said that because the company had begun that way, the connections between Keiō and C-Life had just been passed down from generation to generation through individual human connections.

I: There were a lot of Keiō people inside C-Life because C-Life was started by a disciple of Fukuzawa Yukichi called Kadonoshin. He was the head of Keiō but he changed from being the head of Keiō to being a businessman and set up C-Life. Among people who come into C-Life to work there are a lot of Keiō people. And that trend has continued until now and even now I think there is a high percentage of Keiō people. It is not because we want Keiō people at all costs. We also take them from Waseda, Tōdai, Rikkyō, Kyōdai, Meiji etc. – a range of different universities. But I think that a lot of Keiō people apply and as a result we end up taking a lot on… It is not true that you have to be from Keiō to be a manager. It is unthinkable that there would be that kind of old-school-tie thinking [gakubatsu]. That would be harmful to the organisation and the company thinking is that we should disband those kinds of tendencies. So I always made an effort to aggressively recruit people from other kinds of universities as well. For example, there were a lot of people from private universities inside C-Life so I tried to actively recruit from national universities. From Tōdai, Hokkaidō, Kyōto, Hiroshima, etc., to try to get talented students from those and use them in the company.

However, the personnel head at the time that I entered C-Life – himself a Keiō man – did go on active recruiting trips to Keiō. Two of my dōki were recruited into C-Life during such a trip. Another two were introduced to the personnel section through an introduction from their university professor at Keiō to one of his personal connections at Keiō. And I myself – the first foreign woman to have graduated from Keiō – was also introduced through personal connections stemming from the university. Thus, there was a distinction here between what was said – the tatemae – and what was actually done – the honne.

The Keiō presence in the company is not hard to spot. Once a year there is a party for the Keiō graduates at C-Life. This occasion offers the rare opportunity for younger members of the company to mix socially with some of the most important members of the company – the president, and most of the directors. This highly visible Keiō 'batsu' clique is deeply resented by some of the employees. Many told me that it wasn't possible to really advance in C-Life unless you were a graduate of Keiō. And several of my dōki who were graduates of Waseda University, which is equal to Keiō academically, and often associated with it, like Oxford and Cambridge, actually quit the company in the first couple of years. Our fellow dōki said that probably part of the reason these two quit is that they could see that they would be limited in ability to rise through the company compared to Keiō graduates.

The deep resentment of some non-Keiō graduates towards the Keiō clique is evident in the following comments. The resentment centres around the fact that the Keiō employees create a group to benefit themselves, that it is hard for non-Keiō graduates to advance far in the company, and that graduates from national universities – normally regarded as the best in Japan – are disadvantaged in C-Life.

H: In opposition to that the Waseda graduates have made a Waseda society in C-Life, but as expected they have an inferiority complex. They are weaker and numerically inferior because the directors that are already in place are all Keiō. Everyone knows that.

H: The guys that come to C-Life are all the dropouts from Keiō. So all the dropouts wanted to gather together in the same company... I am from a national university. It is because those guys originally in C-Life didn't have ability that they had to get us into the company and for us as well when they could use our abilities and when we matched... when our needs matched... we could both prosper from the arrangement. I don't think it is bad thing. I think it is OK like that. It is because it is a Keiō company for the sake of Keiō people. Everyone knows that when they get in there. So it is okay to have those kind of companies. But those kind of companies are going to lose to globalisation. It is because they just they don't develop because they are just talking without any actions but that is the road they chose so that is their life. I am not necessarily criticising it.

The Keiō clique therefore forms an important group within C-Life. We thus see how some significant elements of the company's structure are unofficial, below the surface. Awareness of this reality is important: those who realise that it puts them at a disadvantage may quit the company rather than spend their lives fighting against it.

Employees from outside

I now turn to two minorities among the life-long, regular workers at C-Life: mid-career transferees and women. Examining how members of these groups differ from normal 'company men' tells us a lot about the latter. More significantly, the attitudes of others towards transferees and women reveals much about the company ethos.

One rather unusual fact about the international section at the time that I entered in 1985 was that it had four employees who had been transferred from other companies mid-career. This reflected the legislative changes in the industry, meaning that the international section was expanding faster than personnel could be developed internally to carry out the expanding breadth of work. Someone working in the international market needed experience of having lived overseas and a good knowledge of English.

H: I was invited into C-Life by F, who had already got into the international department. I knew F had moved to C-Life and that he was the first-ever example of a mid-career employee being hired by C-Life. At the time the head of the department K had just come in from the Bank of Tōkyō and was department head and there were only two employees from outside so they asked me to join them. They had an ad out in the paper and they were trying to get a number of people in – at that time W also joined. That was what happened.

As I was one of those interviewing the applicants, to test their ability in English, I had the opportunity to see what kind of people were being considered. Applicants came from a variety of backgrounds, some from the finance sector – banking or security companies – but most were from depressed industries such as steel or agricultural machinery. None of the applicants was from the insurance industry. The applicants were required to be around 40 years of age and possess the qualities that a successful manager in a Japanese company would have: an ability to take responsibility, a large number of connections, the demeanour to command respect from kōhai, or juniors, and the maturity to see what needs doing of their own accord and do it successfully. Although a new university recruit might have had the intellectual capacity to do the job, they would not have had the other qualities that the company was looking for.

> H: I went into a trading company first of all – I entered C-Life in 1985 when C-Life had just made an international department for the first time and they were trying to get people together that understood overseas culture and could speak English. It was exactly right for me – it was the international department and there were new assets to manage and so I was able to do a great variety of work and it was really good. I was able to use my abilities and I went from New York to London and I was able to do a large variety of work over there. In that sense I was able to tread the course that I wanted to tread.

The manner in which the transferees began their new jobs was quite different from the experience of most fresh recruits. Their jobs were clearly defined, and what was expected of them was stated. This contrasts with the vagueness surrounding the job descriptions of other company employees. It is interesting to note here that, where there is no time to go through the Japanese-style recruitment, new employees are trained in the fastest, most efficient way possible.

> H: In real-estate investment, the amounts invested are really huge and we were doing things that had never been done before in the company. We had to set the investments up for the organisation for the first time or we had to establish a holding company to expand the growth of our investments and we got income from them. I think that my degree of contribution to the company was really large. By saying that I mean that until then C-Life people couldn't speak English and I was hired because they couldn't speak English. So I worked as a foreign corps in the company.

Loyalty is a major issue for a transferee. It would have been felt that a transferee from a rival company would not have the same loyalties toward his new company as he had towards the old; this meant that they took every opportunity to show that they were in fact loyal to their new company. For example, the company holds an annual campaign for employees to sell life insurance policies, during which time every employee in the company is expected to sell at least one and hopefully more life insurance policies in a one-month period. The purpose of this exercise is to bring the attention of every employee back to the main business of the company. Rare opportunities like this to demonstrate one's motivation and loyalty in objectively quantifiable terms are welcomed by many members of the company, and for a transferee it is an ideal opportunity. The four transferees together sold more policies during the month of their first campaign than any other three employees in the international section and one of them sold the most of any employee.

The transferees were, however, surrounded by an uncomfortable aura. Formally, they had become and were C-Life employees. However, they shared none of the common background and experience of the other C-Life employees. Although they deliberately looked up the year intake that they were equivalent to and sought them out, they were in the difficult position of trying to enter a group of around 50 people that had been a close-knit group for 18 years.

One employee summed up the atmosphere when he said to me, 'Have you noticed that no-one really laughs at their jokes?' Attempts at social integration that the transferees made outside the direct sphere of work were awkward. Their efforts seemed to be met with resistance from the established employees as a group, although no criticism could have been made regarding any one individual's behaviour. One had the feeling that even the lowest-ranked C-Life employee could feel a 'real' member of the company (and therefore somehow superior) compared to the transferees.The four transferees in C-Life during the two-year period I worked there had only entered that year, which may have explained some of the awkwardness. Indeed, on my follow-up visit to the company in 1991, I discovered that three of the transferees had done very well in the company and were more accepted than they had been. Two had, in fact, received promotions to section chief. The fourth, however, had been involved in a car accident and had suffered a serious head injury, which meant that he was off work for nearly a year. Although the man was very enthusiastic about working again, the company did not want him to. I was told that it would be of no use giving this man a survey to fill in, as his feelings towards the company were very negative, and as they did not want me to interview him, I did not push the issue. In 1991 the man had not found work in any other company.

This situation bears some resemblance to the case of another employee. When I first entered the section there was a female employee working under the same terms as the male employees, but she quit shortly after I entered the company. I asked several times why she had quit and the members of the section would laugh and say that her superior at the time had bullied her into quitting. They would say this in front of the section head, who would then explain that she had had badly deteriorating eyesight and had been forced to give up the job, which entailed a lot of fine paperwork. No matter how many times I heard this story the members of the section were never convinced by the section chief's explanation; nor did the section chief cease to feel that he had to repeat the explanation of sickness.

Other employees in the company had also transferred from other lines of work at some stage or another. At one point I was introduced to a man from another section with the words 'He's from — company'. When I asked how long he had been an employee of C-Life, I was told ten years. Even after all that time, the employees of C-Life still associated him in some way with his previous company, even though he was quite accepted by them.

Another interesting case, by contrast, was a man who had worked as a teacher for two years. During that time he realised that this was not what he wanted to do and applied for a position with C-Life. Although he was now two years older than the other employees in the company, he had had to start at the beginning with the other new trainees in the training centre. When anyone mentioned that the man used to be a teacher, it seemed more a matter of describing something interesting pertaining to him rather than implying that he belonged not to us but to another organisation.

The difficulty that the transferees found in penetrating the company socially reflects the very close relationships between many people in the company, particularly between members of the same year group. It seems that to be accepted as a 'normal' member of C-Life it is not essential to have been through the training institute and share all of the background of the other workers – although one is at significant disadvantage if one does not. One does come to be accepted eventually, but only after a period of many years spent demonstrating one's loyalty to the new organisation. Often it is a case of proving one's character to one's colleagues, as there is considerable suspicion that transferees had to leave their old companies because of unresolvable problems.

We will see all of these factors recurring throughout these chapters.

Women

The experiences of women at the company form an interesting parallel to those of the transferees. Like the transferees, the women who were employed as general workers were, in theory, on an equal footing with their male colleagues – but in practice they found life much harder. Here again we see the distinction between honne and tatemae. In this section, I discuss the formal role of women in the company; their experiences in a male-dominated environment, and the attitudes they had to deal with, are discussed in depth in Chapter 6.

Women in C-Life fall into a number of different categories, all sharply different in job content and status. There are general workers (same status and career paths as men); tantōshoku (see below), jimushoku (secretaries or office workers) and insurance sales ladies, popularly known as 'sales aunties' (hoken no obasan). My fieldwork dealt, on the main, with employees in the general worker category, so I did not interview the office workers.

When I entered the company in 1985, women had been employed as general workers (same as men) for five years. This was partly in preparation for the introduction of the Equal Opportunity Employment Law. There were 50 women in this category. By the time I quit two years later, most of them had left the company. Several years after I left, the company revised its strategy on women and introduced another category – tantōshoku – in between the men and secretarial workers. The tantōshoku category was the same as men, but they did not have to transfer to regional posts.

O: Women are hired now on a 'tantōshoku' category which is in between that of the guys and the women employees. They don't have to move out of Tōkyō like the guys if they don't want to. Of course, they are different to E and me because their history in the company is different and their pay scale is different as well. That must have an influence on their feelings towards the company and their work as well. If a woman has been tantōshoku for five years, then she can make the challenge and change into the same category as the guys. If they let her do that, she would go back to the training dormitory and train again with the new intake of guys who were five years younger than her.

The new category was created in response to the fact that almost all of the women general workers quit the company – mostly within the first two years or so. Management decided that the women would be better off in an in-between category that allowed work as a man, but under easier conditions.

I: The category of having women as general workers has now disappeared. There weren't many women who were successful in the general worker category, so we made a category called tantōshoku in between the general workers and the office workers, to bridge the gap and employ people in that category. So, even if those people get married, they can quit the company if it is their wish. In the general worker category it doesn't go like that – when they come into the company, they promise to work until the very end, regardless of marriage. But women in particular have marriage problems, and some don't want to work together with their husbands, and say that they want to withdraw into the household [hikonjaimasu]. In actual practice it's common for one of them to quit. Well, if you ask which one it is, it's usually the woman. So in order to cater to people like that, we opened the door to the tantōshoku category as a new experiment.

C-Life did leave the door open, however, for women to transfer to the general worker category if they so desired. This involved considerable disruption and sacrifice: the women had to go back into a dormitory to train intensively for a year in selling insurance door-to-door.

O: Only one girl has done this [changed to the male category]. She went into the dormitory in her sixth year in the company. So she has two sets of dōki. She did training for sales people at a branch office for two years after that and then she came back to the head office and is doing planning work for new policies. It seems that she calls both sets of dōki, dōki. I just found that out lately. But she must have known much more than the others. The sixth year in the company and the first year are totally different so she must have been looked up to like an older sister by the new entrants. They call them dōki, not because she starts again from there but because she has that kind of close relations emotionally with the other guys that she is doing the training with. Once they get into the workplace the guys know that she is sempai there. But they still have a strong feeling emotionally [kimochiteki ni] that they are friends [nakama] that have been through the same training experience together... It seems it worked out well. But she was the only one who transferred. All the others stayed as tantōshoku.

Additionally, the female office workers, who had been free to dress as they liked at the time I entered the company, had been put back into uniform, a significant reflection of their status as lower than the non-uniformed men. There was a general agreement among the staff of the international department that this was a good thing. One of the members said:

> P: It doesn't matter how much status you give women employees and what kind of clothes they wear, in the end they are just 'enkai yaku' [party hostesses].

It seemed to me that there was very little overt discrimination against women once they were hired as general workers. They were formally equal to men. Behind the scenes, however, as the above comment shows, discrimination was rife. At that time, and even later, I think it would have been extremely difficult for a woman really to advance in the company.

The main reason why women entered in the general worker category was that they didn't see why their working conditions should change from men just because they were women; in other words it was a moral stance.

> O: If I was doing it all again I would still do the same; join as a general worker and take that challenge. All through my student days I was equal with the guys in everything that we did. I couldn't understand why that should suddenly change once we got into the company. I don't think anything really does change.

Working conditions in C-Life were quite tough, beginning with the harsh conditions of the training at that time. Women increasingly questioned whether it was really worth sacrificing other areas of their life to make a stand.

> O: But for a Japanese salary-man life is really hard, so it is a separate question of whether this life is really okay being like this. Because it is really severe and can be cruel. If working like a man means challenging this severe working environment and seeing if you can live through it, I don't know if I would choose that. But that is a separate question to whether I would enter this company again if I were doing it all again. If there were two choices of general worker and tantōshoku I would choose to work the same as the guys.

From the career paths of the women whom I interviewed, however, I think that in some ways they did have a more lenient time in C-Life than the men did.

> E: After I finished with the training, I went to the Ikebukuro branch office and I was a shunin [trainee manager] there. I had to do the rounds with the new people who had been hired to do sales and to educate them. So that was my first job, training sales ladies. I got married after that and became pregnant. So I was sent back to the head office. I was put in the personnel office to do office work there. After my maternity leave I went into the planning department for one year and following that I did roughly the same kind of work as I am doing now in the education department... I moved

around a bit in the company to different sales office as part of my job, educating different sales offices as part of my job… educating people in the different offices.

The above woman was given work transfers based on her pregnancy and only actually transferred out of Tōkyō once, during which time she went alone, without her husband.

One issue that women in the general worker category had to face was going into the head office or into the sales offices as shunin (trainee managers). When men did this, they went in to be managers of sales ladies who were often older than them and vastly more experienced in sales. I imagined that in the case of women this would be more difficult, but this does not seem to have always been so. It seems that the company, in the above woman's case, orchestrated her positions so that she started off teaching inexperienced sales ladies.

E: In the branch office I was educating sales ladies who had just come into the branch office – women who were going to be selling insurance for the first time. So in that sense they were inexperienced and I was more experienced in terms of work. So they listened attentively to me and it was a lot of fun to teach them.

O: How do the secretaries [the 'office ladies' in the head office] see me? Well, there are hardly any of us left now so I wonder. I don't feel anything special about that but when I was younger they used to look at me like I was something really unusual. 'You are a general worker aren't you? That's really incredible… [sugoi desu yo ne]'. Because I am older now they just think she is an older woman but she has been in the company for years and years… I don't feel anything special but that may be just because I don't notice what is going on…

My own experience was sharply different from that of the other women. I was the only woman to be put directly into the head office of the company, rather than doing the year of training and second year of training in the actual workforce. This meant that the other women were removed from the rest of the office until they had been initiated into the company through the training, and thus came back into the company as company members with a whole different experience and knowledge from the women office workers. This resulted in no obvious conflicts occurring.

In my own case, however, because I went straight into the office, I ended up being in the same work section as women office workers who had been at university together with me just the year before. Now, however, we were in sharply different categories with different roles and expectations. These office women were expected to pour tea – the very symbol of women in the workforce in Japan – for me when I dealt with guests from outside companies, a very frequent occurrence as I had to meet with brokers from overseas securities companies regularly to monitor our investments. I found that there was considerable tension in that relationship, which made it more complicated and difficult to do my work. I had to be constantly monitoring the relationship to make sure I wasn't hurting feelings or arousing resentment unintentionally. On the other side, the office women would, on occasion, subtly obstruct my work.

C-Life tried various ways to alter the way in which they used women. At one stage, they decided to hire four-year university graduates and raise them to be sales ladies. The rationale behind this was that compared to the older sales 'aunties', who were often housewives working part-time as sales people, the younger women would present a more professional image. Foreign companies had introduced 'life consultants' to sell. These are young men and women who are trained especially to sell. They use personal computers with especially designed software so they can easily input household data on the spot and produce colourful graphs that show the householder why they should have insurance now, what their investment will bring, and what happens in the case of an accident. However, C-Life's plans for this department did not work well and were later abandoned.

> S: So I think it is difficult to raise a sales woman by training alone. Because they are young women it must be hard for them to get income and they must have difficulties with that. For most of the middle-aged sales ladies in the sales offices, their husbands are the main bread-winners in the family. Although there are some women with a real entrepreneurial attitude that earn more than their husbands, the young single women that are working find themselves earning less than their friends who are office-workers in other companies when they compare their salaries and their bonuses. And they become dissatisfied with that. So when their pay dips they quit. That is probably the main factor.

Interestingly, employees saw no difference between men and women in selling insurance per se:

> O: I don't think it is disadvantageous to be a woman in selling insurance. All of the saleswomen in the general offices are women. At least in selling insurance outside, anyway. Most of the women in the general workers could do it really well. For the generation one year above me, women were top in their year. It was really only me that couldn't sell very well. I got through by getting the support of everyone around me.

However, I observed that when a sales lady was about to clinch a sale, or when a prospect was wavering, the sales office head would often accompany her on her next meeting with the prospect. As the sales ladies were invariably female, and the office heads almost all male, it is difficult to say whether bringing the sales office head in at this stage in negotiations had more to do with the added authority or because he was a man. It is often inseparable. This became more obvious inside the branch offices themselves, which would handle complaints directly from customers arriving at the branches. Most of the women in such branches were secretaries. Therefore, it is easy to understand that an impatient customer would assume that unless he talked to a man he would not be talking to someone in a position of authority.

> O: No-one ever told me to come back and bring a man or anything like that in sell-ing door-to-door. But when I was in the Ōsaka office there was a customer who kept on saying, 'Aren't there any guys here to talk to?' I told him that I was in charge of the particular issue trying to cover up. But there are sometimes really customers who will sit down and wait until a guy comes back to deal with them. Those kind of customers usually have a complaint to air or a grievance. They have come to get money and haven't felt they have been dealt with fairly so they want to talk to someone higher up. They can't understand that insurance is strictly deter-mined and there is no leeway in dealing with customers. They think if they can get us to produce a high-ranking guy it will go better for them. If there is a guy around I get them to go out and deal with the customer. I get them to take them to a room and listen to them carefully. But the amount of money still doesn't change.

Contrary to my expectations I found that the younger generation – especially those starting out in the workforce – were quite conservative in the way they ide-ally wanted to work. They told me that they wanted to be in the same company for life, and to have a secure and stable workplace. I think that this reflected the intense instability and tension in Japan about whether university students will find jobs and whether they can keep them. At the same time, the young students had high expectations of being able to use their 'skills' in their work, developing, and finding work that suited their personalities. The women in C-Life told me that they had observed the same kind of surprising conservatism in young women at university now and coming into C-Life.

> E: I think in my generation there were women that wanted to work, and those who wanted to get married and have a family... there were different types of women... I think the young women now just want to get married and be settled quietly at home... there are more who have strong desires to be like that. They seem not very active, they do what they are told but they are not very interesting.

> E: I have seen in surveys that women who don't want to work are more in number now than there were in my generation. They don't have a lot of aspirations [mamori ni hairu to iu ka], they are in protective mode. They have seen a harsh period, and it is natural to be in protective mode, for companies as well... But if they know nothing else but protective mode they will just go on being in protective mode... they seem very conservative to me.

And those women who do well as general workers – such as this employee, who was the first women to become section chief – stand out as anomalies:

> E: I think that my daughter would be a bit embarrassed to tell the other kids that her mother is a section chief! She is embarrassed about a mother like that! Well, she is embarrassed about a mother that is not normal like that. I don't think it makes any difference to her whether I am a section chief or not. I leave early in the morning and come home late at night and I am a strange mother that works all day

long. And it is not that I have a shop (which is understandable); I am a strange mother that goes off to a company. So that is probably all that she really thinks about it.

One consequence of hiring women as general workers was a number of cases of marriages between dōki – members of the same year group – in C-Life. As a senior manager says below, official company policy was that there was no restriction on both parties continuing to work. However, informal opinion in the company was invariably that one or the other should quit, and that this would always be the woman.

> I: There are no kinds of rules about what happens when two people in the company marry each other. We ask them to be conscious of the fact that they are both working, and to work with that consciousness in mind. But they all quit. It's not a regulation that women must quit, but it's always the women who do quit. Whether we can say it's a custom or not, I don't know. When the company made the new policy of having women in as general workers, the company was mentally prepared for this kind of case. They made sure the individuals were aware of this as well. But if two people suddenly fall in love and get married, it can't be helped.

Again, then, we see a disjunction between what was said and what actually happened. Official company policy said one thing, but the reality was another.

Conclusion

In this chapter, I have briefly described the basic structure of C-Life, looked at some of the more important groups within the company, and introduced the most important themes that will be examined in more depth in this book. None of the discussion in this chapter is intended to be exhaustive – rather, I have here introduced the background against which the subsequent chapters will be set. I continue this process in more depth in the next chapter, in which I follow the stages of a typical career through the company.

4   The company and career

In the last chapter, I described some of the groups of people within the organisation of C-Life. In the present chapter I continue this process in more depth, by following the major stages in the career of the typical C-Life employee.

Joining C-Life

Why do people come to work for C-Life, and what sort of people are they? In answering this question we shall learn something about the kind of ideology and ethos that characterises the company.

As with most other major Japanese companies, new employees are hired as a group in April. The company employs various recruiting methods, including advertising in recruiting magazines or direct visits to universities by company members. The backgrounds of the members of the international section at the time that I entered the company were as follows:

University	Major
Shizuoka	Law
Tōkyō Foreign Languages	English
Kansai Gakuin	Law
Nagoya	Maths
Keiō	Economics
Tōhoku	Economics
Chiba	Mechanical Engineering
Kansai Gakuin	Business
Kyōto	Agricultural Economics
Waseda	Economics
Kyōto	American Literature
Tōkyō	Agricultural Economics
Kansai Gakuin	Economics
Keiō	Economics

According to the responses to the survey I distributed to the international division in 1992, two thirds of the members had had no thoughts other than working for a large Japanese company.

Reasons given include:

- the scale of the work is large;
- Japanese companies are stable;
- they are high status;
- the economic prospects are good.

Some of the reasons were rather vague:

- no reason;
- because I'm Japanese;
- because I went with the 'natural flow'.

These reflected the lack of alternatives at the time other than large Japanese companies, and also reflected the great similarity between one Japanese company and another, at least in the eyes of those looking for jobs. The majority of international division employees had had no real alternative in practical terms other than working for a large Japanese company. We shall see, however, that this vagueness is characteristic of Japanese workers compared to those in other countries. Later in this chapter I shall note the same phenomenon recurring at retirement.

Why do people choose C-Life? C-Life is a large company in its industry. As in other countries, the life insurance industry is seen by workers as a stable industry. C-Life was the seventh largest company in the industry in Japan before the bubble and had a relatively traditional image. Employees seeking work in C-Life could be said to be those people searching for a traditional Japanese large company environment in which to work. The merits of working for such a company were seen to be stability, including the stability of pay, and the seniority promotion system, status, and the fact that the work is on a large scale.

Q: But you knew that C-Life was a very traditional company?

J: Yes, well, actually, every life insurance company was traditional then. It still is. They are all traditional I think.

Q: At the time you wanted to work for a traditional company?

J: Yes, I was a traditional kind of person. And now I am still traditional. I like to work as one part of a big organisation.

T: In working for C-Life, I don't have to explain to the outside world what my company is.

J: From the company the kind of expectations that I had – I was thinking that it was a guarantee of employment for the future and guarantee of livelihood and I thought that probably my own potential [kannosei] would also come out by means of working in the company. At first when I entered the company and all the time since I've been in the company the concept of life-time employment was maintained and I thought that somehow I would just drift on [zuruzuru] in the company.

The outlook for the industry in 1985, when I joined C-Life, seemed very promising to me and others in my position because of deregulation in the industry. Indeed, the industry was one of the most popular choices for graduates in that year. Because of deregulation, new sections were being created in insurance companies dealing with different types of investment. And especially attractive among these were the new international sections, as we have seen in Chapter 3. Because of the popularity of the industry in 1985, the personnel department could afford to be more discriminating in its choice of employees. The intake of that year were consequently of a higher calibre than the older employees, and became dubbed 'The Flowers of 1985'. Among the different sections of the company, the employees of the international section were generally of a higher calibre than those of other sections, because it was one of the most popular sections to work in.

Most of the C-Life employees in their thirties or older, then, had given very little thought to what kind of company they would join, beyond looking for the largest and most prestigious among a very narrow range of well-known Japanese companies. Moreover, they gave little thought to what they would actually do inside the company, or even what company life would really be like. For most of that generation, looking for a company was carried out in the same way that they used when looking for high schools and universities; they made applications to the best schools that they thought they had a chance to enter and accepted places at the best one that accepted them. Almost all of them had taken this same approach in choosing their companies.

> H: What is the company to me? A company is something that a group of people do together that an individual can't do alone – it's a type of co-operation. I think it's that sort of thing. At the time that I graduated and got into the company I just had the idea that it was a group (kyōdōtai), just an organisation and that I would enter and participate in such an organisation as well.

However, there was a sharp divide between the older generation and the present graduates, who have had a much more difficult time in getting into companies in the post-bubble recession. The latter graduates have had to spend considerable time in thinking about skills they will need to get into the industry of their choice. This is one part of the strong sense of the difference between the old generation and the new which is common in C-Life. We will see more aspects of it later in this chapter when we look at life-time employment and the new importance of acquiring specialist skills.

> S: The basis for my loyalty towards the company? I didn't really have a strong reason to come into C-Life. I hadn't really thought that I really wanted to be in C-Life in the beginning so I went around to banks, security companies, and also to insurance companies. If I think about it now I just happened on a certain day to be in Ōsaka because the school that I was at was in Kyōto which was nearby and the company that I had been to to be interviewed at was quite boring. I was wondering if I couldn't find anything better, and I just called a friend, but my friend wasn't there that

evening. So I was wondering what to do, and I was looking through the phone book and I turned the page and there was an advertisement right there for C-Life. And, by coincidence, right in front of my very eyes was the building of C-Life in Ōsaka. So, in some ways it was like fate – the C-Life building just happened to be in front of me. I went in to talk to them – and to the personnel. A really nice person was there so it was the person I was attracted to rather than the company. I'd heard of C-Life but I didn't really know what kind of a company it was, and I hadn't really analysed it carefully. I had already had firm offers from other companies but the guy from C-Life stayed on my mind. The years between 1980 and 1983 had been a little bit tough for this company. But the president had just changed and the company looked poised to take off from there and I thought, 'Why not put my strength into that effort?' I felt this was a company that would grow.

Many candidates went to interviews one after another until they got a clear letter of confirmation from one of the companies, and felt that they couldn't do any better than that company, even if they expended more effort in going on looking.

T: At the time that I graduated, life insurance companies were very popular. They were expanding at a rapid pace towards internationalisation and it was a period where they were expanding towards foreign markets. I wanted to go to a place like that and that is why I came into C-Life. In actual fact, I was trying to apply for foreign banks and I passed the first exam for one of them. But at that stage I got a definite reply from C-Life so I stopped from going any further with the bank.

O: When I was looking for a job in college I remember a friend saying that job hunting was like musical chairs. If you give up the chair you are sitting on then someone is going to take it. I was able to get a job in a place where there is no prejudice against women and was able to work on the same terms as guys so I am really satisfied with that. Being in the company until now looking from the guys' point of view, I was given really good treatment so I am really thankful. The age is becoming even harsher so I don't think that things will go so easily in the future but I am glad that I was able to get into this company.

In many cases it was just sheer chance that employees landed at C-Life rather than another major company. But many other people got their jobs through personal connections of one type or another. Students didn't generally aim to use connections from school to get into companies if they could help it, because that would make them indebted to those sempai – their seniors in the company – for as long as they were in the same company. But they would enlist the aid of such sempai if the situation got desperate – or, sometimes, the sempai would call them of their own accord and volunteer their help. We will look more closely at all aspects of sempai-kōhai relations – the relationship between seniors and juniors – in Chapter 6.

A: I didn't have anywhere to come but C-Life. I actually wanted to go to the mass media field; same as everyone else. I had one company that was decided and I turned down everyone else. It was an advertising agency. I really wanted to go there and I thought that it was okay. But when I went to the interview with the director I had an argument with him and I told him that if it was like that then I would never come back to this company. I let a chair go flying and left the room. But then I was really in trouble for a job. I thought that I would have a year out while looking for a job the second time around. But at that stage a sempai (from my volleyball club at Keiō) who was working at C-Life called me and said, 'I heard that you had a fight with the company that you were planning to go into.' When I said that I had, he asked me what I was going to do and I said that I hadn't thought of anything so he told me to come and see him tomorrow.

In practice, a majority of people do have connections of one kind or another to get into C-Life.

T: I did have connections with C-Life. In practice, almost everyone has connections, don't they? My connection was my father. C-Life was a business partner of my father's company... That company and C-Life had business dealings together since a long time ago; since before the war. For example, they were for a long time a client of C-Life insurance and I heard that they had had such relations from the period of the founder onwards.

But the impact of the connections and the influence that they have on the employee's career subsequently vary greatly. T's story will be dealt with at greater length later in this chapter. Suffice to say now that although employees may make use of special circumstances to get into the company, the initial year of training is a time of deliberate levelling that puts all employees together on the same footing, as we shall see later. If the employee is able to conform properly and follow the correct rules from the beginning, whatever the circumstances of their entry into the company these can be left behind and he or she can go on as a normal company employee. But if the person is unable to do that successfully, they will carry the weight of the failure throughout their company career.

Other employees found themselves being headhunted.

J: I was in fourth grade in Keiō University and I was in the middle of the activity of job searching. And my friend – Mr. S – was also searching for a job in the life insurance industry and we were talking about working for a life insurance company in the Keiō University dining hall. It was summer and there were only a few people in the dining hall and we were talking about life insurance companies. All of a sudden two gentlemen came up to us and told us that they were from the personnel department from C-Life. It was really a coincidence. They showed us their business cards. One of the gentlemen said that he was the jinjibuchō [personnel department head] and the other man said he was jinjikachō [personnel section head]. We hadn't noticed but they had been listening to our conversation. And they said, 'You guys seem to be interested in life insurance companies. As I showed you we are responsible for recruiting. Why don't you visit our head office?' And a couple of days later we visited.

> And the guys from C-Life told us a lot of good things about C-Life, and how promising the company is. Life is kind of fate [en]! I believe in such a kind of fate.

The above recruits (there were two of them together) were, as Keiō economics students, high-calibre candidates; one of them had spent his junior high school years in America and spoke fairly fluent English. Having been personally selected by such a powerful person as the personnel manager – often said by employees to be one of the most powerful people in the company, certainly to a greater extent than would be in a Western company – the recruit would probably accept the offer of employment in this company. As expected, the personnel manager looked after the recruit's career during the two years since his employment, and regarded him very much as his 'own' protégé.

The other employees considered such a route into C-Life to be enormously advantageous. It was felt that the person doing the hiring would feel a sense of responsibility for the student's career. The student would have the feeling of starting off in company life with a mentor.

> J: I thought it would be very good to get into a company through such a contact. Very much so. I'll disclose this. Actually, the section chief (jinjkachō) wrote us a letter before we entered, before we decided to join the company. The letter said 'If you decide to join the company we will treat you as candidates for top management (kambu kōhosai).' S and I didn't believe that, because you know, the company is a company, after all. The company is not for one individual. So we didn't really believe it. But we were moved by such a gesture (kandō shita).

After I had heard this same account from a number of employees in the same year – that if they joined they would be regarded as élite members of the company and management material – I realised that many of the recruits are told the same story. They are lured by the personnel department into the company with a mixture of flattery and promises and tales of the benefits of being employed by C-Life. The employees who told me these stories – sometimes 20 years later – were still flattered to have been told they could be future élite, even when they were not really convinced by the flattery. The employees say something which they now know not to be true, but they are still pleased to have been told it and continue to repeat it.

From the point of view of the personnel department, the company was competing for new recruits against other major Japanese companies, all very similar, and with similar personnel policies and pay systems. The personnel department – especially at the time of the bubble and before – told me they were basically looking for the best minds from the best universities with the best potential to fit into life as company men, to stay in the company throughout their working lives and expand the company. Getting good employees under these circumstances did involve a mixture of cunning and flattery, although the personnel head was hesitant about admitting openly to having said such things.

But what the personnel department was looking for in a 'leadership candidate' was very unspecific and poorly defined. They focused on very general qualities:

they looked for people with energy, a sense of challenge and interest in the business world.

> I: We didn't consider at the time of hiring whether a person would be a good sales man or not. To get good people we needed to look at people who had interest in the world around them and in the economy and people who could aggressively challenge those kinds of problems and have that kind of forward-looking [ki ga mae] attitude. If you ask someone to talk about their dreams for the future you can tell very quickly if they have that or not and we hire them from that.

The personnel department did promote C-Life strongly to the new recruits. We have already seen that the company invests much effort into presenting a glossy image of itself to the public. Part of this is geared towards attracting new recruits. A key portion of the manual includes profiles of 'ideal' employees set up as attractive examples for new recruits to imagine themselves as becoming if they enter C-Life.

> I: The personnel section would also talk to the new recruits about what a good company C-Life is. We would tell them that C-Life was a company that had a new type of attitude and that treated employees very well. That it was a company that would use employees' abilities to the greatest possible extent. And that we would give them great freedom in the way that they worked: that kind of thing.

We may ask how much of the company information the personnel department, who had to attract new recruits, believed. In the case of the former personnel manager, he professed to believe what he told the new recruits year in and year out about C-Life.

> I: I think that is the point in C-Life. If you say that in more detail, we are the number one in the industry as far as developing new insurance products goes. And we were number one in the industry for employee education. We would say that C-Life treats work as of great importance and tries to aim at being number one in this sense. A lot of people with these kinds of dreams are gathered together and everyone can have the same dream of making C-Life bigger and better. We would look for those kind of people and educate and continue to put effort into them... we had in place inside the company the facilities to let people work as they pleased.

Confronted bluntly with the fact that more than half of my dōki had already left C-Life within 14 years of entering, however, he did concede that there were cases when people didn't fit the company.

> I: I would judge that most of the people that I hired are now doing pretty well inside the company. Sometimes they didn't live up to my expectations but there were a lot of people that were hired so among those some changed to another path and I don't think that can really be helped.

The similarities between Rohlen's company, Uedagin, and C-Life are extensive, and they are typical of most large white-collar companies. Rohlen notes several interesting points related to the structure of Uedagin. The first is that the boundaries between each institution are decisive and important; there is a strong sense of 'we' and 'they'. The company label is noted as the most important classifier of people and it is valuable to belong to an important company. Rohlen notes that it is the selection process itself that has determined much of the character of the Uedagin employees. Candidates were excluded from selection on grounds such as undesirable social reputation of the family, unstable background, involvement with political or religious organisations, or an active dating life. The employee expects to have a long and continuous relationship with the bank. 'As in most in-looking social situations, this creates a cautious propriety, a willingness to enter into fellowship, and a sensitivity to the nuances of interaction' (1974: 15). Rohlen notes that the contract that is signed by members entering the bank lists neither rights, nor duties, nor procedures for redress, renegotiation or termination. As we shall see later in this chapter, and in Chapter 5, there is usually no scope in the Japanese company for a detailed contract of this kind.

Rohlen concludes that the two main organisational principles in Uedagin are the community of work and the uniformity of hierarchical distinctions. This can create a paradox by the tendency of the first to unify people and the second to separate: 'In America, hierarchy tends to clash with equality and individual independence. In Uedagin, the differentiation and distance established by rank often appear in marked contrast to the ambitions for a community of common interest and endeavour' (33).

In the next section, I flesh this account out a little by considering the people who were recruited to the international department.

Joining the international division

One natural path into the international division came from the domestic investment department, where a knowledge of stocks and bonds was acquired. After the initial two years spent in the training centre, employees usually do another two or three years of general office (secretarial) work, either working in the head office or acting as head of a sales office. If they are inside the head office they are put in a disciple-style relationship to an older member of the company from whom they learn their initial job. As employees in C-Life do not have personal 'secretaries' in the same sense as Western firms do, much of the routine clerical work is carried out by the new employees. This 'learn by experience' approach is intended by management to allow the new employees to get a feel for the work.

As we have seen, the final responsibility for assigning personnel to sections in the company belongs entirely to the personnel section, although they rely on the advice of the employees' bosses in the section in which they currently work.

To begin with, the company hoped to fill the new international division with employees from within the company. The personnel head at the time that I was recruited recalled:

> I: There are a lot of new graduates that came into the company with the hope of working overseas. And we wanted to grow new internationally minded people up from within. We would choose from among those many people who applied and put them in a dormitory to train for one year and then send them out to the various departments in the second year.

However, having had no experience in raising 'internationally minded' business men and no clear idea of what would really be required, the company was at a loss how to train these people beyond trying to recruit new employees who had a degree of English ability already from having studied it or having been overseas with their parents.

> I: We didn't do anything special in the training to do with internationalisation or have any consciousness of that in the curriculum, because it wasn't everyone who was going to the international department. So the people who were judged suitable to go into the investment department would go there. And among those there were people who excelled at languages and were interested in going overseas. And some of those were able to go to the overseas branches and to acquire international awareness [kokusai kankaku o mi ni tsukete] and advance our internationalisation [kokusaika o don don tsutsumete iku to]. There weren't any employees who were sent off to universities to study. Some of them went to the Foreign Ministry or the Ministry of Finance or the Ministry of Telecommunications [tsūsanshō] to study and work there for a while. In 1985 the kind of students we tried to hire were people who had as broad thinking as possible [haba hiroi kangaekata] and who aggressively challenged things with a new kind of attitude [kise]). We tried to scout such kinds of people.

The company gradually realised that hiring such people and then expecting them to be content to work and advance at the same pace as all the other employees was simply not going to work. That was clear from the example of the female employees. Among my dōki, all of the women who had been hired on the same basis as men had already quit. The women who had been hired in this category were invariably higher-calibre employees than the men, which the men freely admitted. They were from better universities, on average, with better results, and were also on the whole, I think, more motivated and hard-working than their male counterparts. They had more to prove. Several women hired in this way became top in their year in insurance sales in the training centre. One went on to become a business woman with her own company, another went to a foreign company where she would have had more equal treatment, and another passed the difficult exam to become a lawyer.

Accordingly, at some point during the bubble, the personnel department shifted its stance somewhat. Instead of hiring foreigners in Japan, they settled for hiring local staff at the overseas branches. Although this policy remained in place, the attempt to hire specialists in Japan was judged a failure – for reasons that we will see later in this chapter – and the company reverted after nearly a decade to bringing up generalists from within again. The pressure from within the company towards having everyone similar and equal in background was simply too great.

> I: In New York and London and Paris we had local branches and we took on local staff in those branches. We thought that we would stop trying to raise generalists and that we would raise specialists instead. But I don't know what the thinking is about that now. I think that they now want to hire generalists and make specialists out of them. I think that is the policy of the present personnel department. If you try and get specialists from the beginning from outside, inside the larger world of life insurance where we have to sell insurance products and do sales work, there are also people who don't suit that at all. And if that is the case, that causes us problems. So once more we are concentrating on generalists. And we went back to that direction. That is the present personnel department.

What happens to the recruits after they are hired, at the training centre? This subject is particularly important, not simply because C-Life was considered by industry employees to be particularly oriented towards training, but also because the training period is one of the most important stages in an employee's career, establishing the relationships with others which will last throughout his time at the company.

Training

Having entered C-Life, the new recruit goes first to the training institute, where he will spend the next two years formally as a trainee. The training forms one of the most significant experiences in the life of the C-Life man and is most instrumental in removing him from student life and re-forming him in the image of a company man.

> T: Basically, the kind of character that a person has that is able to raise the sales results is somebody who is very social and somebody who is very stubborn and doesn't give up.

For the first month, the trainee studies basic knowledge about the insurance industry in the training centre itself. The purpose of this month is to put the trainees in an intense shock situation where they are thoroughly thrown into company life, and into the company of each other – the crucial 'dōki' same-year intake that will be the core of their inner-company business contacts and friends for their entire working life. The formal purpose of the training is to have the trainees study intensively for the public insurance exam that will give them the licence to sell insurance door-to-door for the company. During this month they are physically and psychologically completely separated from their former lives as students and from the rest of the company.

For the next five months of training, the trainees move into the dormitory in which they will spend the rest of the year, whether they have houses in Tōkyō or not. All trainees must live together communally: this is common practice among Japanese companies. It enables the trainees to get to know one another extraordinarily well and to become thoroughly tied up in each other's private lives and work performance. They are not allowed to stay outside the dormitory, or to visit their homes and stay there during the week. There are random checks to ensure that this is complied with.

For the next five months, the trainees are given separate areas in which to sell insurance door-to-door to individual customers. They are not allowed to sell insurance outside their given areas unless it is as a result of a direct introduction by someone inside the sales area. They are not allowed to sign up personal friends or relations or anyone outside their given area. This is to ensure that all of the trainees are starting out on exactly the same level. Otherwise, those with more extensive contacts, or richer relatives, or more co-operative friends could gain better results than the others without expending any more effort.

It is prestigious to make good sales during this period, and the reputation of the sales record made during of this time does precede the employees in the first years in the company. But the actual amount sold is not really important. The main purpose of the exercise is to have every employee in the company familiar with the company's products and with the way in which they are sold.

The next two months are spent selling life insurance to institutions. The ninth month is spent studying office work such as letter writing and business practice. The tenth month is spent studying finance and investment knowledge. And the final two months of the first year are spent in recruiting the sales ladies who sell insurance door-to-door from the branch offices.

The C-Life training is fairly typical in that it provides a good basic knowledge of the company and an insight into basic business practices, but it is a little atypical in its length. C-Life was referred to in the industry as 'Educational C-Life' (Kyoiku-no C-Life). It will be evident all through this book how very important the first year was in making the employees into C-Life people and in fostering their loyalty towards their organisation.

My own case illustrates this fact. I did not do the training myself, as the personnel department needed an English speaker urgently, and wished to put me straight into the international department right from the beginning. This is an example of the poorly-thought through planning typical of the personnel department. I was extremely sensitive about making sure that my position was equal to everyone else from the start (at least on the surface). I have already hinted at the problems encountered by those who stood out in any way from their colleagues; so I was naturally keen to try to blend in as much as possible. At this time in Japan, foreigners could command a very sizeable salary by using their English skills. However, I knew that having a different salary or conditions would condemn me to an outsider position inside a Japanese company. After lengthy negotiations, during which I insisted time and time again that my pay and conditions must be negotiated to be equal to others, it was decided that I would have exactly the same package and status as every other employee but that I would receive a supplement for 'extra' work, teaching other members of the international department English during my lunch hours. I don't believe that the personnel department were aware at the time of how important it would be in being accepted as a company employee for me to have the same pay and conditions as others in the company. They had never had any kind of foreigner working for them before.

At the time, however, both the personnel department and I overlooked the matter of training. As I had never worked in a Japanese company I did not know the importance of training and its role in initiating trainees as company members. I eventually realised this, and saw that I could never make up the ground lost through missing the training; this was a major factor in my decision to leave the company.

> H: I think it is the same as the world of sumō. If the foreigners have done the training and experienced extreme hardship together with the other trainees they can become yokozuna – sumō 'Grand Champions'. But just by being strong, they can't suddenly come in sideways and become a yokozuna. In the sumō world it is the same as in C-Life. It is like a condensed version of Japanese society. If people come up from the bottom they need to become friends with others by spending a long time together and experiencing a lot of hardship.

The personnel head who had hired me admitted many years later when I interviewed him that he had not realised what would happen when I was put directly into the workplace. He said that, had he realised, he would have let me go to the training centre if I had wanted to. This would have been an extremely difficult thing to imagine, however. Not only was I the first foreign woman in the entire industry, I was the first foreigner many of the employees had ever talked to in person. To do the training at that time would have involved selling insurance door-to-door. It is hard to imagine how average Japanese housewives would have received a young foreigner selling a product as serious and as expensive as life insurance.

> H: I think at that point in time it would have been impossible to have a foreigner do the training. You have to go and sell insurance for the first year. The core of the corporate body is made up from what happens during the training year and all of us had had that experience. I think it would have been really different for Fiona had she done the training.

Most employees' memories of the training were a mixture of how harsh it was, and how good it was being together at that time. They became extraordinarily close to their work colleagues and also to their customers.

> J: It was really hard. Our bosses were really harsh and for example, in the evening, like eight or nine o'clock in the evening when I called my boss, before I even started to talk he would question me. He would ask me if I had got a new client that day and signed him up with insurance. And if I said that I hadn't got one he would sometimes say, 'Okay, don't come back to the office. Keep on selling all night.'

Q: So you did? All night?

J: Well, I didn't. But I couldn't go back to the dormitory or my house, or my apartment. So I would have to ask one of my present clients if I could stay at their house for a night.

Q: Clients that you had already sold to or hadn't sold to?

J: Yes and no. Some of them were already my clients and some of them were not.

Q: So you were that close to your clients?

J: Yes. Right.

Q: Did they feel sorry for you?

J: Yes. So they allowed me to stay at their house.

Q: Did you get any business out of it?

J: Yes. I don't remember for sure, but I believe so.

Q: When you look back at the training now how was it?

J: It had two aspects. The one aspect is just like I said; really harsh. The other is like a really happy experience. Well, people started to believe in me... and to believe what I said about insurance.

   Sometimes all of a sudden the prospect would decide, 'Okay, I'll buy insurance from you.' That is an accomplishment, right?

Q: How did that make you feel?

J: Really happy and... successful.

Q: Did that make you like C-Life, the company?

J: Yes. The training period was only like six or seven months. And we had to leave that particular area when we finished that training period. And when we left the area, some of our clients cried. They told us, 'Please, don't leave. Please continue to be my financial adviser.' So that left a deep impression on me.

All of the trainees – without exception – agreed later that the training year was an invaluable experience in setting them up to be able to manage the insurance sales offices at a later stage. It also taught them a great deal about the actual business of selling. All of the insurance branch offices are staffed by mostly middle-aged sales ladies. It is this army of women that keeps the company alive. The employees said that selling insurance themselves, door-to-door, for those crucial first months made them fully aware of the business of the company, of how it is constituted, and what their role in the company would be. On a more personal level, experiencing for themselves the hardship of selling door-to-door, facing endless rejection and discouragement, equipped them all the better to teach the sales ladies when they became managers themselves. They also earned the respect of the sales ladies by having done this work themselves. The sales ladies to whom I talked were all aware that their bosses had done exactly the work that they had done. They also invariably knew what kind of record their bosses had had in their own first years of training. The record of that year does follow the employee throughout their career.

Having excelled in selling in the first year of training does not necessarily mean that the employee will go on to do sales work. J, who was one of the top sellers of his year, went on to do investment work because he also had English language abilities. S, who had a good but not the top record, went on to become one of the top sales men in the company. He was already seen at that stage to be aggressive in sales and to be talented at it (S broke the rules by making inroads even into the other dōkis' areas in order to maximise his sales!).

Sometimes, separating the trainees into sales or non-sales related work at the end of the first year backfires, because, as we have seen, the personnel department places employees without taking their desires into account. The top seller among my dōki was a woman who had a high degree of ambition and talent. She wanted to go into the international department to do investment work but was left in the sales arena because of her extraordinary record in selling. After a year or two she quit the company altogether in frustration, and went on to establish a high-flying career as a business woman independently.

However, even those employees who went on to areas of the company that had nothing to do with sales still reminisced about their days of training as an invaluable experience in initiating them into the business of the company.

> J: I was transferred to the international department in the second year. My job was… portfolio management. Those kind of jobs have nothing to do with insurance sales, right? But I did have an awareness of how to sell, and how to sell insurance, and how difficult it is to sell a single insurance policy. So because of that experience in the first year I was really careful of investing the company's money.

The new trainees have mixed reactions to selling. Some of them hate the work and do very little in the beginning. The training escalates in intensity, however, so that after a certain initiation period teams are formed and made to compete against other teams. This is designed to introduce a sense of competition and urgency in the selling. Everybody is dependent on the other members of the team for their results, in a very Japanese form of pressure. The motivated sellers in the teams thus automatically act to push the weaker and more reluctant members on. This is, in part, where the employees gain their sense of groupism and community. Twenty years on, training teams would animatedly describe to me, in every fine detail, the stories of their victories and near-misses, the part each team member had played and the favours they did for each other.

> I: The training period has got a lot shorter now. At the time it was a year long and within that year you got a very strong sense of group consciousness [nakama ishiki], and I have the understanding that that was something that was extremely useful working within C-Life for those people's entire working careers.

As might be imagined, the new recruits who hitherto had been carefree students – especially carefree in the Japanese system where, compared to other countries, there is very much less pressure on students to study – rebelled to different degrees at the harsh training. So, we can surmise that the intense loyalty that employees developed to C-Life was not simply a characteristic of being Japanese, nor was it instilled in them in the education system. There were special characteristics in the training itself that moulded these employees to the company. We saw earlier in this chapter that the personnel department looks for recruits who 'fit' the company: now we see that the moulding process that continues after they have been hired is also crucial.

> T: As the policy of our company at the time everyone went into the training centre and lived there for six months. Nobody commuted. I really didn't like the dormitory life at all. No, it really didn't suit me [awanai]. I am the type of person who really hates being constrained. So I remember often staying outside the dormitory.

A strong emphasis in the training is placed on having everyone put back to the same starting line, living in the same dormitory, with the same salary and work tasks to fulfil. The dormitory life is extremely rigid, involving set routines, meetings, rules, and a feeling that there is no stop to work, that 24 hours a day are to be devoted to the sole purpose of selling insurance for the company.

> T: The kinds of constraints that would happen are that they would make surprise inspections without any warning. There would be inspections in the middle of the night and they would find out that someone wasn't there. And if someone wasn't there everyone would start to gossip about it... so-and-so is never in the dormitory, etc. And I remember being asked what on earth I was doing because I was never in the dormitory. If you were not there you got scolded. But if you were doing the training properly it didn't become a very big deal; you just got a scolding.

There was some leeway in behaviour depending on how much insurance the trainees were selling. Those who were selling the required amount had more leeway in breaking the rules. But those who were not, especially as the months went by and competition was channelled into teams, come under significant pressure to conform, not only by the bosses, but also by the group pressure and gossip of the other members of the dormitory.

> T: The first year of training was a year in which you really understood the work of the insurance company. You just had to go out and sell, sell, sell... that was the kind of place that it was. It was training to teach you what kind of place an insurance company was. You had to learn with your body [karada de] how to sell insurance.

One purpose of the dormitory seems to be to remove the new recruits completely from their former lives and the influence of their families and friends in other companies or other industries. Many of the recruits recalled that they hardly knew what had hit them to be suddenly immersed in this harsh world of routine, discipline and selling.

> T: I had a vague notion that insurance companies were going to be like this. I knew vaguely that the basis of an insurance company was sales. But just hearing about it and actually experiencing it yourself is a very different thing. If I had been asked to do sales all of the time I don't think I would have continued this long in the company. But luckily, I was able to go into the finance department and since then I have nothing at all to do with selling insurance. I don't know how much insurance I really sold. I don't think I sold that much during the training. Maybe I was somewhere around the middle.

The training escalates to become more and more intense towards the end. Recruits are caught up in the system before they know it and are given little time to reflect on what it was that they are doing. Many of the recruits recall having had thoughts of quitting. But in the middle of the fury of competition they had little opportunity really to reflect on quitting before the worst was over and they were sent out into the actual sales offices or into the head office to pursue non-insurance related work.

> T: I think that the training was good because you really need to have a lot of education. It is an investment in education but it was really hard at the time. It really has become a great memory for me.

Many employees never do sales work again at all. But they know what their colleagues in the field are doing and have a good understanding of their positions. Employees said that a mutual understanding of each other's work was important in fostering good relations later between different departments. As we will see later, fostering good relations with people in other departments is essential to success.

Mentioning training to any of the C-Life people invariably brought forth a string of stories of sweat, blood and tears in obtaining policies, tales of triumph and satisfaction that formed the very core of the employees' emotions towards the company and their jobs. In these stories, we see how the groupist attitudes of loyalty and dedication of some Japanese employees are rooted in their training.

> T: The biggest memory I have of the training is of selling my first insurance policy and realising what an incredible thing it was to do. I cried then. It was so hard. I remember that I cried in front of the customer. Yes, really! In front of the customer! At the time you had to sell insurance but you weren't allowed to sell to anyone that you knew or to your friends. Friends would always come into your insurance if you tried to get them in. So it wasn't about that. You had to go to a determined area and you had to get the insurance from that one determined area so you had to start absolutely from scratch. You went to the area every single day and finally they would start listening to what you were saying to them. And finally you became

really able to talk about insurance and that was when it really started. It really took a long time to get it to that point. There is that kind of process involved so it was natural that I cried.

You really remember the first time that you sell. Even now, I am still exchanging New Year cards with the person involved and we are still friends. That guy was a person who was working out of home doing manufacturing work. He listened really well to what I was saying and we really hit it off. I went there every day, maybe ten times or twenty times… probably about that many times. At first he wouldn't listen at all. He just said OK, OK… And he just would take the pamphlets that I gave him but that is about all. I cried when he actually took out the policy. When he had decided on the policy. It was really really hard. That is how hard it was – the training. It is hard to describe. It was the most memorable thing about the whole of my company life. It was the hardest period of all.

S: My first customer? In the beginning, there used to be a one-payment type of insurance. At that time it was a high-savings/high-return type of instrument. At the time, if you looked at the pamphlet I didn't really understand what a one-payment insurance was but I had it with me and I showed the customer that. The customer asked me if that was the right one for him and I told him it was great insurance! So it went on like that and I went back to see him two or three times and discussed the return on the insurance and the tax implications. And the customer decided if it was that good a product he would get it. And he had prepared one million yen. It was one million yen; a large sum. But he had one million yen right there with him. But I didn't know how to count it like a bank clerk does, neatly and precisely like a stack of cards. I was so bad at it that I made a complete fool of myself. I was hoping that it really was the right amount. I counted it but after I'd done so I only counted ninety-eight bills. I thought it must be my mistake but because I was so nervous I said, 'Yes, there is one million yen here,' and took it back to the company. When I got back and checked there did turn out to be one million yen there so it was OK but that was my first experience of selling.

When I had to write out the receipt for the customer there was a place where I had to stamp my own name stamp and because I was so happy and so nervous – and also because I was so worried that instead of a hundred bills there might be only ninety-eight – I didn't realise that I was actually holding my name stamp the wrong way up. So instead of stamping the paper I was stamping red ink again and again all over my own hand! When I realised what I had done, I had to cover it up hastily so the customer couldn't see. When I think about this now it is really funny. I was so happy… I was so nervous… I realised for the first time how incredibly important a contract is. When we were students, we bought things like a bunch of cassette tapes or a course of English classes. But I had never had the experience of being a participant in a real contract myself. And especially not a contract that involved an amount of money as large as a million yen right in front of my very eyes! So although I laugh about it now, I thought at the time that I was an incredible fool! When the customer went home – because it was my first experience, and because the customer had left his money with me and trusted me – I felt incredibly happy. I thought that I was a genius. It is not a really big deal. Everyone can go and get an insurance policy. But because it was the first time… My first sale was in May. It is the time of year that the new company workers are wearing their shiny new work shoes for the first time and everything is bright, just one month after the start of the financial year. I thought it was such a relief to have got a policy and that my seniors would be really happy with me. I was so happy!

O: I couldn't get my first sales for a really long time because I was so bad at it. By that time, everyone had good results and I was the only one left behind. My boss at the training centre supported me by coming along with me to visit my customers and introducing himself as my superior. He helped me to be able to pull off the deal and make the sale. It was a bachelor guy that I sold to; a hairdresser with his own salon. I still send him a postcard once a year just to let him know how things are. That is all the contact we have. But he answers the postcards so I know that he is doing OK too. It is a bit of a strange feeling.

I was surprised again and again during the fieldwork at the depth of emotion that the C-Life employees showed about the training and about their clients in general, and particularly the first clients. Many of them pulled out photo albums full of photos of themselves with their clients. Many kept in touch with their clients by means of New Year cards. The trainees were obliged to go to each of the households in their area at least three times. Regardless of whether they seemed likely to be able to sell insurance or not, they were still obliged to go so they ended up just idling time at various houses or becoming friends. One of the trainees in my year became a volleyball coach for housewives in his area – signing them all up on insurance policies by the end of the year!

Another one married a customer whom he had met during this first year. His wife tells the following tale of their first encounter:

R: My mother really liked salesmen – she would always bring out tea for them, so it didn't take long before she brought tea out for him as well. She thought that he was a fine-looking young man so it was my mother who liked him first. My mother would say, 'Come in, come in, you must be tired!' and bring out tea for them. So we would talk and although the talk would mostly be about insurance that went on a couple of times. My mother would look at the salesmen as if she was looking at her own sons. She would look at them trying so hard and would want to support them.

Japanese have a soft spot for young people striving to meet a goal – as is evident in even a cursory glimpse at day-time soaps or popular cartoons and movies. The young salesmen striving their best to achieve in their first year on the job attracted sympathy and support from a lot of the households to which they were selling. However, it must be said that they also went through a lot of frustration as well. In the worst cases, some employees reported that they had salt thrown at them as they departed from the doorstep – salt being a purifying agent in Shintō religion to ward off evil spirits!

What kind of person is a top sales person? Employees praised those who combined aggression and drive with a trustworthy, likeable character. One of the famous incidents of my dōkis' training was when S not only made inroads into other trainees' assigned areas, but actually sold policies to members of the family of another dōki!

> T: One of the people who was the most incredible was one of my dōki who went and got an insurance policy from MY family! I really bowed my head [was full of admiration towards] that kind of effort. It was S who did that. During the training period he was a really social kind of a guy. And he was good at talking to people. Well, good at talking to people probably isn't the right expression. He had the kind of talking style that really drew people in – both before men and women. He was really an attractive personality to them. So he really made use of those skills. And made his circle of acquaintance wider and wider and got insurance out of that all of the time. His sales area was the neighbouring sales area to mine. So I heard a lot of feedback about him. And we were quite close, he and I. The incredible thing about S was that he would come into my area! To sell! So that kind of thing went on... He would get an introduction to someone in my sales area from someone in his sales area, which was allowed. So he took really a lot of insurance from my sales area as well! I thought well, OK...[mā, ii ya to]. If he really wants to do it that hard, then he can! I thought, well, just go ahead.

Aggression and drive are important, but if the person is not likeable as well, such behaviour could well have caused a severe rift inside the dormitory and among the teams. Ambition is essential to success, but there is an unwritten rule that one cannot be seen to be ambitious or competitive – one must dress it up as super-loyalty to the company. This is a widespread and clear example of the use of ideology to promote personal ends. S was successful at sales and became an important member of the company, whilst T, who meekly allowed him to sell in his own territory and to his own relatives, never did as well and eventually left the company. Yet there is always a formal or stated emphasis on co-operation. The fact that selling is conducted in teams for the majority of the training ensures that a balance is kept between competing and maintaining good relations among the dōki, a balance that is crucial in the relations between dōki for the whole of their career.

Towards the end of the training, as competition escalates, the trainees are given a new objective: the eight-eight club. They must get eight households within a month signed up, and sell 80 million yen worth of insurance. The candidates have to announce that they are consciously aiming to become members of the eight-eight-club; they cannot join it, even if they have made the required sales, if they did not say beforehand that they were planning to do so. This ensures that they concentrate on a set task and achieve a target that they have set out to achieve. Much prestige is connected to achieving this goal inside the training centre. Indeed, correspondents showed me prizes that they had won for joining the eight-eight club whilst training 20 years earlier, still displayed on their desks at work. This included people who had since left the company, such as this one:

J: I have a pen here... this was an award given to me during training. It says '1985 – Eight-eight club award'.

Q: So you still use it every day?

J: No! But I keep it. Eight-eight means eight accounts... eight insurance policies... so I had to sell to eight customers... and the second eight stands for eight tens of millions of yen – 80 million yen worth of insurance. So by getting that I got one of the best records in training.

Because team results were made so important, there were many examples of team-led sales efforts. Many employees told me of nightly visits of stronger sellers to the households to which the weaker sellers were trying to sell insurance in an attempt to help them secure the sale. An entire team of ten or twelve earnest young men might turn up at the household of a potential client who was wavering on getting a policy. They would all bow in unison, saying that they had come on behalf of their dōki, and earnestly beg the householder to help their friend clinch his sale. Thus, the intense loyalty, or group co-operation, which I discuss in detail in the next chapter, were forged during the training period. In Japan, where 'giri' and 'ninjō' – duty and emotion – are key values, householders are very susceptible to the combined display of ten people having made an effort to help one of the weaker members of the team. Of course, not all sales are made on the basis of emotion, but when the client was wavering, the sight of ten young men all having made an effort to come out at night to help their comrade was sometimes enough to push them into buying the policy. They would say, 'Well, it can't be helped... if this many people have come out to support your cause, I'll have to get the policy...' The ties that were cemented between those who helped, and those who were helped out, bonded these dōki relations through years and years of work in the company.

In the final crescendo of the training, recruits were put into pairs – of more or less equal selling ability – and made to compete against each other. This brought the focus back onto individual selling – the purpose of group selling having been attained – and sharpened the focus of competition. All through the employees' lives in the company, the tension between dōki, continually wavers in this way between competition and comradeship. I pay special attention to this feature of human relations in Chapter 6; here we can see that it forms an interesting example of honne and tatemae – ideology and practice. Everybody speaks of the comradeship of the dōki, but there is always a varying degree of competition underlying this. The ideology of comradeship remains constant, whilst the actual feeling about the relationship varies between individuals. So it is very hard to judge what is really going on.

Training at C-Life has now been cut down to just two months from the original near-two years – a concession to the recession and changing times. Employees who had been through the training had mixed feelings about this, although most of them accepted that the training they received was not efficient, and the company does not have the leeway to do such training any more. But they agreed that the shortening of the training would inevitably result in a loss of loyalty to the company and a weakening of the ties between dōki. They were not all sure, however, whether this was good or bad. Here we see the uncertainty of many employees in the face of change.

> X: I heard that that the training doesn't happen any more in C-Life. The training itself was not really efficient. So… well, I understand why the company ceased to give training to new entrants. But I think the new entrants will be different now if they don't give training. I think they will be.

> I: The new entrants now? How will they feel about C-Life if they haven't done training? I think they could be less attached to the company or the group. But as to whether I think that is better or not… well, the world is changing. Well, it is meant to be.

In this section, we have seen how the foundational experience of training laid the roots for many of the attitudes typical of C-Life employees: loyalty to the company and to each other, close relations between the dōki, and great competitiveness. All of these will reappear in the following sections and chapters.

Sales

The experiences of the training centre prepare the employees for the primary business of C-Life: selling insurance door-to-door. The 'sales aunties', overseen by general employees, normally do the actual selling.

The relations of C-Life employees with their customers show all kinds of characteristics typical of Japanese society. The C-Life sales personnel go far beyond a purely business relationship in their relationships with their customers: relationships are very personal and depend on a long-term development of trust. The personal characteristics of the sales person are immensely important in selling. The sales person must be seen as upright, diligent, and above all, trustworthy. It is because of this factor that it is virtually unknown in the life insurance industry for salesmen from one life insurance company to change to a sales position in another company. They would be seen as untrustworthy if it were known that they had transferred. This reflects the general lack of trust surrounding employees who change companies.

> S: If you think about it, insurance is a very expensive product. Basically it's a product that you buy from someone you trust. People are paying about 50,000 yen a month in insurance premiums which is about 600,000 yen a year and if you count that over 30 years it adds up to 18 million yen. That is pretty expensive shopping. So it's not easy to buy from someone who just turns up on your doorstep and that you don't know at all. So you have to stress human relations. You have to start things off with a trustworthy senior.

A: Basically, the products of all of the insurance companies were the same for almost all insurance. So it is the same as now when companies take out the insurance of a company based on the company and not on the product. So the point is which life insurance company you are going to have a relationship with – the judgement comes down to that. When people buy a car they decide do they want to buy a Toyota car or a Nissan car. But if all the cars were exactly the same car and they were going to buy a car then the point would be where you want to buy the car from. It would be somewhere that was nice to them… if you were talking about petrol stations, you go to a station where they wipe your windows… Basically, where all the products are the same, the judgement about which life insurance to buy comes down to who comes round to sell it and what the differences are between them. If you don't educate the salesmen well, it won't work. So education is extremely important. I think that that is the same case now. Basically the field itself hasn't changed. Selling hasn't changed either. Well, it might have changed a little bit according to the period. But basically, it starts with saying, 'Hello, how do you do? I am so-and-so from the C-Life company!' and the basic idea of it hasn't really changed.

We have seen how, during training, trainees were not allowed to sell to friends: they had to go from door-to-door. This taught them how to build up good personal relations with strangers, an essential skill to successful insurance selling. Sales personnel try to get to know as many people as possible and become involved in the society of the area in which they are based, while initially keeping the business of insurance sales in the background.

S: It's really important to make contacts with the local people if you want to do well in sales in the provinces as well. At first I thought that because I came from Tōkyō, the people in the provinces wouldn't want to deal with me. If you are stand-offish in any way they know that, though. I knew that I had to love the area and so I went to see as many customers as a possible. I went all around the area… there were a lot of customers who supported me because I made the effort to enter their society from my side… Rather than connecting with C-Life, I got them to see S first as a person, and because I did that, those few years were extremely fulfilling years both in terms of work and for my family.

Relations go far beyond a simple business transaction of insurance and money. In endlessly complicated arrangements, some of which amount more or less to bid-rigging, the sales personnel try to win favours from the company for their customers. They will arrange company dinners at local restaurants, use local construction companies, or arrange for goods to be delivered from local suppliers.

S: Of course I want to get the local people here to sign up for our insurance but I think it's also important that the shops that are doing business in this area are happy in their business – that way we're happy as well, it's give and take.

For the C-Life salesmen, this kind of give and take relationship was so natural that they did not think of such behaviour as bid-rigging, or see it as harmful in any way. Because of the intertwining of the personal with business, it was difficult to separate the two at all. And indeed, in the normal process of life, the employees saw no need to try to separate the personal and the business sphere.

> S: Obligations: what does that mean? For example, if C-Life is going to build a new building and one of our clients is in the real estate business or the construction business I would tell the client that we were proposing to build the building and suggest that he put in a quote. But I would suggest that, in return for that, I would hope that he would take out some insurance with us: that's give and take. Or I would say, 'Do you remember the favour that I did for you a year ago?' I would bring that up. Whether that insurance is really necessary for him or not is irrelevant. If I introduced the president of a small company to something I would think, well, whether it's not really necessary or not – that might be the case. It might not be very rational and the insurance might not be really necessary for the family but that one insurance policy is necessary for us. There are many cases like that.

Although some employees agreed, when discussing the topic, that taking out policies in order to get business or because of personal relations was not very economically rational behaviour, they did not believe that the sales people would try to sell in any other way in the near future. On the clients' side, however, things are changing:

> S: However, in the present climate, over-insuring is a problem. There are too many people who have taken out insurance in order to fulfill different obligations and now in the bad economic climate they can't pay their insurance premiums. So they are turning in their policies and that's a fact – that is what is happening.

A very important aspect of selling – and one that came up time and time again in conversations with the sales people was the concept described below.

> S: We say in the insurance industry that business is all about Giri-Ninjō-Purezento – obligations – human relations – and presents! It's not 100 per cent the case, but if you also keep it in mind that that is important... I try and make efforts not to leave those things out.

In practice, 'obligations' for the C-Life salesmen means the kind of exchange relationships mentioned above. 'Human relations' refers to the intense personal relationships salesmen develop with their clients whereby they exchange presents on festive occasions, eat at the clients' houses, and even, on occasion, attend weddings. 'Presents' refers to the common practice of salespeople taking small presents around to their clients, as seasonal gifts of food or drink, or as souvenirs from trips.

S: If you get transferred and don't go around to all the clients and tell them about the transfer and say something before you go they say to you, 'How come you never said anything before you went?' You have to fulfil your obligations before you go.

S: The second factor that I mentioned – ninjō or human relations – is like the example of my wife's mother who would say, 'S comes round here a lot, so why don't I do him a favour and take out an insurance policy with him?' There is a lot of that kind of business done in Japan, whether it's men or women.

The word 'ninjō' has connotations of warm emotional ties. An example would be friends taking out policies with the dōki that they graduated from university with. Another is the scenario in the training centre where ten young men would go to a prospect's house with the salesman who had almost clinched the sale.

Life-time employment

It is appropriate, in discussing features of the typical career of a C-Life employee, to consider the ideal of life-time employment, since this ideal underlies what most employees hope to achieve in their careers. We have seen something of this already; life-time employment is, in fact, one of the most frequently discussed characteristics of Japanese employment. But, in many cases, life-time employment in a Japanese company is more an ideal than a reality.

I have described the status of female workers at C-Life in Chapter 3, and briefly discussed their disadvantaged status compared to the men. They are paid considerably less than their male counterparts and act as a buffer for the élite male workforce, since they are the first to be encouraged to leave in economic downturns. And since they are usually only employed for a period of three to four years, it is easy for the company to protect the jobs of their male workers by regulating the intake of the female workers. Life-time employment is thus rarely assured for women. But, conversely, their perilous state makes it easier to assure it for men, because they know that they will not be the first to be laid off in times of economic hardship. This gives most men a good sense of security, which can sometimes adversely affect their performance:

J: So what does a Japanese company put the focus on if it is not work performance? It is a rough and ready kind of answer, but people can't be fired. The job security is guaranteed even if you don't work very hard. It is not the case that you can get a really good salary if you work really really hard, but it is also not the case that your pay goes down if you make some little mistakes and it is a good thing about Japanese companies that you don't get fired.

Even in normal times, however, there are many methods by which a company may divest itself of unwanted employees, as we shall see later in this chapter.

Life-time employment never really existed in any Japanese company to the extent that the nihonjinron literature claimed. But life-time employment was firmly associated with large Japanese companies and remained very much the 'ideal' for many of the employees that I talked to. In practice, it was also associated with the extensive company-based welfare system. One employee at the time that I was working in the international department had a car accident and was unable to work.

> H: In the old C-Life, they looked after employees like this. A guy called F joined the international department from outside and met with a car accident shortly afterwards and was no longer able to work. But C-Life looked after him by paying his full salary for three years although he never turned up to work at all.

We will see more examples of this sort of treatment of employees by the company, especially later in this chapter when dealing with employees who leave the company. It is part of the general feeling that the company should look after employees, rather than simply employ them. Thus, the life-time employment ideal and the welfare benefits are connected to the idea of the company as a family or group.

Most C-Life employees said that the 'ideal' would be to start in one company and to finish one's working life in the same company. As I had expected, this attitude was especially strong among the older members of the company. But I was surprised to hear from younger people that, although they no longer expected to be able to be employed by one company for life, they wished that they could be. Life-time employment, then, is really an ideal, and reality falls short of it – especially now. At one point I interviewed several dozen young university students looking for jobs at a large job fair. Again and again these 22-year-old men and women, about to be employed for the first time, expressed their desire to get a 'life-time employment' position. They think of life-time employment as an easier system, as not involving as much competition to succeed. As we have seen, this is a rather naïve view. But the following comments illustrate how the ideal it reflects is associated with positive Japanese values:

> Y: I think Japan is changing towards the West. What kind of Japanese things will be lost? Well, I think they are trying to change without losing the Japanese parts that are good. They are trying to make efforts for example to keep the good parts of the life-time employment system. There are demerits to life-time employment but there are lots of merits too. They want to keep the merits going. Loyalty and stability are two such merits.

> E: As far as loyalty to the company goes, in that sense I wonder if I am an old-fashioned kind of person but I think that my loyalty is quite high. As I said before, as far as my generation goes, because I was employed at a time where once you entered the company, you worked there for a long time was the normal consciousness. I would like to be here until the end.

At the same time as life-time employment was described as an ideal, it was also spoken of as an icon from a past age, or a vanished good that might be resuscitated if the economy improved. It was recognised to be an 'old-fashioned' value. The employees who spoke with longing for the bygone days of life-time employment spoke apologetically, admitting that they were probably behind the times, or old-fashioned. Employees did recognise the present reality to be sharply different from the ideal. Here the reality is admitted, in contrast to the company ideology of the life-time employment period. However, it is done so only in the context of recognising that times are changing.

> O: When this company hired me I thought that I would work here for life. I was very serious. Previously, once you were hired, to work until you retired at the same company was normal Japanese perception although it is totally different now. There might not be any companies left now where you really can stay until retirement, even in Japan.

But people also recognised that there might be individual choice in the decision to be employed for life or not. Employees seem to be thinking about different patterns of employment now that everything is changing and different patterns have become possible.

> A: The best pattern would be to come into C-Life and to go into retirement from C-Life. And I think that that is the best working pattern for the individuals as well. But whether that should be protected or not protected is not really the issue. If a person wants that, then it should be like that. But if they want to move somewhere else, then it is best if you can make that kind of chance for them as well.

For some employees, life-time employment is inextricably related to their feelings of loyalty to the company. It is because the company hired them and has 'raised' them to be fully-fledged members of the society that they feel a debt of gratitude that prevents them from changing company. Working for the same company all one's life is in part an expression of that debt and a symbol of an ideal reciprocal relationship between mentor and disciple, or senior and junior.

> E: So far I have come with the intention of being here all the way through although that is starting to break up because the present environment is the present environment after all. At the time that I got into the company it was really hard to get into any company at all. Even while I was looking for a job I couldn't get any positive answers from any of the companies I applied for. I really felt the harshness of society as I was looking for a job. And among those companies, C-Life opened its doors wide to me…

> E: As long as there are people in the company whom I can never thank enough for what they have done for me… as long as they are still in the company I feel that I want to be there too. I feel that I need to be there to repay my debts. It is probably rather old-fashioned thinking but that is the way that I feel.

Employees who spoke of such values would invariably follow up their remarks with a confession that their values were 'old-fashioned'. There was a very strong consciousness that values changed according to the age a person was in the company. If someone's values were out of line with their age they would describe themselves as 'old-fashioned' or 'forward-looking'. There is a strong consciousness that the 'younger generation' (which meant roughly under 30 years old, and especially those recently entering the company) had sharply different values from both the 'older generation' (those about to retire or having retired) and the middle generation which constitute my dōki.

One of my dōki said:

> H: So the thinking of the younger generation is really different now. They say that half of all employees change companies within the first three years now. That is very different from my generation.

In fact, ten out of 50 dōki had quit the company within the first five years, and 30 by the time they were 38 years old. Few foresaw that they would definitely remain within C-Life for life. Thus, their perception that attitudes are changing seems, for whatever reason, to be justified.

> Z: The young guys now take certificates and licences of different kinds; securities analysts' qualifications and such. So they can sell themselves as specialists. In my generation you had to climb up the ladder and cultivate your character and it wasn't until you had established a certain level of trust that the company let you advance. But now with specialist skills you can move diagonally forward. It is a sign that there has been a real shift in consciousness. So you can't make a mistake here. The generation until around 35 and the group the generation above that are completely different. And another thing you need to realise is that in the Japanese case it is only really possible to move company until around age 35.

> H: If you're more than 40 years old then no company wants you at all, so there's no possibility of being hired basically. Even in foreign companies you have to be under 40 even if you have ability – that's the fact of the matter. Japan is still an age-oriented society where employment discrimination is allowed. If you look in the newspapers you can see the ads that say up to 30 years old – this is strange but if the labour market is to be flexible normally you shouldn't have male/female discrimination and you shouldn't have age discrimination either: you should abolish it. It should have been abolished but it hasn't been. That is a very one-sided affair and I think it will become a problem in the future.

Job advertisements in Japan are not banned from specifying age. So almost every advertisement for mid-career job transfers mentions age – and invariably only people under the age of 35 can apply. This barrier was mentioned again and again by those correspondents of mine still inside C-Life who were uncomfortably aware of having 'missed the boat' (to change company), of 'approaching the point of no return' and so on.

Despite this feeling of a wind of change blowing through the Japanese employment system, most companies are still somewhere in between life-time employment and whatever will take its place. Companies are being rocked by being unable to keep employees that they have invested a lot of time and money in training, as they head for higher-paying jobs or jobs that will allow them to be promoted faster. Nor can they now tell what their staff needs will be at any time in the future.

> H: We are in the middle of a transition – a partial transition – away from life employment and toward the American style of employment. Before now companies hired according to what they thought their needs would be ten years into the future. So there are a lot of employees still that are older. But now they have started to hire less because they will hire if they need to hire when the time comes. That has changed the entire face of employment.

A number of respondents echoed some of the recent media opinion by saying that they thought that the real crunch for life-time employment would come when the Japanese economy recovered. This could change the employment situation suddenly from one where companies are retrenching dramatically to one where they are short of staff and desperate to hire – somewhat akin to during the bubble. In that situation, the rigid character of the employment market is likely to be greatly loosened. There is still considerable uncertainty about which way things will move.

As the unemployment rate rises, students are opting to take practical certificates while still at university. When I interviewed fourth-year university students, many of them were taking extra lessons in the evenings after the university day had finished so that they would have the practical skills that would make them stand out from other candidates when they went to find jobs. The most popular skills to acquire were computer competency, accounting qualifications, and English ability.

> C: Under seniority employment pay rose with years of service so there was not a lot of difference between people. When I entered the company the difference between the highest paid and the lowest was only one or two hundred yen. But now there are significant differences. In bonuses and such. And in service allowances for doing special types of jobs. Such service allowances inside the seniority system are a special Japanese phenomenon. In Japan there are few companies that have the system where you get so much money for doing a certain type of job, but change is happening now. The service allowance allows different jobs to carry different salaries.

Even in C-Life, which still maintains the outside form (tatemae) of life-time employment to a greater extent than other companies, it is true that jobs have already become quite differentiated and pay scales have become increasingly different. My dōki reported that, by 2000, there was greater discrepancy in bonus size amongst them.

As the comments below show, the demise of life-time employment is due to a mix of factors: first, the state of the economy, second, the change in values, and third, the change in the state of the job market as a whole. It is the combination of factors that is affecting companies, each to a different degree.

In the case of C-Life, I believe that the dismal economic state of the company has been most responsible for the change in employment patterns. As pay cuts have been initiated, the more talented members who are able to move have done so. It is also a matter of skills. Among the talented members of my dōki, it is clearly those who have been mainly engaged in investment or finance-related work – transferable skills – who have moved. We shall see this particularly in the next section.

> C: The wave [of restructuring] hit America first. Because the economic climate was bad before it got this good again. There is a sense in which they had to do what they had to do because of the economic climate. In Japan, because results were going up they didn't have to go that far. However, in the present economic climate in Japan we do have to do something and there are two parts to it; changing because we are conscious that we have to, and changing because there is no choice. Maybe we won't need to go as far as America did. But a lot of the new middle managers now have been brought up with a different set of ideas to the old school. There are quite a few that are moving around horizontally between companies. I don't think that Japan will go as far as America, not because Japan has a Japanese society to contend with, but because there isn't that flexibility in the labour market yet. Even if you want to quit, often there simply isn't any place to go. Even if you have the ability... that is also a large factor.

The breakdown of life-time employment in C-Life has massive implications for the structure of personnel. It is clearly the most talented members who are leaving the company. Indeed, it is often the most talented employees who are asked to leave, because they will have the least difficulty in finding jobs. The company's attempts to look after its employees as much as possible, which we saw earlier in this section, thus negatively affect its own economic performance.

> Z: The kind of people who are going to stay in this company for their entire lives are the people without any special abilities at all [yoppodo no nōryoku no nai hito], and it's actually the case that we don't want people like that.

> Z: If only talented people can shift and those without talents are left behind? Firstly, in the process of the breaking down of life-time employment, the people who are still under the life-time employment system are mostly over 35 years old. And the companies have a surplus of people now. Normally, in a recession such as now they would be cutting people endlessly. And when the economic climate improved they would have to re-employ a lot of people. However, are the new Japanese venture capital companies using them? No. Why is that? In Japan the unemployed are protected inside the companies; that is why the unemployment rate is so low. That

is the real situation. However, since the bubble, companies have only taken on the bare minimum.

Employees disagreed about what they thought would happen to life-time employment if the economy recovered. Some told me that when the economy recovered the company would be able to reinstate life-time employment practices. Others felt that once the changes had been instituted and the drastic restructuring completed, the values of the employees would have changed so radically that there would be no going back.

> C: I think that when the economy improves there will be a huge need for staff and hugely increased mobility as a result. Companies will be hard done to secure the staff that they need. Companies may try and retain the staff that they have but once those staff have a changed consciousness they won't be able to keep them, and it would take an enormous amount of money to keep people anyway. You have to provide various social welfare benefits and retirement allowances. It is cheaper to hire from scratch. This is especially so since the population itself is shrinking and the labour force with it. I think that this will be the biggest instigator of large-scale change in employment. So it is a return to good economic times that will precede that change.

Another possible reason for the decline of the life-time employment system is changes in technology.

> H: Who knows what will happen. I know from working in labour management that putting contract workers in the workplace doesn't mean that they can produce when they first arrive. But then they didn't have common computer systems company to company.

Technology has made an enormous difference to the job market. When I entered C-Life in 1985, there was not a personal computer on a desk, although they were already commonplace in Western companies. Forms used to process life insurance by hand were unique to each company in the life insurance industry, making it impossible for employees to transfer their skills in that area from one company to another. Now, however, there are a number of skills that are very transferable and there are also certificates that are industry-wide. Standard computer applications are as widely used now in Japan as in the West, and investment-related skills have become much more uniform. Transferring company is therefore easier from a purely practical, technical point of view.

Quite apart from the economy, people's values seem to be changing in many respects, and this has also affected the life-time employment system. In Chapter 3, I briefly mentioned the suspicion felt by many employees towards people who transferred into the company mid-career, as it was felt that they could not be loyal to their company. But this is becoming less and less the case, because people no longer expect to serve one company for their whole lives. Transferring companies is now, therefore, that much easier in terms of human relations.

Employees who had already quit C-Life told me that their own attitudes towards life-time employment had changed.

> H: But at the time to change your job or to change your company was something akin to a major crime, but now that's no longer the case so I think that Japan has really changed. I wish that I had quit C-Life sooner – that's my judgement now.

The values of Japanese-style management or life-employment – including close human relations and communication – were taken for granted in 1985 when I entered the company. In 1999, however, employees were openly questioning why these values were relevant. In other words, they were, for the first time, looking at the relation between these Japanese values and profitability. Their attitudes had become more profit-conscious.

> P: The plus factor of having been in the company a very long time is that you know everyone really well, because you know each other. You know the company customs very well (fūsyū), and understand the culture. I think that's a very large factor. But if you're asked whether culture and customs actually come in use anywhere, it's a strange thing to say, but no, they don't.

Life-time employment directly relates to the whole system of the personnel department and evaluation in the Japanese company too. If employees are unable to leave, personnel strategies can be a lot more long term. Although an employee may be unhappy for a while in a certain position, or be unfairly compensated, the life-time employment system ensures that situations can be evened out over the employee's career. The power of the personnel department is therefore waning as the system of life-time employment recedes.

> V: If you say it with a bit more sarcasm – life-time employment is probably good because you don't have to think about things too hard if you've been in the company a long time. When you go to evaluate somebody or make a judgement, you already know the basic standards of evaluation without even thinking about it, so it's easy on the evaluating side, or it is because it's much more secure to evaluate that way.

> P: Basically, it's the most secure or comforting [ichiban anshin nan desu yo]. You can have the confidence that somebody won't do anything really weird. If you look from the point of view of the top guys in the company who have come up in the seniority system, after 10 or 20 years they become section chiefs and then department heads. People move up in the company because they know people in the company, and because they understand people.

The concept of trust is crucial. The life-time employment system relies on the body of the workforce being average and solid employees with a proven record of not having made major mistakes in past positions, rather than having unpredictable geniuses. We have seen earlier in this chapter how the recruitment system favours this kind of employee in the first place: employees should 'fit' the company.

> P: If you promote people in just two or three years because they've done good work, and that person has only two or three years' career, the argument would be that you wouldn't necessarily know how they'd go in the future. But in the seniority case, somebody comes in at 22 or 23 years old, and they work all the way along the company, and you see them in various different positions and there are numerous evaluations. Whether the evaluation is well done or not, you can say a lot about the person himself. So they feel a sense of security about that. More than anything else, it's because it's comfortable or safe [anshin]. So they know that somebody wouldn't suddenly do something strange. They might say, 'This person isn't very adventurous, but he is solid at doing his work [katai]. And this is why he got this evaluation.'

There are other, more complex, factors behind the wane of the life-time employment system. One element is that, as other aspects of the company change, conditions may sometimes become less bearable. For example, we shall see later in this chapter and in Chapter 6 that the seniority system of advancement is not as fixed as it may have been in the past. Employees related that C-Life had already changed in the 14 years since I entered the company in 1985 to the point where there were some actual cases of seniors being employed under their juniors.

This change has resulted in a change in the amount of emotion that employees invest in their jobs and in C-Life the company, because notions of seniority remain sufficiently strong for such a situation to be unpleasant to most Japanese – as it would be to many Westerners, too. Their attitudes turn from 'wet' to 'dry', that is, they take what is perceived to be a more Western attitude towards the company – less loyal, more prone to change companies if conditions are not satisfactory. However, most employees shuddered when I asked what they would do if they ended up in such a position.

> P: I think that human relations in that kind of situation would be very difficult. I think you would just have to see things from a very rational point of view... make things very clear-cut [warikiru]. So seeing things in a very clear-cut stance is something that is here to stay. The need to keep things clear-cut is something that is necessarily taking root. From a few years ago, that trend has increased little by little.

The dōki parties that I attended in 1999 involved the same small group of relatively élite employees coming again and again. At the parties, the very same dōki who told me how close they all were as dōki would also say, in hushed voices, 'Well, so and so could hardly come because he hasn't yet been made a section chief.' It was a sensitive time for the dōki as they had reached the age when they might be made section chiefs. At the same time that life-time employment is disintegrating, the competitiveness among dōki remains. The intense desire for status in the company is still the main motivator for employees. So the present situation and values contradict each other and cause considerable stress.

> P: For the first people [who found themselves working under a junior], I think that it was a considerable shock: for both of those parties; the senior and the junior. But quite a few years have passed now since it first began happening. And there are reassignment orders [jirei] in all kinds of places in the company like that now. So if it happens to you, you just have to take an objective view of it. You just have to take an objective view and just carry on with it, both of you. Although you have to be very careful of each other's feelings, both of you. There are actual cases like that around us in both the sales offices... there is a sales department head like that... underneath him there is a guy that is older than him.

In practice, making considerable effort to be careful of each other's feelings means always using honorary language to those employees older than oneself, regardless of position. This significant aspect of the seniority system has never changed in my observation.

Although employees told me that these cases were increasing rapidly, which was confirmed by the personnel statistics that I saw, they could relate every case like this among their dōki or within their direct experience. These cases were tainted with the atmosphere of scandal, and related with the air of gossiping about a forbidden topic. As we shall see in Chapter 6, the relationship between senior and junior is an important aspect of life in the company. If that relationship becomes unbalanced, such as by the junior being older than the senior, there is likely to be tension.

The changes, once again, were inevitable because of the situation of the company. Employees were uncomfortable with the fact that such cases occurred and many of them felt it was very tiring to have to deal with the additional care that was needed to ensure that people's feelings were not ruffled.

> P: It is still not really widespread for the order to be really mixed up. So I don't know how much it has changed the situation regarding people's loyalties to the company. I don't know about people's mental state. I have never been in a situation where my boss is younger than me so I don't know, but if I had to imagine it, I wonder if the person involved would be able to keep their loyalty to the company intact. I think it would probably drop quite a bit. It is all about your pride. If you have been working for 10 or 20 or 30 years, it is all about your pride. If you had worked all that time and suddenly your morale plunged, you would have to ask yourself why you had been working until now, and you would find yourself in a really difficult situation, so you would just have to go on doing your work. If you weren't resolved to do that then I think you'd have no choice but to quit.

Although many employees felt that once life-time employment broke down the system would turn completely into an American-style system, I found it was mostly the middle and younger generations who would say this. Older people hope for a return to life-time employment. Here, then, we see another difference between the generations, symptomatic of the real change taking place in values and attitudes.

> P: If there was another bubble, the organisation might expand rapidly. And they might reorganise it so the seniors come out on top again and everybody would be happy.

They would be happier, it seems, because there would no longer be the danger of somebody's feelings being hurt by having his junior promoted above him.

> P: If it was like that [if the company were to expand and the seniority system to become stronger], in one sense, it would be happy. As I said previously. Because for salary-men life is all about status and pay.

For the personnel department, it is therefore a difficult decision to appoint a senior under his junior because of the risk that he will quit. So the seniors who are appointed below juniors tend to be very much below where they should be in terms of ability for their age, and not just slightly deficient. The following con-versation outlines the real dilemma for those involved in not being promoted at the same pace as their dōki.

> P: The people who came into the company in my year and those older knew they would go into a seniority system from when they were students because Japan was that kind of society. So they worked really hard for a really low pay…This is because they did it on the premise that that low salary would gradually go up and that they would be promoted automatically. That is why they undertook to suffer that hardship in the beginning without questioning it. So as they became 30 or 40 their pay gradually went up and they looked forward to a happy retirement at 60. And now the situation has changed dramatically and they are saying, 'Hey, wait a minute! This wasn't the plan!' So now they are perplexed and at a loss [tomado]. It is the people in their fifties who are most confounded by the situation, isn't it.

> V: Yes, me included!

> P: Me too. I have just turned 50. That is the worst age. We wonder what we can do.
> Nobody really calculated things carefully as to how their career would turn out. But they did have general assumptions. For example, if you have kids you might plan it so that they become independent before you turn 60. And that you would like to go on an overseas trip with your wife after you retire. In the case of some of the 'old boys' of C-Life, their wives go off on overseas trips without them. And the guys go with their buddies somewhere else. That is a good idea too. Sometimes that kind of independence helps a relationship last for a long time. The plans have changed now. Their pay didn't go up as much as they expected it to. And in some cases it has been scaled down. So there is a continual sense of insecurity towards the future. So the curve as to how your work was supposed to go doesn't go as

expected, the way it was supposed to go according in Japanese society. And where normally it should be really setting off now, there is nothing to fill in that hole that has been created.

V: People think it is a bad joke.

P: The line is different to how they thought it would be. Even if I think that it should be different to this, I look at the figures that the company presents me with in terms of my pay and realise that it can't be helped on the part of the company. But I wonder also what it is going to be like from now on, and how I am going to manage.

All employees who I talked to said that any disruption at all to the Japanese management system as they have known it – and to life-time employment – will inevitably result in a loss of loyalty to the company and thus increase liquidity in the job market. That is, they think that the decline of life-time employment will cause a decline in loyalty, rather than vice versa.

V: The guys after us might get a good deal themselves in the company. But because they are seeing seniors like us in this situation they come to the conclusion that they better not rely on the company. Like people did before. So the employment market will become really liquid, I think.

Employees pointed out that loyalty is not the only issue. Company employees are highly reliant on the company for all kinds of benefits, including pensions and the ability to get housing loans. Being unable to rely on the company for life-time employment will result in far-reaching changes to the whole pension system.

P: I think it will really change in the future. There are already quite a few companies that have stopped the system of providing pensions. Even large companies. This is really an 'epoch making' issue here. Japan is a country with a corporate pension system. Welfare annuities and national pensions are an issue of the government so that is okay, but the corporate pension is something that the company and the employee builds up together, and is the very example of a very Japanese custom.

V: The standard of those was very high, too.

P: Because there was the corporate pension, the larger the company the more solid an institution it was.

As we will see in the next section, changes in the life-time employment system also have enormous implications for the education system.

Skills

With the decline of the life-time employment system, many employees are busy acquiring new skills to help them as the economic conditions become ever more unpredictable. Even whilst still at university, people are trying to give themselves an edge in the job market in this way. Many people regard the new importance of specialist skills as a symptom of the great changes that Japanese companies are experiencing.

> E: The sections that I have been in have mainly been in the sales sections. At one point in time, I was the head of a sales office: just one place. So in that sense, sales is probably the main area in which I contributed to the company. I really want to remain a generalist though. When I say that I mean I don't have any special ability so I can't become a specialist.

When I joined the international division, specialist knowledge was required in several areas: international real estate, investments, international loans, international stocks and bonds, as well as knowledge of English and competence with computers. So specialist skills have always had a place in some areas of the company. Indeed, almost all of the respondents to my survey in 1991 stated that they were using specialist skills in their present work.

But not everyone is aware of the skills that they are using, especially those employed in the sales offices. When I asked them about what kinds of skills they had, they invariably said that they had none at all, that they were generalists. When I asked if they were sales specialists, they would look bewildered. They seemed to have a concept of 'skilled' that included professionals with fixed certificates of one kind or another, or people with very defined jobs, like investment expertise. To have 'skills' always seems to be linked to the concept of job transferability. The sales employees are basically unable to transfer to other insurance companies to follow the same line of work. Therefore, they see themselves as 'unskilled'. On reflection about what kind of skills their jobs really involved, some of them concluded that they were actually personnel management experts. One dōki said that if he were to go on to another job from C-Life he would manage a large retail store of some kind that involved managing large numbers of relatively unskilled personnel.

> C: With the exception of young people who are different – life-time employment is the norm, right? If you analyse that, Japanese guys could expend their efforts in the context of the company or the organisation until now, so they don't really have individual abilities or specialist skills. There is nothing that they have that is common to all companies, their skills are specific to one company. So the structure is such that they have to stay in the same company to make use of the skills that they have. That is all changing now of course. If they are just working within one company the whole focus is on getting up the ladder there, so they have no ability to make dramatic new changes. That goes for the president as well. There are really no cases where the president is recruited from outside in the Japanese case. They all come up from below. They can only express their abilities in one context. They know the thinking, organisation, structure, way to proceed, methods of one company like the back of their hand.

The salesmen were very conscious of the fact that they were unable to transfer jobs easily. It was the main factor that heightened their tension about the situation of C-Life.

As I indicated in the last section, many people are now starting to learn as many specialist skills as possible. Some of my dōki were studying after work in preparation for a possible job change. One dōki in particular was studying every night at a specialist school to learn to draw cartoons. He quit the company a few months after my fieldwork to follow full-time what had been a passion since his high-school days.

> J: I think that the people in C-Life still don't change jobs because it is a matter of skills. Unfortunately they don't have the skills to change. If they only did sales all the way along or if they have only done clerical work all the way along in the present Japanese environment they don't have the skills to change.

The employees are aware of the hand that the company has had in choosing the careers of employees who have turned out to be 'lucky' or 'unlucky'. But on the whole, apart from commenting on that fact, employees had little to say about the matter. There was an air of resignation; that was simply the way each person's career had turned out.

Interestingly, in discussing this issue with the NHK crew while I was filming C-Life, they noted that in NHK, where the life-time employment system is still followed to a greater degree than in C-Life, and which has a more rigid bureaucracy, the question of skills had caused great conflict with the life-time employment system. When television first began, NHK hired university graduates from the best universities by means of exam, and assigned them randomly to be camera crew or to be directors and producers, as these were seen to involve equal skills. It was not foreseen at the time that the industry would divide into blue-collar technicians (cameramen) and white-collar directors. Although the policy of taking university graduates as cameramen had long since changed, the very first generation that had been taken on were still inside NHK, working as cameramen under the direction of university graduate directors, who were in some cases 20 or more years younger than them. In such cases, the directors had to exercise endless care in terms of language, and treatment of the older men, whose careers had been entirely a matter of fate.

> J: It just happens that, if by chance, there is someone like me who speaks some English and knows about overseas and knows about investments they have some chance to change jobs. It just happens to be that kind of world now. I don't know how it will change from now on but people who have done office work all the way along might become valuable assets in another age. The kind of people who can do the accounting for the back office – practical management for security companies, etc., those kind of people that I just mentioned – are in demand so in that sense I think there are people who have been lucky and people who have not been lucky.

The C-Life salesmen were not only less able than other employees to transfer easily to other companies, they also had increasingly less chance of being promoted to the very top of the company. In 1985, it was advantageous to have a good sales record in order to advance to top management. But this had changed, and employees seemed to think that now it was better to have been in a number of different positions inside the head office. In other words, it was now better to have a number of skills that would allow one to transfer jobs easily than to have a good track record that would allow one a better and more secure position in one's current company.

> W: Top salesmen have a low chance of getting ahead in the company; they lose to generalists (employees inside the head office) in the end.

> T: I think it is really difficult to have a management person or a business person [keiei man] at the helm of the company. But I think that this age is a little different now in that it is hard to just have a salesman at the helm. It is not an age any more where you can just sell and that is enough. Although, it is true to say that how much you sold during training does determine your path inside the company in the future. The people that were moved to the sales areas straight from training are people – not necessarily those who could sell a lot themselves – but the types of people who could get the sales people in the offices to go out and get a lot of insurance in. And increase their results. Those kinds of people go up in the company. I think that that is quite clear.

Employees who were connected with the union told me that the issue of employees' skills was one of the union's concerns. As we saw in Chapter 3, one of the C-Life's union's main priorities is to ensure that employees have stable employment, and, if they are unable to do that, then to find new jobs for the employees who have to leave. The union was concerned in 1999 about how to train employees in C-Life in such a way that their training was not company-specific. In this way, they could protect employees from redundancy if they were forced to leave the company.

> A: The theme now is how to make people that are useful no matter to where they are transferred. It would be the best if people inside C-Life were equally useful wherever they went. It would be really hard if it were the case that people who had been working in C-Life were no good anywhere else. So the union asks the company how best to educate employees really well. I think that that is the present style.

The company has been forced to begin to hire specialists from other companies in response to the need for these people, especially in the investment field. This is partly due to the general, sales-related nature of C-Life's own training, as we saw earlier in this chapter. During the recession the employing of skilled transferees has been put on hold to some degree while retrenching is carried out. But it is generally assumed that any recovery in the economy will sharply increase the need for specialists once again. One employee commented:

> C: It takes about ten years to raise a specialist inside the company. And over 100 million yen. So even if you have to pay 30 million yen to get someone to join you, it is still cheaper for the company. In the case of a Japanese company, the pension and social insurance that the company has to pay on behalf of the employee adds up to more than twice as much as his yearly salary. So if someone is getting 10 million yen in salary they are costing the company over 20 million yen. In the first year in the company the salary is around 200,000 yen or 3 or 4 million yen a year. So for the company from day one it is already costing them 8 million yen a year to keep that employee. And that adds up over ten years to at least 150 million yen or so. So it is much better to get specialists from outside.

The changes in life-time employment promise to have enormous implications for the education system, which is no longer producing the type of people that companies necessarily wish to hire. Students are now looking ahead and predicting that getting into a top-name school will no longer be sufficient to ensure employability on graduation.

> P: Now there is more weight on increasing emphasis on practical business skills or specialist knowledge, so they are looking at how, in good training schools, to make people more skilled, and by which methods. And even if it is great to get into schools that are prestigious, like Azabu or Kaisei, it is now the issue that that isn't all there is in life. And that is true. Things there have really changed.

Promotion and demotion

More changes are taking place in the life-time employment system in the area of promotion. The breaking down of the seniority system means that the employees feel great pressure not to be left behind their dōki. But how do people actually get promoted or demoted?

> H: It is the special characteristic of Japan that they want everyone to get the same results together. They organise things so there are no laggers [ochikobore]. They bring up the guys who are falling behind. The talented guys help the ones falling behind. They want everyone to get equal results. It is a primitive kind of communism. But in actual fact the guys that can do that are the ones that can already fulfil their own work quota. In reality, it is the guys who can do it should be getting more pay but they just do more and more work to cover for the guys who can't do it. The guys who can't do it can just hang about. If you ask them about the company, they say what a great company it is. They say it is comfortable like a warm bath and they are dependent and indulgent [amai]. There are a lot of people hanging about but the pay is the same even though the able guys are working their hardest [gangan yatte iru no ni].

Promotion often accompanies a transfer to a new division. For example, when the company needs an employee to handle the new area of international loans, an employee of the appropriate age with experience in planning, finance and sales is promoted into the international section. The company needs to co-ordinate the career ladders of all its employees carefully with promotions and the availability of new positions. As the company generally tries not to promote younger men above their elders, the co-ordination of personnel movements is a very complicated business indeed. Now that employees can no longer be relied upon to remain with the company indefinitely, this is becoming even harder.

Promotion is often associated with showing initiative, or using one's special skills in a selfless way, to help the company without thought of reward. The mid-career transferees in the international department had particular scope to do this, as they had skills that other employees lacked. They were relatively competent in English already, as were the new graduates entering in 1985, and English conversation classes were attended by all members of the international investment division, including the female office staff. Very few staff in the company as a whole had any familiarity with computers or word processors, and there were very few machines available for use in 1985, but employees were praised for developing new computer applications for their work. One employee, a graduate of American Literature, developed a program for the international department into which share prices were input daily and which produced a table displaying profit and loss details. In 1985, the development of programs like this was left entirely to the initiative of individual employees, and self-generated ideas like this were a large factor in promotion. The bosses in the international department did not have the expertise to design such new programs themselves. Therefore, new innovations in work invariably came up from the bottom ranks.

At the beginning of their careers in 1985, all my dōki made the first promotion after two years of training; but, as time goes on, the gaps between the dōki who are the first to be promoted and those who are promoted last to the same level become wider and wider. This is caused by various factors: the differing degrees of initiative shown by different people, differing ambitions, differing abilities and so on. For the international department respondents in 1992 the following career gaps between dōki were reported:

For someone who had been in the company for:

3 years	No difference
7 years	2 years' difference
10 years	3 years' difference
12 years	5 years' difference
19 years	10 years' difference
24 years	16 years' difference

Although the nihonjinron literature at the time largely gave the idea that Japanese are promoted automatically, the actual figures for C-Life showed a different picture.

In the survey I conducted in 1992, five members of the international division at that time said that they would like to end up as department heads and believed they would be able to reach this level. Seven said they would like to be directors or department heads but thought they would only be able to reach the level below the one they wanted to attain. This reflects the reality of large numbers of people vying for the same positions. Rohlen estimated that at Uedagin one in thirty would reach the position of chief, and only one in a hundred would become department head. The case in C-Life was similar at that time. Since then, the situation has become even more severe. The enormity of the task a new recruit faces if he wants to make this level was reflected in what one respondent said when I asked what level in the company he would like to reach. His despondent answer was, 'I have 80 dōki. I have no idea what level I can reach.'

As in many large Japanese companies, C-Life's president in 1985 was the oldest man in the company. The vice-president was two years younger. This in effect means that the president was the only 'survivor' of his year's influx of recruits. Competition in the C-Life hierarchy leads to one either being ousted at the minimum retirement age or being promoted to department head, being ousted at some time beyond that or being promoted, being ousted or finally remaining to become president. The minimum retirement age in a Japanese company is very young compared to most Western countries. This gives the company the earliest possible opportunity to ease out workers who do not merit higher office. The vast majority of workers do not want to retire at such a young age and devote a great deal of effort to being considered for promotion so that they can stay beyond retirement age. The resulting competition is fierce. This competition begins the day an employee enters the company, and goes on until the very end, intensifying as the numbers of dōki dwindle and the pyramid gets more and more narrow. However, this competitiveness is rarely evident on the surface, an example of honne and tatemae I have alluded to already. This implies that the 'harmony' so often mentioned in the literature is nothing more than a tatemae to conceal the ruthless competition beneath.

My dōki freely spoke of who among them was still a top leadership candidate. After the large restructuring in 1999, they occasionally described one employee as the 'sole' remaining candidate for president among the dōki, the other potential candidates having all left the company. When I interviewed him, though, he emphasised the fact that everyone has an equal chance to become president:

Q: Does top management tell leadership candidates that that is what they are?

A: Well, everyone that has entered in the general worker category is... but, not everyone is aware of being a leadership candidate. But there are some categories of work where it is impossible to become leaders. That is one point. So at least all the general workers are on the same start line to be leadership candidates at the beginning.

The employees now accept that the promotion system is becoming more flexible, giving talented people more scope to be promoted ahead of their contemporaries.

This is in part due to the influence of foreign management systems. The following insightful comment, for example, is from a former employee who spent considerable time in America.

> J: In Japan, the concepts of 'fair' [this is in English] and 'equality' [kōhei] are completely different. In many foreign countries apart from Japan they start out at the same starting point. They say that fair is when the environment is the same for each company but in the Japanese case fair means everybody shares the same amount after something has been achieved. Because everyone is dōki he and I should have the same amount. Dividing things into equal portions is called fair and that is the concept that is still in place. And that can't be overthrown easily. It is difficult to emerge from that situation. If everyone came to the same understanding that fair means that the starting point is fair and that people who try really hard get more as the result of that and people who don't try can't get money. People with ability can get lots; people without ability can't get much. They have to. If they are able to accept this kind of thinking, Japanese society will become better... Japanese companies will become better. I think that the management will become better; that the earnings will increase, that companies will acquire competitive strength.

What of demotion? This is a subtle matter in the company, and may have been overlooked in earlier literature. Employees do not actually have their rank reduced, but they may be shifted to jobs that, although equal in formal ranking to their old jobs, actually carry less status. For example, C-Life has one department with jurisdiction over such employees as the drivers, cleaners, security people and so on. The manager of this department was frequently pointed out to me in 1985 as an example of what happens to unmotivated employees. By being made manager of this unglamorous department, the man was not demoted formally in terms of rank, but the section itself signified demotion. The manager concerned might be transferred back to a 'better' department once he had done his time.

Transfers to highly undesirable positions have not always been recognised in the literature for what they often clearly were – demotions. By 1999, the situation had changed as large-scale restructuring was brought in, but the point here is that even in 1985, demotion did actually exist in large-scale Japanese companies like C-Life. It was concealed by the tatemae of retaining the same formal rank even though one had been moved to an inferior post.

Leaving

Having discussed how employees enter the company and change ranks within it, it is natural to turn our attention to methods of leaving.

Employees leave C-Life for a variety of reasons. Of my dōki, all of the five women hired in the same category as men left within five years, as we saw in Chapter 3. Some left because they had got married (two of them were married to fellow company men). But by 1999, fully 30 of the original 50 dōki had left the company. Employees who left the company were very careful about how they went about it. In many cases they told nobody until the last possible moment. They invariably turned down their colleagues' offers to hold goodbye parties for them. And after they left the company, many of them – especially those who left of their own accord – were careful not to be negative about the company. We have already encountered the negative attitudes many employees held towards transferees, and this goes some way to explaining this – they did not want to seem disloyal. Employees may also feel betrayed by their dōki who quit, because of the strong bonds formed in the training centre. We have seen that these bonds are very personal: trainees feel personally indebted to their colleagues with whom they struggled through the harsh conditions. In such circumstances, we may suppose that it is not unnatural for some to feel betrayed by those who choose to leave.

Q: It is very Japanese that you won't say anything bad about C-Life clearly!

J: Well, it is difficult to say because a bankruptcy for C-Life would be a very bad thing and I most definitely don't want to say anything bad about C-Life. And also it is a matter of human relations. Because I was in C-Life for ten years there are a lot of people who I am really really close to. And when I came to quit I felt in some sense that I was betraying those people by quitting. I felt it hard to tear away – a strong reluctance to leave.

Other members of the company had the following to say about this former employee:

Q: How did everyone take it when J left?

T: Well, I had already heard about it. When he came back from New York, I knew what kind of work he was doing. And I knew that he was doing a different kind of work from what he really wanted to do. As far as our company goes, when he came back from New York there were positions that he would rather have been in – he had been in New York for four years – but they wouldn't let him do what he wanted to do. So what he had been doing in New York, and what he was doing when he came back to Japan, were completely different. So, in that sense, I think that he wanted to go a little bit more to achieve in the area that he had already been working in. I think that was the issue. He saw me before he quit. I don't know if we really talked about it that much, but I think that what I just said was the point. I don't think that he quit because he disliked our company. I think that he quit because there were other things that he wanted to do. And that is why he went to his present company. And I think that is a good thing because he is doing something that really motivates him [yarigai no aru shigoto]. However, if we had used him a little bit differently, I think that we could probably have kept him all the way through in our company.

X: He [J] is a really talented guy. Well, I think that it is really true that to let guys like him go is a real waste for the company. I think that is really huge. Among my dōki, there are now 31 or 32. But because really talented guys are disappearing it has been quite tough [kitsukatta]. But they have their lives to lead and things that they want to do [yaritai koto ga]. If you ask how you can stop them, well, all of them have found things that they really want to do elsewhere. So, I think that all you can do is respect their feelings. I think there are a few people that quit the company because they didn't like the company. Well, there might be some like that... But even among other companies... but if that is the case, it is better for them themselves that they go to a company that matches them better.

P: In five or ten years in the future – well, maybe there aren't people that think that far ahead but without exaggerating it could easily become like that – there is a lot of talk about whether we are actually going to be able to get our pensions, and I am of the generation that is right at that stage so I really do have insecurity on that level. So what do I think about people who are leaving C-Life and have places to go, people like J? Well, I think there are people who feel a lot of discomfort about that [fuyūkai]. He was really very careful in his dealings about the way that he quit [ki o tsukatta]. He didn't want to tell people openly about where he was going until he actually quit. I think that is the same in everyone's case. There are no people who actually walk around the company and talk about where they are going to go next after they quit, so in that sense so I think that J felt that he was doing something underhand or of a guilty conscience; but as far as he himself goes it is like he has crossed a new border. So I think there are both positives and negatives about moving. Towards the company and towards their acquaintances [nakama] I think people like that feel quite guilty. If you try and give them a sending-away party they say, 'Thank you very much,' but they turn it down out of respect for people's feelings [enryo suru].

At the first dōkikai, or party for the dōki, that I attended when I started negotiations to film C-Life, I found out that one of my dōki had had a serious rift with some of the others who had left the company. He had actually refused for five years to talk to two dōki who had left the company in their third year, because he saw their action as a betrayal of the company. The words used were invariably 'we feel as though we have been betrayed by dōki who quit' (uragirareta yo na kimochi da). Accordingly, there was a big issue for a number of years about whether people who had quit the company would be invited to the dōkikai. To begin with they were not, and they responded by organising an 'uradōkikai' – a 'shadow dōki gathering' only for themselves, and didn't invite current company members.

However, since then, as we have seen, employees have become a lot more tolerant of other members who quit. And management no longer feel so strongly that these employees have betrayed the company and squandered the investment that was made in them. Instead, they accept that some people do not 'fit' into a certain environment and should find one in which they do fit. This concept of 'fitting' with an environment is a very crucial one. It poses a key question for the middle generation, and indeed, it is their stance on this question that divides the older generation from the younger generation in C-Life. Does one attempt to search for a working environment in which one 'fits', or should one make oneself 'fit' the environment one is already in? To realise that some employees may not 'fit' the company was a major shift in a fundamental attitude for the C-Life employees of the middle generation.

> T: People who are really talented can show their talents wherever they go, basically. It is part of the company's strategy or strength to have talented people, I believe. You have to gather them together, then bring them up, then use them, then bring them up some more... And it's a continuation of that. In order to bring people up in the company [ikusei saseru tame ni]... well, it is not just a case of putting the right man in the right post. If a person fits then that is okay, but if he doesn't fit [hamaranai], then it would be increasingly hard for him to develop.

The younger generation's opinion is more clear-cut. If the company they are in does not suit them, they will go and find somewhere with a better 'fit'. This attitude is accompanied by the idea that work positions and personal development can proceed at different paces, creating a gap between expectation and reality.

> J: I had the idea that I would quit the company for a long time. This was probably two or three years after I got into the company. I thought I would quit if, after absorbing various things from the company, I reached the stage where I could no longer absorb anything new from the company. In the recruitment talks that they do for new company employees, I remember saying something like this to one of the students I had to talk to. I said it is possible I might not be in the company six months from now. If I can't grow any more from being in this company I would go to another company that would stretch me more and would develop my strengths, if there is such a place. It is something that you really shouldn't tell students, but I would say things like that without hesitation.

They are sometimes impatient with the slow and long-term pace of development in C-Life. They realise that the world is changing, and feel great pressure to be in the right place at the right time. The pressure of being able to move only when young adds to the sense of urgency. Here, we see again the feeling of change and uncertainty in the younger generation.

> J: The reason that I switched my thinking was because Japanese management – not only limited to C-Life but all Japanese financial institutions regardless of which one and which company – they are all old-style thinking. Life is short and 36 or 37 is the last chance to move company, so I pulled out the pegs and changed [omoikitte kawatta to].

> J: As to how the remaining dōki in C-Life think of me, perhaps – and while I have not asked them directly – they probably think that I was successful in achieving a magnificent job change. The place is good – well, it is not really magnificent – and I would not want to say it in a loud voice but my pay has not changed a lot from

C-Life. Normally, for investment banking in Goldman Sachs or Salomon Brothers, if you go there you would get two or three times the C-Life salary at the least or maybe even more. Where I am now is not that kind of world, but perhaps my dōki think that it is like that anyway, and they are jealous.

Other reasons for changing are simply because of the environment and the company's position. The insurance market is totally saturated, with more than 90 per cent of Japanese households signed up with life insurance. The salesmen are being given quite unrealistic sales targets. C-Life's income from new policies had been decreasing by as much as 20 per cent per annum in the period immediately preceding my fieldwork. And consumers are simply not spending, having become deeply distrustful of the finance industry in general since the bubble.

> I: I think that the main reason that people started quitting is because the environment for sales in the life insurance industry is extremely harsh. So there were probably people who couldn't handle that. It is really hard to get by in the sales world. So some people, for whom work didn't go as expected, gave up and changed to other paths.

However, personal position is crucial in deciding whether one has the practical ability to leave. In particular, housing loans are closely tied up with the company. If employees own their own houses, they have usually had their loans guaranteed by the company or have borrowed the money through company-related institutions. Leaving would mean having to transfer the loan to the new company, so they would need to have the next job decided before quitting C-Life. Marriage, children, and the financial ties to the company create additional hindrances to changing companies.

T is one of my dōki who quit the company shortly after he divorced and found himself with no ties once again.

> T: I was in the company until July of 1999. I quit the company cleanly and abruptly [assari to iu kanji desu ne]. I quit the company of my own accord for personal reasons [jiko tsugō]. There wasn't any special reason. It just somehow happened... [nan to naku].

> T: C-Life actually pulled out of the work that I was doing last of all in the company. So I thought that if I quit at the same time that C-Life had just pulled out of the job, I wouldn't cause them any trouble by suddenly pulling out. So I chose that time to quit. Well, it is a lie to say that I have security now but I am a bachelor and I have no loans at all so it was easy for me to move. I knew that it would be really hard to change jobs but I thought that I could do anything if it means doing that to survive. So because I felt happy doing anything I was able to come to the decision.

Moreover, the ability to leave is very dependent on age. The older employees in C-Life were, the more they realised that C-Life was their only practical choice.

Y: I don't know if I would move if the conditions were better somewhere else. At this age it is almost certain that those better conditions don't exist anywhere else. There are definite age limits.

There is extremely strong family pressure to stay inside C-Life. My respondents gave in to this pressure to varying degrees. In some cases, as is common in Japan, parents were living with employees in a three-generation family situation. In these cases, pressure was stronger. Wives, on the contrary, seem to exert much less pressure. Employees reported that their wives were generally uninterested in the type of work that they changed to, provided that the disruption to the family was minimal and the quality of life didn't drop. We shall see later that employees typically keep their home and work lives quite separate, and wives rarely take much interest in work affairs. The following is representative of the attitudes of C-Life wives.

J: I have one daughter and my wife said that if what I am doing is going to be good for her and my daughter then it is OK with her. She didn't ask about any of the details.

Firing

Not everyone chooses to leave the company voluntarily. The peculiarities of Japanese firing techniques illustrate very well some of the themes we have already seen, such as groupism and the ideal of loyalty to the company.

We have already heard about the major restructuring plan announced in 2000 by C-Life's management. However, this was simply the latest in a series of moves responding to the worsening economic climate. This began half-way through the 1990s in a number of steps. The retirement age was successively lowered and there were a number of bonus reductions and actual pay-cuts of increasing severity. In 1999 there was the largest pay-cut to date – 6 per cent across the board for all employees. Finally, in 2000, towards the end of my fieldwork, a vast restructuring happened in which a full third of the workforce was laid off. Large-scale restructuring had already become commonplace among large Japanese companies, but one on this scale was virtually unprecedented.

At earlier times, employees who had been judged superfluous were encouraged to leave. Various degrees of pressure existed: being sent to subsidiaries, being asked to retire early, and eventually being asked to find one's own job if the company went on paying the bulk of the salary for a certain period (kobetsu shukkō). Now, however, the process occurred *en masse*. The restructuring of C-Life at that particular time smelt of panic. It was very sudden and large-scale. The brunt of the restructuring fell on those who were older, who had higher pay-packets, women, and those who had transferred into the company mid-career.

H: I really didn't think it would be like that at all – to be suddenly asked to leave. It was unexpected. I think that it was probably decided in a hurry as far as I could see. They suddenly decided that they had to reduce personnel and that they had to reduce personnel in the head office. So in the head office if there was someone who had reasonable results and wanted to go to the investment subsidiary they thought that they should let him go there, but in that case there would be too many people in the investment subsidiary and they had to start thinking about who had to leave the company altogether – it was a case of last in first out that occurred.

On the whole, both those employees who had been asked to leave and those still inside accepted that the company had to restructure. The company president had announced in speeches that it was inevitable, and there was a general realisation that it had now come to this, and was unavoidable.

Even those who were now out of C-Life and happy in their new jobs told me that they would not have changed jobs unless there had been pressure to do so. This was especially so for those older than 40, almost all of whom had hoped to end their days in C-Life. This reflects the fact that the system of life-time employment is still retained as an ideal, even when it no longer entirely matches reality, as we have seen earlier in this chapter. It is connected to the feelings of loyalty to the company that we shall see recurring throughout these chapters.

> H: The reason that I changed to a venture company like the one I am in now is because of outside pressure. If there hadn't been that kind of personnel order for me to leave the company, I would probably have gone on doing the same kind of thing inside C-Life. Because I was doing that and getting paid I thought it was okay like that. But there was outside pressure and I had to go and look for my own job. So I said OK and did as they asked.

Where resentment was expressed, it was invariably at the fact that, because of the role of the personnel department in employee transfers, it was impossible to tell why exactly any one person had been asked to leave, or who had made the decision. That made it impossible to seek any kind of recourse, or to argue against the decision. Also, respondents reported that there was considerable pressure placed on those who were tardy in submitting their 'voluntary resignations' as the company asked. Such pressure often took the form of being asked to transfer to departments where most people would be unwilling to work. For example, we heard of one employee who was given a transfer to a branch in the northern-most island of Hokkaidō, to a remote country branch where the official job title was sales branch head, but the actual job was door-to-door sales since there were no other employees in the office.

Employees expressed frustration with these strategies and with the lack of responsibility shown by management who failed to be open about the reasons for decisions. Those who lost out in the restructuring invariably wanted clear standards applied and explanations offered as to why one person was fired, and under what circumstances they should be allowed to remain.

> V: It would really be the best situation if salary men got their salary and were doing their work simply in return for that. It would be much better if you knew clearly what

kind of costs a person was incurring and against those costs what kind of pay a person needed to get or was able to get from the company. Without making anything difficult or complicated. Rather than because a person has gone up through the seniority system, chasing and forcing them into a windowside seat. There is no need to do complicated or weird [kiki] things. It is bad for the mental state of both sides [seishin jōtai]. You should just determine who is equal to how much money. So if you leave, then I think it would be better if you determined the costs of a job and told a person if they wanted to apply for it they could and if they didn't they could leave. And from the people that applied for the job you could choose one. I think it would be better to make the standards like that.

The company still only 'requested' resignation. However, there was considerable pressure to comply, including emotional blackmail. The person is often 'requested' to quit in order to protect the company, in order to protect others, because he is in a stronger position than other employees in the company. Appeal is thus made to the employee's sense loyalty to his company and his friends, the loyalty that was inculcated so strongly during the training period.

> V: From the beginning, there is no such thing as 'cutting' people in the company [kiru to iu no wa nai no de]. They say, 'If you could possibly, could you not please quit?'

> P: They actually say, 'If this and this are the conditions, could you possibly consider quitting?'

> V: It is not as if they nominate a name and tell them that they must quit. It is after they advertise for candidates wanting to quit in a Japanese corporation.

> P: At such a time they would sit someone down and say, 'Well, you are living in a very large house, and you won't have any problem eating, isn't that the case?' That is actually a common way in which they say it.

> V: Are there any Japanese corporations at all where they name people and fire them?

> P: I don't think there are any like that. It is called 'requested resignation' [kibō taishoku]. So requested resignation... when they talk about who might be able to do that, then it is people who might have the ability to provide for their own livelihoods or people that have the ability to change jobs. So it is people who are 'travelling light' [kigaru]; without accompanying families or obligations.

Thus, until the very end, a kind of groupism prevails, with the departing members being asked to be sacrifice themselves for the sake of the group. Far-fetched though it may sound, one employee who was asked to quit because he was 'travelling light' told me that he felt that his sacrifice would be worthwhile if the company as a whole survived. It does not follow, of course, that he really felt this; perhaps this was tatemae, unmatched by the underlying honne.

What of the point of view of the personnel department and management? They have quite a different view of the lack of clarity surrounding who is on the restructuring list. Being faced with someone who is not up to the job and who cannot be directly fired puts management in an awkward position.

> I: If someone's really bad, and impossible to evaluate at all, then it's really difficult to do anything with those people, so it's a big problem. You can't make them quit. If the guy himself wants to quit, it's OK, but if he has no ability and produces no results and he goes on sitting in the company, it's a big problem. Until now, in the seniority system, I think it was unavoidable that there were people who sat there without ability. But the concept of seniority employment has become weaker [usurete iru]. So there are people who retire from the company early, and there are also people who remain in the company. And it's probably a question of the difference in ability.

Previously, such people were just left inside the company in peripheral positions where they retained their positions and pay-packets but were given a minimum of work and responsibility . They were known as 'madogiwazoku', or 'window-sitters'. But in the present climate, it is no longer possible to allow madogiwazoku to remain in the company, and there is considerable pressure on management to ensure that the quota of people to quit by a certain date, which has been decided by the personnel department, is filled.

> X: If someone won't quit of their own accord, we discuss things with them, and listen to their feelings. And, on the basis of those feelings, they quit the company [hanashiai o shite, honnin no kimochi de motte kaisha o yamete iku to iu ka]. They talk directly with the personnel department, or a discussion ensues when that person has come of their own accord for advice. We can advise them that they are not very suited to the company, so it would be better if they went elsewhere; but it is left up to their own decision. The company can't say, in a one-sided statement, that they should quit. So some of them cling on to the company [shigami tsuku]. I wonder what should be done about that. Should we do the kind of restructuring that has been done lately? Well, maybe not something of that scale. But maybe something that takes each individual case by case... now that it's an age when the company must be able to use its employees efficiently.

Retiring

The third way to leave the company is simply to reach retirement age. I have noted already that the retirement age in Japan is younger than in many other countries, and so most employees are very keen to advance to a higher position in the company to avoid having to retire.

Retired employees of C-Life range from maintaining very close relations with the company to having none at all.

C: After retiring there are guys who stay really closely involved with the company and those who don't, like me, and just do what they like doing. I have had nothing at all to do with the company since I retired.

I: I still have quite close connections with the company – there is an OB (old boys') group which meets together, so I go to those events and hear about the company's present condition, and the latest news. Or we deepen the friendship among the people who used to work together. So the gatherings are for that purpose as well. They have such gatherings about three times a year. I wonder how many per cent of the OBs actually get together for those? In Tōkyō perhaps about 30 per cent? A short while ago, there was an end-of-year party, and 250 people got together for that, to deepen their friendship and to hear about the conditions of the company from the president.

When I met with some of the retired members of the company, we met at a company 'club'. The doorman addressed the ex-employee by his former title in the company, and so did other company employees and ex-employees whom we met inside the club. Status in Japan is intricately tied up with position inside a company, and it seems that the men enjoy being able to re-live their former lives.

I: There are a lot of people who keep their relations with the company going even after retirement. Even when they go to play mahjong it is with ex-company members. I don't know if that is a good or a bad thing. I have a lot of other people around me so I don't know what to say about that... Those people are eternally anchored to the company. There is a real family ideology going. I personally am not really into that but I don't feel that it is a bad thing, either.

How best to spend the years after retirement is a big issue in Japan, and one that is constantly covered by the media. Retired people in Japan hold a large proportion of the country's savings, and retirement is long because they are one of the longest-living peoples among advanced economies, yet retirement age has become younger and younger since the collapse of the bubble. The older respondents have often been rather surprised by retirement. They have not really thought about stopping work, and lack well-formed plans about how to live the rest of their lives.

It is a well-reported phenomenon in the media that newly retired men keep getting in the way of their wives, who have formulated their own busy lives at home during the years that their husbands have been away working. These men are dubbed 'washimozoku' ('me too men') because whenever their wives prepare to go out they say, 'well, I'll go too,' since they have nothing else to do.

H: There is a phenomenon of wives divorcing their husbands as soon as they have retired and got their lump-sum pension payment. That is because they are in the house all the time. It is unfortunate that most people who have been constricted in the company for a long time don't have any network outside the company. And there are limits to how positively they can create such a network. For a person who has been 100 per cent involved in the company – when the company says, 'Well, it is the end of your employment,' and they have to retire, their social network was only in the company so if that disappears they have nothing at all. So they don't know what to do and they are just lounging around the house all the time. So they are nuisances to their families and their wives and their families get irritated with them. And they begin to fight with, and part with, their wives.

However, the present generation who have just retired or are preparing to retire seems to have more clearly thought-out ideas about their retirement in C-Life. This retiree had in fact contributed to a book on the subject:

> I: I retired from the company last year in July. Retired people are usually going to spend from about 60 to 80 years old in retirement. People usually live until about 80 now. So if you think about that, people live about 20 more years after they retire, so the big question is how are you going to live meaningfully during those 20 years? If you take away the time that you need for your daily life – for eating and sleeping – you still have ten hours of free time a day and if you count that over 20 years then you have a 100,000 hours. How are you going to spend the hundred thousand hours in a healthy and enjoyable way? I decided to live my second life in a country house and I moved down here [to a house on the sea coast an hour or two from Tōkyō].

Evaluation

One theme which has recurred throughout this chapter is the way in which the company evaluates employees, and here I consider what the employees think of the system.

Employees were ambiguous about the place of skills and ability in evaluation. Invariably, employees who liked another employee would praise him in terms of skills, and denigrate those they disliked in terms of luck. In other words, they would see people they liked as getting ahead in the company on their abilities, and those they disliked as getting ahead on their strategies or human relations or by manipulating bosses.

> H: The reason I evaluate Q highly is because even though he was in the domestic section for so long, when he came to the international section he made a vocabulary list and studied it earnestly. I think he is really talented so he was able to catch up really soon. But most people are not like that; they can't do that. I'm a meritorian [nōryokushugisha]. I don't think that companies should ever try for anything else.

In practice, as we saw in the previous chapter, the formal evaluation of employees is made by the personnel system in conjunction with the department heads in each department. The records of evaluation remain in the personnel section and only personnel section staff of a certain level or higher have access to people's records.

People who are working in the personnel department are obviously in relatively powerful positions, but few employees told me of information concerning evaluation coming out as gossip from employees working in the personnel section. It seemed to be a code of honour for those employees not to speak about records. The employees whom I asked about this told me that they had never directly asked dōki working in the personnel department about people's records, ostensibly because they knew it would put them in a difficult position.

Also, because of the system of rotation, most employees working inside the personnel section are moved every two or three years. So even though these employees might have an insight into other employees' careers at the time they were inside the personnel section, their knowledge quickly loses currency once they are stationed outside again. So no one person in the company is in a strong enough position substantially to influence any other person's career single-handedly.

Because employees in C-Life are accustomed to lack of clarity in evaluation there was a sense of resignation even from those who had been laid off without clearly knowing the reasons why.

> H: What did I feel about the fact that my results for three years were not at all recognised by the personnel department? I thought they shouldn't do something really stupid like that. As a management move, however, because it's a Japanese company, after three years they change everybody because that's the general timing of it. That was the Japanese way of doing things until now and in that sense it wasn't really an unnatural move.

I found, however, that C-Life employees were quite vocal in their criticism of a system where evaluation criteria are very unclear. This was the same almost across the board, yet the criticisms were voiced with an air of resignation as most realised that they could do very little about changing the situation. But at the same time, they also admitted that from the standpoint of being bosses, it was much easier to have a vague system than clear-cut standards. They often expressed to me, however, a certain envy of other professions or even of the sales staff for having clear criteria against which to perform.

The system of evaluation is not uniform throughout the company. In some departments, the criteria are clearer than others.

> Y: It is not only investment-related work that is very logical in C-Life though. I was in the section where they calculate salaries and that was also very logical. They had strict standards as to how they calculated each person's worth and applied it to their salaries.

Some of the branch heads also said that they preferred being in the branches to the central office, since at least the insurance sales each month were charted and clear and they knew how their own performance was. This reflects what we have already seen in discussing the union and people's reasons for entering C-Life: they hope for security.

In the limited situations in C-Life where pay was clear, the employees found satisfaction in this system.

> E: Bonuses differ by some tens of thousands of yen from the best to the worst in dōki. That is a difference of about a million yen per year. We know roughly because the bonus is at the level of A to E. There are five different levels so you know which one your own bonus is. People don't work in order to get a bigger bonus but it feels good to get a good bonus. It is the feeling that your work has been evaluated highly that is good.

Criticism centred around the fact that, in practice, evaluation often depends on such criteria as how long a person has been in the company.

> P: It's really impossible in the Japanese system, to push someone talented up [more quickly] and make him assistant department head, for whatever reason. It's really difficult. I wonder why we can't do that? I think it would be better if we could do that, but for some reason we can't do that.
>
> V: I don't think we're used to evaluating people or being evaluated, both of them. It's probably because it's just easier to evaluate people on age.
>
> P: Yes, that's probably the case. In that sense, age is probably easier. There's quite a strong focus on how long a person has been here in evaluation. That's probably the strongest focus. So being in the company a long time equals loyalty. The company thinks that, although that's not necessarily the case.

Employees – especially those who had not been valued highly – complained bitterly about the subjectivity of assessment in C-Life.

> H: Stupid guys would get to be section chiefs ahead of us. I was the last to be promoted. I was beaten by W because I was overseas. If you are overseas, you aren't directly under the eyes of the department head in Japan. Your results don't matter if you are in Japan. The department head can like you and promote you but if he gets replaced then you are thrown out. It is really subjective. That is the same everywhere.

But the employees also recognise that, even with strict standards governing how a person's worth is measured, the ways that those standards are actually calculated and applied, in terms of job transfers and so on, and when deciding which section to post a person to, are ambiguous. In other words, even when evaluation is purported to be quantitative, employees recognise that bosses' evaluations are biased.

> W: There are two things in evaluation: qualitative and quantitative. That is a true evaluation. The qualitative part is subjective but the quantitative part also involves the subjectivity of the person who does the analysis. In quantitative analysis, there are figures involved so it is clear, but because the subjectivity of the department

head doing the analysis comes into it the qualitative part becomes really large pro-portionally when you consider promotion... It is the philosophy of the person who is doing the management and you get evaluated on those kinds of things where there are no figures involved. In the investment world it is said that the qualitative part is seven tenths and the quantitative part is three tenths. The Japanese com-pany has the same system but companies that are growing evaluate people more objectively.

What the qualitative part is actually about is detailed in the comments below.

Q: So what is the qualitative part about?

H: It is about a person's potential ability.

W: [It is about] personality, and if you are the organiser of the dōkikai you get a double tick because those people seem to have an ability to gather people around them or to unify people [torimatomeru]. In other words, they are people who are growing in terms of possibilities.

H: So the kind of guys that get ahead are the kind of guys who do the organisation at the dōkikai of their own accord because they know that is the way to get ahead. So although they don't have much ability, because they are good at getting the dōkikai together they get ahead.

Q: Like P who has been doing the organisation of the dōkikai for 14 years?

H: Yeah, it's guys like him who are comparatively fast to advance.

Here we see the importance of human relations for success in the company. This topic is discussed fully in Chapter 6. Here, I simply note that human relations are extremely important not only to smooth communication in the company but in order to set oneself up in a position to be advanced quickly. The more connections an employee has, and the more people who speak well of him, the more influence he gathers in C-Life. Where people move position every three years or so, almost everyone has either worked closely with a particular person or has worked with someone else who has.

C-Life employees tend to attribute the demise of Japanese management to the fact that it is not merit-based. This is particularly true of those who have been fired. Devaluing Japanese management serves a vital purpose in reducing psy-chological dissonance for those who feel that they have been hard done by. Thus, as the company adapts to changing economic conditions, so the attitudes of its employees change in response to conditions in the company.

H: But it is because Japanese companies weren't merit-based that they went down [dame ni natta]. If they had concentrated on being merit-based they would have become profitable... Because I was ahead in my ability at work it should have been easy to evaluate me but for Japanese it is the whole character and the person's whole life that come into the calculation. So I just couldn't be bothered with that. I thought that I couldn't go along with that [yatte irarenai]. Japan doesn't really accept differences. It would be better if they accepted more different kinds of people.

But from the point of view of management, it is easier to evaluate people who have been in the workforce their whole lives, on the basis of their characters and their overall long-term work performance. Management – and especially the personnel department – feel responsible for the performance of their juniors. Evaluating people on a long-term basis provides security that, should something go wrong, responsibility will not be directed back to the bosses who evaluated them.

> P: It's actually the people who are flitty [charan poran], but who do really good work, who are most difficult to fit into a mould. And it is being able to fit people into a mould or box [kata ni hameru] that gives people the most comfort or sense of safety [anshin]. So if it's a normal person, even if he does make a mistake or two, you can say that he's this kind of person, and that's why he was put in this kind of place in the company. And you can escape feeling responsible about why the situation ended up with him doing something silly.

The literature has often equated life-time employment with conformity, but, as will become increasingly clear, the most conforming members of C-Life are by no means the most successful. Being regarded as a member of the élite, or being a 'leadership candidate' (kanbu kōho), requires a curiously delicate balance of conformity together with qualities that make the employee stand out. Standing out usually means to stand out among one's dōki, because, at all levels of the company, this is how I found respondents referring to their colleagues. When I asked if they were good, or bad, or talented employees, people would answer, 'He is talented among his dōki because...'

> I: The basis for going up in the company was seniority because it is Japanese society. So you couldn't suddenly advance in the company just because you had good results. You had to advance while gathering a certain amount of experience [keiken o fumaenagara] and you were evaluated on what kind of results you had inside that framework and you advanced up the posts gradually. So in that kind of framework people with individuality and people with a concept of challenge towards the future were highly evaluated. We wanted the people we hired to work for all their 37 years inside the company and to finish with the company. We wanted them to work for the company for as long as possible so they could fully develop their abilities and be useful in developing C-Life. Those were the kinds of people that we wanted.

In actual fact, originality, and the courage to create a standpoint and stick to it, are highly valued. There has been a widespread concentration in the literature on Japanese management as a 'bottom-up' system where ideas are created by junior members of the company, and then presented to their seniors and implemented up through the ranks of the company. But I found that in C-Life this is the case only for some work. The majority of the work is routine, and the work practices surrounding this work are already put in place. This must be the case in any workplace. These previously set 'rules' and practices are mostly related from boss to junior and down through the ranks. The ideas that go from the bottom upwards, being approved by an employee's seniors, tend to be new and novel ideas that would change something already existing in the workplace. Implementation of the ideas goes by order from top to bottom. Because the bottom-up practices are generally new ideas, or ideas to improve or alter present practices in the workplace, originality and the ability to think ahead and to strategise is paramount. Also valued are the abilities to study other companies or trends in the industry and transfer their practices into the company.

However, having said that, getting innovative plans that come from bottom-up actually approved and implemented involves a lot of 'Japanese-style' strategies. As one employee related, it is crucial to introduce the idea to the right people at the right time through the correct routes. He pointed out that the idea has to appeal to the boss directly above; it can't go to a higher boss, skipping several levels, because then it would be difficult to gain the acceptance of those who had been bypassed. The idea is more likely to be accepted if it is to the advantage of the direct boss to accept it, and if it enhances his career and standing. The question of responsibility in the case of disaster is crucial. Ideas are more likely to be accepted if responsibility for an idea that backfires is diffuse or can be directly taken by a single employee willing to take the risk.

So to stand out and advance through the company, an employee must have more than just good ideas. He must be able to surf the complexities of the human relationships in the company and promote his idea in the correct fashion. Those who were pointed out to me in the company as examples of leadership candidates invariably combined these qualities of originality, individuality and strength of character with the ability to recognise and use the rules of the Japanese company correctly and, especially, to manipulate the rules to their advantage. In other words, they have to be able to strategise, and, in order to do so, be conscious of the rules that they are using.

However, because bottom-up ideas become changed and often unrecognisable as they rise through the company, and as responsibility for the ideas becomes diffused, it is then difficult to evaluate the ability of the various individuals who have contributed to them. As one employee said:

> I: So the real difficulty is how you find and pull out ability among that. If somebody has succeeded in a certain type of work, you have to find out who put that plan forward, and who co-operated in the plan, and who took the plan into effect. If the results of the work improve, and if the results of the section improve as well, you have to find out whether it was because the section chief was good, or because the assistant section chief was good, or because the people doing the actual clerical work put forward a good plan and everyone worked together to make it a

success. To see that kind of thing very clearly and to make that the basis of your evaluation – I think that should be the basis of standards of evaluation, to find out properly how results were made.

It is true that, as the life-time employment system disintegrates, evaluation has become more difficult because the time frames of employment are that much shorter. Employees expressed anxiety about this, and about the possibility of harsher and more random evaluations happening as the system changed towards a more Western system.

Conclusion

This chapter like Chapter 3 has not been intended as an exhaustive survey of most of the subjects covered. It has continued to introduce us to the most important elements of the company and company ideology, by examining in more detail some of the characteristics of a typical career in C-Life. In the next two chapters, I re-examine what we have already seen in more depth.

5   The company and life

In the last two chapters, I have described C-Life and the career path typically followed by its employees. In the process, we have learned about working life at the company. In this chapter, I examine working conditions in greater depth. What is it actually like to work at C-Life? What kind of hours are worked, and what do employees do in them? How do employees balance work and leisure time, and are they really happy in their work? Why do they work they way they do, and what do they hope to gain from it? In addressing these questions, I look ahead to Chapter 6, where I discuss human relations and the company ethos.

The C-Life employee

> H: As to what kind of person C-Life wanted, they want someone who has come in as a fresh graduate, who has been in the training place for a year and has done life insurance sales by going around door-to-door and house-to-house. Someone who has experienced great hardship during the training, and worked hard and studied finance, and then gone into the finance department; that is probably the most ideal type.

The employees devote much thought to the kind of employee that the company is looking for. But despite the ideal, the average employee in C-Life is not of a superhumanly dedicated worker who is prepared to give everything to his company. Rather, he is an average human being making the best of the situation in which he finds himself, looking positively towards finding meaning in his own existence, and doing a certain amount of rationalising about the negative aspects. Much of the individual's motivation can be explained as an attempt to find and maintain security. Insecurity is an important determiner of behaviour. And the best way to remain secure, as we shall see in the next section, is to attain as much status as possible. Status in the company does not apply only to the employee's position in the company – it determines his status in life. To gain status and to keep it, most C-Life employees are prepared to work hard.

Insecurity is however, ultimately also an economic threat as well as a psychological one. C-Life employees do not, on the whole, perceive themselves to be well off, because of both the exorbitant cost of living in Japan and the fact that most families have a single income. This has been exacerbated by the recession, and by the series of pay cuts that C-Life employees have had to endure. Because of the low level of state welfare, employees must ensure their own financial future – through company pensions – after retirement. In the international division survey, employees said they felt they had to work 'very hard' to support their families. Most Japanese now have cars and every possible appliance in their homes. What they don't have is the security of owning the roof over their heads, a result of the phenomenal housing costs in the larger cities. Thirty-year housing loans are quite common and the repayments can take up to 25 per cent of the monthly salary. Moreover, as previously mentioned, housing loans are often dependent on company guarantees and thus on continued employment with the company. Since the recession, many companies have lowered minimum retirement ages, with the result that it is not unknown for employees to have mortgages that they will still be repaying after they retire.

When I entered C-Life, employees had relatively little choice other than to toe the company line or to leave. There was no real chance to voice one's complaints until one had spent years in the company and advanced to a level where one's opinions would be heard. In comparison to these Japanese employees, foreign employees had no such perceptions that they had to stick with one company. This is well illustrated by the attempts of Nomura Shōken, Japan's largest stockbroker, to hire foreign employees (Alletzhauser 1990). In 1982 they experimented with hiring 28 graduates from Ivy League colleges and from Oxbridge. They planned to train these graduates in Japan as they would train their Nomura employees and have them go out to work in the foreign offices around the world as 'true' Nomura employees. However, the graduates 'were horrified when shown the antiquated Nomura concrete cell-block dormitory in Funabashi, 40 minutes north of the Nomura headquarters'. They had only come to Tōkyō to get a background in Japanese business and then planned to go on to other jobs. 'They were happy making $1,541.66 per month at Nomura until they discovered friends earning similar figures per week at Western firms.' By 1985 all had left of their own accord. As we saw earlier, C-Life's experiments with hiring women as normal employees (same status as men) ended with precisely the same results.

Throughout the fieldwork chapters, we can see how these economic worries and concern for status affect the way that employees behave in their relations with each other. An employee's status is directly related to his place in the company hierarchy. In the next section, then, I examine in more detail the importance of status in the context of the hierarchy. First, however, I conclude this section with a brief case study of an employee who represented many of the qualities looked for by C-Life. Industrious and loyal, S fits into the pattern of the good employee with which we began this section.

The career of S

We chose S to be the hero of the English documentary. He was a very personable man who had been a top salesman from the very beginning of his career in the company. His whole career had been a series of positions from one sales office to another around the country and he was currently the branch head of the Naka-Meguro sales office, which, being situated in the same suburb as the head office of the company, is an extremely important sales office. S was earnest, hard-working and old-fashioned. He personified the attractive elements of the employee at a Japanese company, those qualities we have seen as associated with the ideal employee, although, as we will see, he had his strategies for personal gain, as did everyone in the company. My film crew likened him to a brave and earnest sailor trying desperately to rescue the Titanic as it went under.

> S: The sales targets are quite strict and hard to achieve but I want to try to match them to the best of my ability. I think that the person in charge should be someone who is very honest, who is very yielding and obedient. No matter how big the goal is I think that the people who say that they really want to do it and keep on saying that to the end, the turnover does get achieved.

We went to have a look at S's sales office. Brand new blank sheets of white paper adorned the walls; some of them had orange calligraphy sprawled across them: 'MILLENNIUM 2000: Each Person's Sales Add Up to a New Tomorrow!' Another wall was covered in maps marked with red dots for each separate sales area. A poster proclaimed:

> If you just live a normal life, you will only be able to grasp a normal life. If you want to achieve happiness, if you want to achieve your dreams, the only way is to make a lot of effort, a lot more effort than others; you have to sweat. You can do it! Even now! Live with all your strength!

One of the sales ladies had written the poster on her own initiative.

The office was extremely colourful and there were lots of women buzzing around doing insurance sales work. The assistant branch head was writing another huge, brightly coloured calligraphy poster: 'The year 2000 – let's put all our strength into it!' The walls were covered with the sales results of each of the sales ladies. They were in the form of a line graph, with the names at the bottom and the sales in a vertical line up the wall. There was huge discrepancy between the results of the different employees: the top-selling lady's graph went up the wall and along the ceiling.

Loyalty and apparent dedication were important for S, and certainly must have helped to motivate his sales force. We spoke to him later on New Year's Eve as he prepared to spend the night in the office, guarding against the ravages of the 'millennium bug'.

> S: Our branch was number one among the group. We reached our targets – even for the recession our results were quite good. It's good that there is at least one healthy organisation. The targets were 20 oku in cover. November and December are the bonus season… so this month we have to fight for another two months for

results. This is a period where we really get going. It's almost the year 2000, so this is the last part of the twentieth century.

S frequently went beyond the call of duty in his work for C-Life: always the first to arrive in the morning, he would usually work on Saturdays as well. Indeed, it was he who, during training, sold insurance to a member of one of his dōki's family. S's work philosophy was that, like a soldier, he should work hard for the sake of the company, regardless of the economic situation. Like many other sales staff, he didn't want to think too deeply about the company situation or analyse it. For a C-Life employee, however, he put a considerable amount of effort into his home life and family. He believed that it wasn't possible to be happy in one sphere of life without it reflecting on the other spheres.

Like many of the successful branch managers, S saw the ability to manage the sales staff, particularly to motivate them to sell more, as the key to better sales results. And a central element of that leadership technique was to show that he was working harder, and had more confidence, than any of them. The best way to lead is by example. Where a direct order to exhort the sales staff to sell more would have been unlikely to work, and where extra bonuses were not an option in the system of fixed percentages, the main ways of motivating staff were personal. The women working for S would work harder because they liked him, and wanted to help him succeed in his goals.

> S: Managers who are unable to show how much the turnover is in their sales offices as a whole, especially when their aims are large compared to the goal – that is the same as showing that you have no ability. And I don't think that is on. It is better to confess, to say frankly as the manager, what the situation is. And maybe because it is a women's workplace, often they will say to me, 'Well, in that case, if it is like that, we will try our best to get more.'

> S: If you say things like, 'Hey, what the hell do you think you are doing!' to women who are the same age as your mother, you need to think carefully about how you are going to say that and you need to think about the nature of women before you say it. Or otherwise they will refuse to do even things that normally they would be able to do. Well, I am a human too so there are some types of people that I am not very good with either.

While I heard C-Life sales managers say again and again that they had no skills, the actual skills used by the successful branch heads were considerable. They were very talented at spotting personalities, and being able to relate to each employee in such a way as to help them to enjoy their work and to succeed in it.

> S: The real job that is demanded of a sales office head is to pull out the abilities of each person under him. I think that I have been influenced by women. I don't think I would be able to do what I do without being influenced – both in the way that I work and in the way that I speak. However, my branch office head says that the

company is like this and the branch is like this so I do have to do that much. That much has not changed. A sales head is like a pitcher who has a number of balls and the baseball field ready and throws the balls to people. When I was in the field I only threw straight balls and shouted encouragement and I thought that work was all about energy and I still do think that. Different people talk about how much guidance you should give to people… whether you should encourage someone who already likes arithmetic to study some more arithmetic or whether you should show them that there is different ways to do things. I think that it takes a lot of skill to be a sales head; it takes a lot of management skill.

Hierarchy

In describing the structure of C-Life in Chapter 3, I introduced the topic of hierarchy, illustrating it with the importance attached to the seating plan. Here, I discuss the prevalence of hierarchy in detail, focusing on the great importance attached by employees to status in the company.

In general, the ordered character of Japanese society is reflected in its hierarchical structure where each person has his determined place in the hierarchy. Iga (1986: 196) states: 'Hierarchy promotes the co-ordination of Japanese institutions and individuals because their behaviour is regulated by clearly specified norms in accordance with status, and this regulation eliminates unnecessary misunderstanding and friction.' The hierarchy is all-encompassing and permanent. Japanese will be ranked in some sort of hierarchy inside every institution they belong to, and the institutions themselves will also be ranked against other institutions.

Self-identity is closely intertwined with one's position on the social hierarchy. As we have seen in Chapter 4, the first stage in climbing the hierarchy is to choose which company to enter, since some companies are considered higher in status than others. Ambition as a student is generally directed towards entering the group with the highest social value that one can. Once inside C-Life, employees' energies were largely directed towards obtaining the highest rank that they could inside that hierarchy. So, in other words, education determined the hierarchy (workplace) to which employees could enter, but then work history within C-Life determined the place employees would come to occupy within that hierarchy.

In terms of status, most employees consider the company that one works for, and one's position in the hierarchy of that company, to be far more significant than the kind of work one actually does. Name cards are the primary identifier of position and symbol of status. Whenever people are promoted, their name cards are pulled out and given out anew to people outside the company (who already have the old ones). When employees give out new name cards there is a lot of 'oohing' and 'ahhing' as people congratulate the employee on his promotion and admire the new card.

There has been much discussion in the literature on the relative lack of a 'class system' in Japan. A class system in the Western sense suggests a system in which one group of individuals is positioned over another group of individuals. This implies that within each group, the status of each individual is roughly equal – for example, there may be two classes, managers and workers, consisting of a group of roughly equal managers who all have higher status than a group of roughly equal workers. But this is not the situation in a large Japanese white-collar company. There is no clear dividing line between two separate groups. Rather, individuals are continually in transition throughout their lives from worker up through the ranks into management status. The only groups of people with roughly 'equal' status are the dōkisei groups.

The hierarchy in C-Life at the time that I entered was a strictly pyramid-like system with a broad base of new recruits and a narrowing top of older executives. Employees slowly move up the pyramid as they progress through the company. The actual hierarchy in C-Life when I entered in 1985 was as follows:

Trainee	22–23 years old
Shunin (assistant manager)	24–26 years old
Shusa (manager) or Kakaricho (assistant section head)	27–29 years old
Kachō (section head)	30–46 years old
Fukubuchō (assistant department head)	47–48 years old
Buchō (department head)	49–57 years old
Torishimariyaku (director)	53–58 years old
Jōmu (3rd highest position)	
Senmu (2nd highest position)	
Shachō (president)	

The strictness of the hierarchy means that if an employee reaches retirement age and hasn't made the next grade he must retire. This is repeated at the next level up, and so on. So achieving a promotion to the next level at the upper echelons of the company is much more than just promotion: it is equivalent to a ticket allowing the older employee to remain in the company, to keep his job, his name card, his status and the bulk of his social contacts.

In C-Life the status inside the company is still of primary importance in determining the life status of the employees. A person's home background or personal wealth are of very little importance in his company life. Employees of a 'rich' background entering C-Life may have advantages in getting into the company through their connections. But having got in, they are not necessarily advantaged for the rest of their careers in the company. On the contrary, if they have been able to get in on connections but are unable to prove themselves to be worthy of entering by normal means, they are especially vulnerable to bullying.

As we have seen, the confusion surrounding the restructuring in C-Life has produced exceptions to the normal rule that everyone is senior or junior to everyone else with the sole exception of members of the same year-group. Japanese company life has begun to change. Nevertheless, status is still extremely important within the company. This will be seen throughout the rest of this chapter, and again in the next chapter, when I consider relations between different groups of people in the company.

One of the most easily observable effects of the competition for status is the enormous amount of overtime undertaken by many C-Life employees.

Work and overtime

Virtually everyone at C-Life engages in what, to a Westerner, seems an excessive amount of overtime. The amount of overtime reported by international division respondents on the survey ranged from 20 to 70 hours, with the older people doing 20 to 30 hours and the new recruits 50 to 70 hours. The respondents in the overseas offices reported less overtime than those in the head office. On top of this, the employees often also participated in after-hours socialising or tsukiai, usually with company members and in the environs of the company, which they did not record as overtime.

C-Life employees, on the whole, work extremely long hours. Company employees often talked of the hours that they worked, comparing notes and boasting about sacrifices they made for the company. The official working hours of regular employees in the international section were 9 am to 5 pm. In reality, however, all regular workers work from about 8:30 am to about 7 or 8 pm. Sometimes workers go out to eat around 6 pm at a neighbouring restaurant and return to work later. It is not unknown for a worker to return to the company to recommence work at 10 pm after a section drinking party, and most people express admiration for those who do so. C-Life is slightly unusual in this respect, even by Japanese standards. Employees work many more hours than the company officially requires them to work. One wife of a C-Life employee says:

> R: Sometimes he puts the company ahead of his family. Well, normally Saturday is a holiday. He almost always goes off to work as usual. People who have made a firm decision that that is what they'll do – take Saturdays off – they take both Saturdays and Sundays off but there aren't very many like that, whether it is because they're Japanese or whether because they're C-Life employees – I don't know – but even though Saturday is a holiday they still go off to work. I think that is a case where he puts the company ahead of his family. Well, that's the way I think but I'm already used to it.

Her husband comments:

> S: Well, there are employees of other companies that live around here as well and those fathers are playing with their children on Saturdays when I'm waiting for the bus dressed in my business suit. I see that, but I still have to get on the bus and go anyway. At those times I wonder… I feel sorry for my own kids but I end up going to the company anyway.

> S: People in the company often say that they do 'Seven-Eleven' – working from 7 am to 11 pm. Another thing they say is 'satsugoe'. When it passes midnight we call it satsugoe. We would call around our friends from our student days to try and get

insurance. But most of our ex-classmates were out drinking or they would be late from work so we would have to wait up till 11 or 12 at night to catch them. We'd say, 'Hey, it's been a long time – how have you been? Have you got any insurance, by the way? You should get some insurance! You should change your insurance!' We would call those kind of phone-calls 'satsugoe'.

Why do they work like this? Where an employee is in a company for life, and constantly competing against a group of individuals with almost exactly the same qualifications as himself, any way in which to distinguish oneself is avidly grasped at. And the only acceptable way to do this, that will not result in being ostracised by colleagues, is in serving the company.

However, even at the time that I entered C-Life, there was considerable variation in working hours and attitudes to work among employees, usually depending on whether they still considered themselves to be in the running for leadership candidacy.

Employees also differed dramatically in their attitudes towards overtime, depending on whether they were still in the company or not. Those who had been ejected from C-Life were generally scathing towards this aspect of 'Japanese management'.

H: I'm the type of person who tries to fit in half of the time but half of the time I try and protect my own way of thinking. I have a lot of loyalty towards my own work – because our company is a co-operative body that has gathered together for the purpose of doing work, it is already enough to know whether you are making money in terms of the results of the company or not. Apart from that nothing should matter [hoka wa kankei nai], but in a Japanese company 24 hours a day they try to bind you even on Saturday and Sunday. If you won't go out and amuse yourself with other people in the company they say that you're a bad guy [yatsu wa dame da to]. If you won't go drinking at night they say that you're no good. That's really strange and the proof of that is what is happening now.

What, however, are they doing during all this time? Many people are engaging in 'extra work' of their own devising. Some of the tasks undertaken by the regular workers, especially new employees, of the international section are repetitive, low-skill tasks that in a Western firm would be done by secretaries. A great deal of such work fills the 9 to 5 official office hours. If one wishes to develop a more rational way of doing one's work or to do something non-routine or outside the regular company work, the only time one has in which to do it is after hours. And this is the way to earn praise and early promotion.

Often it is the only time that the creativity or special talents of the younger workers are put to use at all. Some workers seem impatient for 5 pm to arrive so they can start work on what they want to work on, rather than what they have to work on.

Otherwise, some workers remain after hours 'for the sake of their colleagues' or 'to uphold the morale of the section'. For some, this is a case of being psychologically unable to leave until everyone else does, or simple peer pressure to stay the longest. This kind of peer pressure can and does reach ridiculous proportions. At one stage when I was employed in the company, there was a train strike scheduled to begin early in the morning, which meant that C-Life employees would have been unable to get to work. Several members of the international section spent the night at the company, while others, leaving home before 5 am, walked for several hours to get to work on time. Fourteen years later, as 1999 turned into 2000, employees were still vying for recognition as having made the most sacrifices in staying over at the company – in case there was an emergency – during the New Year period.

Inevitably, the immensely long hours adversely affect employees' private lives, an area I examine in more detail later in this chapter.

> R: S's style of working – well, he's busy all the time. At the time we were living in the provinces we used to go out most Sundays. He was quite serious about doing things like that. It really changed when we went to Fukuoka. Until then, we'd been in Tōkyō for three years. In Tōkyō you tend to get tired out between commuting and working. It seemed that he always came back with a frown on his face. He would come back around 11 o'clock at night and just eat and then sleep.

Her husband says:

> S: At the time the department that I'd been entrusted with was a new department. I felt a really strong mission to get the department up and going and make it into a success. But at the time it was a period when the world was in a lot of turbulence and it wasn't going as I wanted it to. So day after day I had a lot of worries to contend with. But I really wanted to win at all costs so, for those three years...

Thus, we see the great importance attached to status by many employees. This is reinforced in the next section, in which I examine the employees' attitudes to their work placements within the company.

Attitudes towards work

We have seen that employees have very little say over what job they actually do in the company. They are, as a rule, assigned positions according to the personnel department's evaluation of their skills, not according to their desires. Even if employees write in their personnel evaluations, year after year, that they want to do a certain type of work, they may spend all their lives in C-Life without being able to do it. Here, I focus on the varying attitudes of employees towards this state of affairs.

I found an interesting variety among the C-Life employees' work attitudes. On the surface they seemed quite uniform, which is the situation that is generally presented in the Japanese management literature. But it should be noted that their attitudes do not necessarily coincide with their work behaviour.

C: I was in charge of long-term planning for the company at one stage. I also did labour management in my student days, and when I went to the personnel department the theory of what I had learnt was really put into practice there. I studied economics originally and I like economic work. I was lucky to be able to do the kind of work that I wanted to do inside the life-time employment system.

Most of the C-Life employees are aware that they have little personal say in what work they are assigned to. As a result, they do not expect to be able to enjoy each and every position they are in, and feel lucky when they hit upon a position that does suit them. I was struck by how many people had fallen into work for which they had no particular liking, and were resigned to the fact that they had spent so many years of their lives trudging through it. When asked, they would just shrug their shoulders and say, 'It can't be helped (shōganai). Because it is a Japanese company.'

E: The content of my work was really different inside the head office and away. Inside the head office I was in the position of supervising planning and giving orders. In the branch office, I was in the position of getting orders and being one of the army that was carrying the orders out. It was always more interesting to be on the side that was giving the orders out. When I was getting the orders, the experiences that I had were much narrower and had smaller scope. I just had to do what had been decided for me to do in the way that it had already been set down, and that was the kind of section that that was, so I wasn't really keen on that kind of work. Rather than that I wanted to be in the head office where I had a sense of motivation [yarigai]. That was more suited to my character.

When they are able to do the work they want to do, employees generally attribute it to luck, rather than their own efforts, and express gratitude to C-Life for allowing them to do as they want. Employees talk a lot about 'luck' in connection with their careers, as they do not have a lot of self-direction.

Z: When I look back on my career in C-Life, I don't know if I was lucky or unlucky. I have really hard [tsurai] bad memories as well, but looking at it on a total basis I think I was very happy.

Some employees are less aware than others of their own lack of control over their careers. When I left C-Life, for example, I told one of the middle-ranking members of the personnel department that I was leaving to do a higher degree. He told me that he was thinking of doing the same kind of thing himself. In fact he had already drafted a letter to the personnel manager about it and he was certain he would be overseas in one capacity or another very shortly. The man was very enthusiastic about his intentions, but the fact was that he was dreaming. Not one of the employees around him thought that he had even the slightest chance of entering the international department, an essential prerequisite to being posted overseas. Very often in C-Life one can see the position of others more clearly than one can one's own position, and we will see this graphically illustrated later in this section in the story of T. The man in this particular case, eventually realising the reality of his own situation, would probably have had to accept it at that time (1987), since, given his age, he would have no other option.

In contrast to this case, many employees who do not get to do their preferred job give up trying to change their work, and instead get motivated about the work that they have been assigned. In a kind of resignation and refocusing, they decide to double their efforts to do the best possible within their immediate work environment. Employees realise the value of resigning themselves to their transfers and working hard in each section because they do not really know how that experience will influence their work in their next post.

> I: I was working in C-Life for 20 years. I did work mostly related to planning and personnel or to marketing, and at the end I did some computer system work as well. I was the computer system department head and then I was an auditor. And C-Life had a foundation that it created, called the C-Life Health Development Business Foundation and I was a director of that. In total it was 37 years. I worked with all my energy no matter what job I was given, though I think I put most of my energies into personnel-related work: how to keep new talented staff at C-Life and help them to play a role in the development of C-Life.

> E: As for which section of the company I would like to be in now? I would like to see it become a really good company … and towards that end … well, I have always done sales work and within that work I have had the opportunity to meet with a lot of the sales ladies. All over the country there are more than 10,000 sales ladies. I would like to be involved in some capacity with helping them to see the company as a good company. If I can put my strength into that task I will be really happy with that.

As we see, most employees do have dreams in connection with their work. Others, however, become frustrated at not being able to do as they wish, and quit the company. They often have more clearly defined views on the subject of work placement, having had to think about it when they chose their next jobs. As a rule, they are much more critical of work patterns in large Japanese companies like C-Life. One man who left the company said:

> H: What I really need from the company in my life is opportunity – the ability to be able to actualise my own skills. If you asked normal C-Life people they would say that they want job security – I think that that would be the main answer. I don't have any job security in my present life. I don't get that from anywhere now. I think that that is challenging.

This attitude contrasts sharply with the following comments made by an employee still inside C-Life. He questions criticising the company because one is unable to do the work one wants.

A: Because this is work, you are given things to do. You have to respond to that with effort and produce results. So the people who achieve those results, they say, 'Well, next, where would you like to go?' And they have hopes of where they would like to go... all of us do... and so you get to be able to go to those places basically. But then there are also people who say, 'I shouldn't have been put here. This is not how it was supposed to be [ore wa konna hazu ja na katta].' But if you ask me, I think that they just haven't made enough effort. It wasn't the case that they were bad because they couldn't do it; they were bad because they didn't do it. They say that they couldn't do it. But it is actually that they didn't do it. That is the case for everybody. Some people really do things properly [yaru yatsu wa chanto yatte iru].

A: I have been able to do whatever I wanted in the company. What I wanted to do in the company and what the company wanted me to do matched perfectly. In that sense, I have been really happy.

According to this employee, who was universally described as a top leadership candidate, the company will let employees go where they want if they have put in enough effort. There is some truth to this, at least in this employee's own experience, as the company is certainly more accommodating to the desires of leadership candidates than to those whose results have not been as striking. But it is a matter of patience as well. The increasing numbers of young people quitting C-Life in the first few years of employment indicate a high level of frustration with the necessity to bide one's time until one is assigned to a more desirable job.

On the whole, though, C-Life employees are resigned to the fact that they are shunted around by the personnel department. Because of the relative arbitrariness of the job movements, gossip about job changes is rife in the company. Reassignment orders come out once a year, and speculation over who will be promoted, who will be transferred where, and who will meet with unexpected moves, rises as the day approaches. Each employee is informed verbally by the department management where his assignment will lead, and the official list is published a day or two later. So the time in between the informal knowledge of the moves (when some people choose to tell others near to them where they were going) and the release of the official list is a dramatic one. The days after the official list comes out are filled with speculation over the meaning of the transfers, and their implications for the person concerned and for the departments that he moved out of and in to. We have seen that employees are aware of the criteria used by the personnel department to transfer people; thus, few expect to receive the job changes they wished for each time.

Y: I wanted to change from investment and applied for a job change. I didn't know what the work would be like in that section. But I wanted to change so I was really happy about being able to experience a different section and different kind of work. If you just do investment for 10 or 20 years you get tired of it. I wanted to do something different for a change. The company allowed me to do that.

Another reason why many employees are resigned to their lot is that they recognise that being moved to a variety of possibly unpleasant assignments is essential to advancing up the company hierarchy. And it is never clear whether someone has been moved to an unfavourable position because they are on the way up, or because they are being shunted sideways. So employees can always justify an apparently negative movement to themselves by believing that they are still on the way up.

Before the bubble, the company seemed to prefer all-rounders who had worked their way up inside the company in a number of different areas. This could be seen by looking at the diverse careers led by the presidents of the company up until the bubble. It was striking that after the bubble, the company appointed, for the first time, a president who had been primarily an investment specialist rather than mainly grounded in life insurance-related business. Some employees therefore try to strategise their moves up through the company, applying for those job transfers that they think will give them a maximum chance to move up in the company, rather than those jobs that they feel they are suited for, or that they enjoy the most. But even those employees who do this are unlikely to be able to influence their own direction to a very significant degree. Moreover, because of the changes in the economic environment, employees see that they cannot be sure which skills the company will value many years into the future.

> Y: I'm not particularly glad that I didn't do sales all those years. Actually, I would have liked to have done some sales work. If I was going to do that next time I would like to be the head of a branch office. I like the dynamism of working with human beings. You can see that more with sales work. Investment work deals with an object rather than with human beings, so it misses out on that dynamism.

Here again, then, we see the importance to the employees of status. People are willing to be posted to a variety of uninteresting or unpleasant jobs if they think it will increase their chances of rising through the company ranks. Moreover, they are aware of the situation and prepared to exploit it to their personal advantage in gaining status. The following conversation encapsulates very well the employees' attitude to work and postings.

> P: As to whether people are becoming more individual in the present changes – I think that depends on what kinds of values you have. From a long time ago, there were always some people for whom, if they had an individual hobby, work for them was just a place where they got their pay, and they were living just for the sake of their hobbies or interests. And in any society there are those kinds of people.
>
> V: I think for some people, work is the most interesting thing apart from their families.
>
> P: In the end, that is really the case. Among 24 hours in the day you have to work for eight of them and you sleep for eight of them. So half of your waking life is at work – so if your work is boring then I don't think you would have any value in living.

V: It's because work is important that we do it.

P: And we want money!

V: We want money as an expression of status. But in the end, even though you did-n't get that much money, and, in an unfortunate case, if someone whose status was below you became your boss, if work was really interesting you'd still do it. I think that humans have that kind of character. And I think that's even more true of Europeans and Westerners. There are heaps of cases like this in other companies.

Here, the employees mention several factors as motivation for working hard in whatever job the company places them: the feeling that their work is important; financial reward – primarily as a symbol of status; and inherent interest in the work itself. Almost always, employees mentioned financial reward as less important or secondary to the inherent interest and enjoyment they had in the work itself.

Z: I was able to do the work that I wanted to do inside this company so I think that is the biggest factor. Unfortunately, there wasn't a large pay-off from doing it. That is how I feel. But I was able to do what I wanted [jibun no yaritai koto o yarasete moraimashita yo].

Employees often express gratitude to the company for chances that they had in their careers that they could not have had alone. One employee near retirement reminisces about his overseas experiences at a time when overseas travel was extremely expensive and very unusual in Japan.

Z: When I came into the company I was first in the loan-screening department doing corporate analysis. In other words, when someone comes to us to borrow money we decide whether or not we will lend to them. I did that the second year I was in the company and did that all the way along and then I said that I want to go overseas. Because I didn't have confidence in my English ability and I had no money, it was better to use the company's money and go overseas that way, so I applied to the overseas education department. Whether I was lucky or unlucky I don't know, but I passed and was able to go overseas to train once or twice. The purpose of that was to study international investment, so in that sense, I think the company let me do really interesting work [yoi shigoto o yarasete moratta].

As with so many other aspects of company life, however, things have begun to change with the harsher economic climate. We saw in the last chapter that many people no longer expect to work at the same company all their lives. They there-fore do not see why they should put up with doing boring work in the hope that it may improve their status years in the future. People are re-evaluating what work means to them, and especially the balance or importance that work has in their lives in comparison to other areas – like family or leisure. These remarks, for example, are made by a former C-Life employee who left to join a much smaller firm. He now expects his work to help him improve his own skills.

J: As far as the balance between stretching myself and stretching the company, I don't think the company as a whole really matters [kaisha zentai wa amari kankei nai]. For example, this company that I am presently in is a company with about 30 people. My company now has 30 people but C-Life had 3,000 people. This company is one hundredth the size of C-Life. Here it is an issue what each person does. In this company what each person does is a real issue. For the company to become bigger and the scope of our investment to increase. But regardless of the results of the company, the issue for me is how many more skills I can acquire for myself, and I don't think that is a very common way to think among my dōki.

To illustrate the points we have seen in this section, I here briefly discuss the career of one particular employee, which he interpreted in quite a different way from his colleagues. T was not very aware of how others perceived his situation, and his attempts to manipulate it to achieve the postings he wanted did not gain him the coveted post.

The career of T

T: After the training I went into the company. In 1985 I got into the company and in 1986 after the training I went into the international department, and that lasted for two years and then I went to the life insurance association (an external posting) for two years. And after that in 1989 I went into the domestic loans department for two years and then again for two years I went to the international department and at that time I did foreign loans. Two years later I went to the individual loans department for four years and three months and then I quit the company. So the individual loans department was the last department that I was in in the company. The individual loans department is as it says – we give loans to individuals: housing loans, consumer loans or loans to buy golf club membership. Also cars. Those kinds of loans to individuals. I think it was one of the departments that has got in the most trouble since the recession… it is an age where bad debts have become extensive and that department is the department where you have to collect; forcible collection.

If we consider a case like this, it is very hard to tell exactly what each job change meant at the time. Different people evaluate the individual at each step, and both the circumstances of the company and the performance of the individual change with time. I could ask the individual their interpretation of their situation, and the dōki around them, and the personnel section. But still, there was no ultimate truth about why the employee had advanced in the direction in which he had.

To attempt an interpretation in this instance, T was sometimes referred to as a 'hostage', someone who had entered the company on the basis of his connections. As such, it was hoped – but not entirely expected – that he would be a valuable company member, and it was recognised that, once in the company, he was there for life if he wished to stay. Here, I contrast T's own interpretation of his career with that of others.

T said his experience of the training centre was abysmal and he tried to quit, but was dissuaded by the trainers. It was T whose sales territory was invaded by the model employee S, who sold policies even to his family. But during the training, T did learn how to sell insurance and became motivated to learn what he could from the company. He requested a transfer to the international department, which he got. As it was the most coveted position inside the company at that time, there was some resentment about his appointment from the other dōki, who thought he had only got it as a result of his connections.

One woman, the most talented seller of insurance in the training period, eventually quit the company because she had not been able to advance as she wished. The dōki saw this as stemming from her reaction to T's appointment into the international division. Had T done well in the international division, the C-Life employees agree that he might have stayed there and eventually got the next transfer that he wanted, which was to an overseas office.

However, his dōki report that he was not exceptionally good at the work, and, although he did the routine office work tasks satisfactorily, he did not show the kind of talent that would have allowed him to stay in the department. He was transferred instead to the life insurance association, the outside body that co-ordinates the stance towards the bureaucracy and other industries of the life insurance industry as a whole. All the companies that participated in the life insurance association had an obligation to contribute a certain number of employees of the appropriate age and status for the positions vacant. T's appointment could have been seen either as a strategic move for a talented young member of the company, or as a move sideways to remove someone who was not terribly useful anywhere else. T's dōki saw his appointment as intended to remove him from the international department and allow another employee to have a turn there. Employees from the personnel division said that at any point of his career, it was possible for T to have excelled so that he could have improved his passage through the company and perhaps worked back to where he himself wanted to go: the international department.

His next move, to the domestic loans department, was a very progressive one. It really gave him the specialisation that he carried all through his subsequent career in the company. The experience he gathered there was then carried back into the international investment department to apply to international loans. By then, he had become in some sense a loan specialist. C-Life employees interpreted this move as motivated by two things. It was a concession towards his incessant desire – expressed in the transfer request forms submitted by each employee to the personnel department annually – to be transferred back to the international department; it satisfied the need to have him somewhere in that department that was not too strategic to the company and where he could do work at which he had already specialised. T also received concessions in the form of being sent overseas on temporary assignments accompanying senior members of the company, on which occasions he would have acted in the capacity of a secretary.

When he was transferred from international loans to individual loans, his dōki interpreted this move as his having reached the limits of what he could do in the important international division: in other words, the peak of his career. The individual loans department was very much less popular, less important to the company, and involved work related to the recovery of debts from individual customers, a rather depressing aspect of the work of an insurance company.

T's own interpretation of his career, however, was rather different. He had resigned himself during the training period to learning the basics of life 'as a businessman' (shakaijin to shite no). He was satisfied with his appointment to the international division first. He was mystified by his appointment to the life insurance association, but was able to cope with it as it lasted only two years. Being sent to the domestic loan department was relatively satisfying since he realised that he was gaining valuable specialist knowledge, and when he returned to the international department his hopes rose that he was on the right track for a successful route to the overseas offices. When he was sent to individual loans, he took it much as he had taken the life insurance association appointment – as a temporary appointment that would eventually translate into a return to the international department. At this point, his view of his career and others' perceptions of it had clearly parted ways. During all of this time, even though some of his dōki say that it was perfectly obvious to them that he would not be offered the highly desirable overseas office appointment, which, indeed, also seemed obvious to me at the time, he had gone on working there for 14 years in the hope that he could still achieve this.

In some ways, then, the lack of clarity in appointments and evaluation in C-Life that we saw in Chapters 3 and 4 serves a vital purpose in keeping employees motivated and involved who would not be if they knew the reasons behind their career moves. On the other hand, as we saw above, in the case of one of my dōki – a fluent English speaker, graduate of a top university and top of the year in sales in the training centre, a very highly motivated and talented woman – the lack of clarity served to make her so frustrated she quit the company.

It was when T had been in the individual loans department for four years that he realised he was no longer likely to make it back to the international department. He realised that his career had been derailed from his desired route. His primary reasons for quitting the company at that point were that he could see that he could no longer go overseas, since employees in the branch offices were either young – up to 35 or so – or branch office heads of mid to late forties. He told me that he knew that he was too late for the first category and that he would have to wait a long time for the second. It was still not clear to me whether he had really realised that he was very unlikely ever to become a branch office head at all, or whether he was just putting it like this to me in order to save face. In his own words, he said of his decision to quit:

> T: I had had a lot of experience in different kinds of departments. There were also cases where money was in arrears. Also there was work that was general clerical work. Practically, I would have to go to the debtor's place and try to collect the loan. Well, that did happen but it was not that common. Well, I just did it as part of the work. It wasn't that unpleasant. I think that I learned a lot from being in that

department. But I had been there for four years. I thought that that was enough. I am going to be 40 soon. And I had never had the intention of being in the same company all my life. So I thought that this was my last chance to change.

As the desire to quit grew stronger, he began to really think about the life that he had led inside C-Life, and openly recognise frustrations in himself that had otherwise lain below the surface.

T: There wasn't any happiness in spending my entire life as a company man. I think that anybody has that kind of feeling. I can't say that it is the case 100 per cent or that 100 per cent of people feel like that. The income is stable and if you put up with it and do the work you can have some kind of a life [sore nari no jinsei]. But I started feeling that that was incredibly empty.

T: The company policies themselves – I didn't ever like them or become used to them [najimenakatta]. It is mainly because your own wishes were not heard. I wanted to live overseas. That was my wish from the beginning. I wanted that all the time, yet I was approaching 40 years old. And I felt that there was no more hope of doing that. To go overseas with C-Life, you either have to do it when you are young or to go as branch office head. The hope of going when I was still young had disappeared. So because that chance had disappeared I quit. Within the investment department we had branches in both London and New York and I wanted to be able to experience overseas life while working and getting more knowledge about investments. I was interested in being able to experience overseas life. When I was young, when I was really little, I spent two or three years living overseas for my father's work. That wasn't the only reason I quit the company but it was one reason. I had been thinking about quitting for three or four years. But I really decided it in my own heart since about a year back.

Once T was stuck in the individual loans department, he had a number of options. First, he could maximise his skills in order to change jobs. He did this by tackling the American Accounting exams that would qualify him to do investment-related accounting work for Japanese companies with dealings in the US. This – along with the American investment analysts' exams – was a popular but very difficult qualification which assured those who were successful of adding significantly to their value in the job market. Unfortunately, unlike other dōki in the process of changing jobs, who had gone through considerable hardship to study for and pass these exams while still working at C-Life, T was unable to pass the exams before he quit. His dōki believed that he quit in order to get the time to do the last stint of study before he passed.

T: It was difficult for me to think of the future – where I would work in the future – while I was still in the company. If you decide where you are going to go then I would have had to go there straight away. And I wanted some time for myself. I just wanted to live life slowly for a while [yukkuri suru]. I know that I am not of the age that I should be doing things slowly. But within a long life, I thought that it would be okay to have one or two years like this.

T: I really don't know what I am going to do about looking for a job. I was in the finance department inside the insurance company so I will probably go to a field where I can use those skills rather than go to a completely new field. Well, I am thinking of various things now. I would really like to live overseas for a while. I think it would be too hard to go back to university in the West now but if it were a short programme of some kind that might be okay. If there were a good place… if I find a good place to work inside Japan then I might just go to work inside Japan. I have decided not to decide anything about the future just yet.

The NHK crew were totally enamoured of T. They saw him as personifying the Japanese salary man's existential crisis. They called him a 'moratorium man' (moratoriumu ningen) – a person who is lost without a purpose in life. T had no firm idea of what he really wanted to do in life, no clear idea of how to market himself, or which direction to go in. Luckily, he could still make use of his personal connections to make a company himself or to go into another company if the worst came to the worst.

T: I was in the company until July of 1999. If I knew the answer to the question of what I really want to do… Well, I might still be groping for what I really want to do for the rest of my life (mosaku). It is not that easy to produce an answer to that question. Well, I think at the very least I need to be independent and I need to get income. And then thinking about what I really want to do with myself is the second step after that.

T: I think that I am really lucky though. Well, I think the Japanese are really lucky. Anyway, there is no chance of starving in Japan. There are some homeless around but a lot of those are people who chose that themselves. Well, lately there is more and more restructuring and I think more and more people find themselves homeless without being able to help it. But with a normal body… with normal physical strength you should be able to live in this country.

This disregard for status was really unusual among C-Life employees.

The last time that I met T during my fieldwork he had narrowly failed the exam and was preparing for the next attempt several months later. In the meantime, he was, incredibly, working as a day labourer – a very tough physical job normally undertaken on a casual basis by students and others in need of quick cash.

Quite apart from being assigned various jobs within C-Life, many employees also have to cope with being sent around the country on transfers, which can be very disruptive to family life. An examination of the varying attitudes they have towards this will therefore illuminate further the range of attitudes towards work held by the employees.

Transfers

> O: Ōsaka was a transfer [tenkin] for me. It was the only one that I did. The guys are doing a lot more than that. They are really actively into their transfers. I think that they are thinking about the fact that I am a woman. I went to a large branch office when I did move, and I think that they chose work that they thought I would be suited for.

Transfers are common for employees of large Japanese companies in general, but this is especially true of those in the insurance industry. C-Life has many branches around the country and employees are shunted between these roughly every three years. As we have seen, most prospective employees don't think too hard about what kind of work they will be doing when they get into the company. So, for some, the frequent transfers are something of a shock.

Transfers out of Tōkyō are often considered risky, as they remove the employee from the centre of things, from the gossip and tsukiai, and from the direct sight of the people who will be promoting them next. In general, the further from Tōkyō the transfer is, the greater the risk, and the greater the feeling of banishment. Because the transfers are frequent they are regarded as inevitable, but a transfer from Tōkyō to a remote place and then back to Tōkyō again generally gives employees the feeling that they have fulfilled an obligatory duty, whereas transfers from one remote region to another seem much worse: an indication that management is trying to keep them out of harm's way.

For example, S had spent a very hard three years at a certain post, and received a transfer notification that sent him to the distant south of Japan. As we have seen, immediate transfer to a very remote place is often, to all intents and purposes, a demotion, even if it is not officially described as such. And transfer to a remote place when the company knows that the circumstances of the family will make it very difficult for the employee to take up the transfer can be an indirect means of firing. S comments as follows:

> S: I got through those three years and was at the point that I was wondering where I would go next. I was told Fukuoka and, at that point in time, when I was told that, I really wondered what on earth I had been putting all that effort into all those three years. I thought, 'Why do I have to go as far as Fukuoka at this stage in my life?'

I found some differences in my correspondents, according to age, over whether they saw remote transfers as positive or negative. The older generation more often saw it as negative because they were generally more career-oriented. Amongst the middle-aged respondents, however, we see that some, like S, although initially interpreting a transfer as very negative because of its effects on status and the career path, discover the positive aspects of living in the countryside because of the effects on their private life and family.

S: But when I got to Fukuoka, I realised that it was actually quite a large city, that the sky was really, really blue, that the city was really beautiful and I was really moved by the beautiful nature.

R: It's really grand nature – it's not nature on a small scale – it's nature on a grand scale.

S: But the economy is still a shop-style economy. It's a place where they really accept people from different places so our family ended up really loving that place. The people there were great as well. We changed our car into a camping car and on each holiday we would go out as a family.

R: There might be another transfer for us but for me it's much more stressful to be here in Tōkyō! It was much easier to live in the provinces as far as living standards went and I certainly want to stay together with my family.

The main difficulty with transfers is the impact on the employee's family. When employees are newly-married, a transfer often results in the wife being landed in a place where she knows no-one and has no work to keep her occupied. Often the wives have not considered the impact that their husband's career will have on their own lives.

R: Before I got married, I had no idea that people who worked for life insurance companies had to transfer so much. I was born and bred in Tōkyō. So I had no idea that I would get married and have to leave for the provinces where I knew nobody. I had never had any idea like this at all. After our marriage was already decided he suddenly got transferred to Nagoya. I really wondered what to do then but we had fallen in love and I went on and got married without thinking about the transfer.

R: So I went to Nagoya – it was an incredible culture shock. In the subway and on the streets the language that they speak there sounds almost like a foreign language to people from Tōkyō. I was so surprised but now I've moved so many times.

When such a transfer comes up, families are faced with the choice of moving to the new location together as a family or having the husband move by himself for the three years or so of the transfer. The choice often comes down to factors such as whether the wife is looking after aged parents in Tōkyō, or if there are children who do not want to move schools. Children often need to stay in their present schools in order to take the crucial entrance exams to junior high schools, high schools or university. Often the families do not want to disrupt the children. As has been well documented, Japanese schools are not very receptive to transferring children, and bullying is rife.

H: Japanese society is a fairly harsh society. By that I mean Japan is the only country where men have to go off and live by themselves while they work for the company and leave their families behind. In other countries the family is number one but in Japan if you didn't make the company number one, everyone would be fired.

E: I don't want my husband to go off by himself to work in the provinces. My children are still small so I'm not thinking of that option. We ask our children – we ask our oldest girl what she would like to do – she says she'll go with her father. If the children get bigger then the problem of their having to take entrance exams comes into the picture and then it might be more difficult, but we'll go as far as we can like we are now.

The company does take some of this into account. At many locations there are company dormitories that are used by the transferring employees, making it cheap for them to live.

R: Because we were living in company housing I was able to make a lot of friends there, and although I went to the provinces where I knew nobody it wasn't really the case that I didn't know anything or couldn't find my way around – there was always someone to ask.

Some families have also discovered positive benefits of the moves for the family.

R: When you go to the provinces there are lots of families that have moved there so, contrary to expectations, the family gets bound together more because you're landed together in a strange place as a five-person family and you have to live there. If the children get sick there's only my husband to help me – there's no-one else to ask for help so you end up becoming much closer.

R: At first, I was really concerned about moving but after I moved I discovered it was really fun and I discovered the quality of life that can be had in provincial cities. And I was really glad that I got married. Especially Fukuoka and Nagoya were great. They were really easy to live in, and until March this year we lived in Fukuoka for three years. I was in tears when I had to come back though I was in tears when I had to leave Tōkyō in the beginning as well! But I really didn't want to come back.

Talking to female employees who were employed with the same status as men, I found that some of them had transferred but they invariably had negative views of transfers. Indeed, this was the main reason why the company changed its policy of allowing women to work as general workers (same as men) and introduced the tantōshoku category that allowed them to work as men without the obligation to transfer.

E: At the moment I have just come to my present section so I am not thinking of moving yet. So I would like to do this work for a while. And in the future? I'd like to move somewhere else inside the organisation… perhaps back to the area where I am carrying out orders. But as far as far away places go, because I am married now I don't want to go somewhere by myself. I would like to go somewhere where it is possible to go without leaving my home.

O: My husband is an auditor; he does accounting work. He doesn't have to move unless he wants to. I can't say that I won't have to move again with C-Life. If there is the order I will have to move. I wonder if the company thinks about the circumstances of my husband's work when they ask me to move. In the bad economic climate they probably don't have the leeway to do that any more, I should think. I think in any company it will be more and more difficult from now on. Just because you are a woman general worker won't mean that they will do anything special for you because they just don't have the capacity to do that now. I get a little anxious thinking about that. But if it came to that and I wasn't able to go on working I would have to just think of another way to go on living. We are lucky that both of us are working so if something happens to one of us we will be okay as long as nothing happens to both of us at the same time.

In one case, a woman working in the general worker category was asked to 'voluntarily retire' as part of C-Life's restructuring moves. She told me that she imagined that if she rebelled and refused to do as the company asked, the first thing that they were likely to do would be to ask her to transfer to a remote place, knowing that because her husband's work made it necessary to stay in Tōkyō, she would be unlikely to accept the transfer and stay in the company.

E: There is an association of women general workers from different life insurance companies that has been going for years. I heard there that there are some cases of marriages inside the company and continuing work. The husband in one went to Nagoya to work by himself while the wife stayed behind in Tōkyō. I heard that and thought that must be really difficult. There is no guarantee as to when he would come back and I wonder if it is really necessary to sacrifice that much. Especially in this industry where job transfers are so common. If it was another industry the problems might not be so large.

E: Because I am a general worker I did get transferred once: to O-town. And I was by myself there for quite a while. It just happened to be O-town that I went to and it was to a branch office. In the branch office I was a deputy head. It was the first time that I had been away like that and it was a really good learning experience. Well, maybe I shouldn't call it study but it was a really good experience. In the end I applied to be transferred back to the head office and I was able to do that so I was really lucky.

We saw earlier in this chapter that employees who have left the company tend to be more negative about its management policies. This applies to transfers too, as this comment indicates.

H: I don't think Japanese corporations have really thought a lot about the happiness of the people who were working for them. For example, in insurance companies they move people around a lot. Every few years they move and move and move. From Hokkaidō to Okinawa, moves like that are a common occurrence... It is something that you wouldn't even be able to think about in America. But Japanese companies have been doing this all along. So a large problem that has arisen because of that is when children become high school students and it is hard to change Japanese high schools. In that case the company man has to leave his family behind and go off to work as a bachelor. It is a custom that is special to Japan and that has only been done here. Is moving to different assignments actually about getting profits? No, it is not about profit. It is about maintaining the organisation as it is, rather than looking for profits. And another factor is if you leave financial institutions for a long time they establish relations locally and there is a tendency for them to do bad things [bribes, etc]. So they tried to abolish that. And they tried to stop things becoming too settled or institutionalised. If the employees become too attached to one place then bad things can start happening like bribes.

Leisure

So far in this chapter, I have focused on those employees who work extremely hard, above and beyond the call of duty, putting up with unpleasant work place-ments, in the hope of gaining status. Some, like S, are successful; others, like T, are less so. However, I have pointed out that the degree to which employees work like this does vary greatly. There have always been some employees in Japanese companies who have made the decision to work only during required hours and give up on the struggle to advance. This was true even in the immediately post-war period. Often such employees had hobbies that were the primary interest in their lives. A few C-Life employees in each generation firmly believe they are leadership candidates; a very small minority have clearly given up advancement in favour of their hobbies, and the rest lie somewhere on the spectrum in between. Here, I briefly consider the relations between work and leisure; the discussion is only brief, however, because a full study of employees' activities outside company time falls beyond the scope of this book. I include it here only inasmuch as it sheds light on life inside the company, and how much time employees typically devote to company activities.

Many employees expressed a desire to devote more time to their hobbies but were prevented from doing so because of their commitment to work. One way around this is to use company facilities or clubs. The company has various sports clubs that are very popular, mostly among the younger members, both male and female. In winter there is a weekend ski trip to a nearby resort. These sports occa-sions are relatively informal and voluntary, and, as such, differ from the occasions, discussed in the next section, in which the whole company is involved and which imply obligatory presence. Some of these clubs are well attended because it is easier for employees to participate in company-run activities than ones outside the company.

T: I really like running marathons. I have had the experience of running several full marathons. And I like running hundred-kilometre marathons and triathlons. I like to challenge myself by doing triathlons as well. There are people that go on doing things like this while they are working. But if you have a competition on Sunday and you have to get up and go to the company the next day, then that is really hard.

I did not observe that there was a big difference between the generations in the proportions of hard workers and those with hobbies. However, I could see that the older the employee was, the more likely that their hobbies and work were less clearly divided. In other words, for the older generation, hobbies often *were* their work. This connects with what we have already seen regarding overtime; many employees spend their spare time on company-related projects of their own devising, which are almost like hobbies.

C: I wanted to play the flute while I was working at C-Life too but I never had the time. There was no time to be involved in hobbies. I had to keep in touch with what the market was doing and I didn't have time to study at the company itself. So I had to study at the weekends. I read books mainly and got information in a variety of ways. Reading newspapers, magazines, books. You have to try and keep an eye on what the Japanese economy is doing and what the world economy is doing. And also what the outlook is for interest rates, foreign exchange, Japanese stocks, bonds. There is a lot to cover. You have to study in order to be able to make good judgements. I did a lot. Almost every weekend. And I also wrote a lot of articles in magazines and newspapers too. I couldn't write those at the company itself. Because people would be there. I mainly wrote about Japanese stocks for newspapers like the Nikkei. And I participated in panel discussions as well. I did all that for around 20 years from 1974 to around 1999 when I retired. So for all that time my work equalled my hobby.

But the same thing can apply to the middle generation too.

H: I don't have any holidays at the moment at all – I am so busy! So for me, my hobby equals work – that is the kind of feeling I have about it. But I don't think that is in a traditional sense. It is just that for me there is no distinction between the two. I work 24 hours a day. Since I was in London, I have been like that and whether I am disliked for it or no matter what happens, even if I am at home I am still working. It doesn't matter what time I get phone calls in Japan either. If somebody comes to Japan then I go to the airport to meet them 24 hours a day, even on Saturdays or Sundays.

The long hours worked by most employees, then, means there is little time left over for leisure activities that are not connected to the company. So there is a blurring of leisure and work in C-Life to a degree that would be unusual in a Western company, where more people would be likely to distinguish sharply between work and leisure. In the next section, I examine in detail some of the activities that are neither exactly work nor exactly leisure time. We shall see that here, again, there have been changes over the past 15 years – but some of these practices remain central to Japanese company life.

Tsukiai

'Tsukiai' (or 'getting together') refers to all of the company leisure activities. Before the bubble, the company organised many activities and trips, some of which involved the entire workforce and were therefore, essentially, mandatory. During the time that I worked at the international department, during the 1980s, there was a variety of official social functions in which we participated. These included evenings to commemorate certain dates (end of the year parties, Christmas parties), or to celebrate promotions, retirements, engagements, occasions where members were to be sent overseas and so on. C-Life also participated in the traditional summer festival of the town in which the company was situated. As many employees as possible were encouraged to participate in this event, as it was seen as an occasion for the company to involve itself in the community. There are many of these formal events throughout the year in C-Life, including one occasion where the entire company gathers together for a party. The company provides food and drink for the party, and there is a variety of events, games and shows throughout the evening. This is the only occasion when employees are encouraged to bring their wives and families – although not many of them come.

Like other supposedly informal events in the company, the occasion is considerably strained. The many events that go on throughout the evening create a formal structure designed to make sure that there are no awkward gaps or silences. Nevertheless, middle-aged and older employees reminisced frequently to me during my fieldwork about how enjoyable these activities had been.

> P: There was one time that we went on a big trip with the finance department, about 200 people. And as I said before, Fiona got up and sang a song. We all wondered how she knew a song like that! She changed the words of the song – she'd only just got out of university, and everyone was surprised. It was a really fun trip. We went to Yugawara: the hot springs resort. Everyone went by car one by one, and we all gathered together in the large banquet hall, and everyone sang a song one by one.

The financial department organises an annual trip: a group of 80 or so employees spending Saturday night at a hot springs resort near Tōkyō. On the occasion that I participated, which followed the usual pattern, everyone ate together in a large banquet hall and drank late into the night. Dinner was quite formal, with speeches by senior members in an arranged order, and a structured period after dinner was spent watching people get up and sing or perform. Having a talent of some kind is an asset at such occasions, as employees are called on to do something as part of the entertainment at these kinds of functions. If called upon to perform by a sempai it is generally difficult for juniors to refuse. Good performances are duly appreciated, but hesitant performances and performances full of mistakes – especially amusing ones – are appreciated in a different sense. Participation symbolises unity at these functions, and performers who have given bad performances are as accepted as those who have given good ones.

Some people are very good at these performances and obviously want to be called on, while at other times, as Rohlen found, the room must endure a horrible performance by a miserably nervous soul. As the performance is concluded the performer sits down with a huge sigh of relief having done their duty for the evening. After some time in the company, they will become inured against embarrassment or humiliation, as they will constantly be forced to participate in this way. I hated performing at company functions and generally avoided it as far as I could. But on the trip referred to above, my direct senior took me aside about a week beforehand and warned me that I would be asked to perform, and that this time there really was no getting out of it. I sang a very traditional Japanese love song, changing the words so the song referred to different people inside C-Life. Luckily, the song was a great hit and the occasion passed without incident.

In sum, these kinds of occasions never seemed to me to be really relaxed because they were still in the arena of company life, with pressure from seniors always there (a pressure that I discuss in Chapter 6). But I was one of the most junior members of the company, so I may have felt this particularly keenly. I think that most of the senior members of the company did enjoy themselves, probably the more so the more senior they were in the company. But, nevertheless, the atmosphere seemed to me on the whole rather as if the employees were working hard at playing (Doi 1973).

But in C-Life, as we have seen, many people do not distinguish between 'work time' and 'leisure time', and are never really off-duty. Company trips and similar occasions are therefore work, so they can relax to only a limited degree. Doi explains the Japanese inability to relax in terms of psychological compulsion. Without going this far, I think one can say that it is easy to see how, in the structure of the Japanese company, with the strict sempai-kōhai hierarchy, examined in the next chapter, it is impossible for the more junior members to forget their standing and relax. While sempai are present one is at constant attention, literally, for one must light cigarettes, pour drinks, anticipate desires, run errands and always speak formally with care to what one says.

In this sphere, as in so many others that we have discussed in the last two chapters, there has been significant change in recent years. In the 14 years after I entered the company, there was a dramatic reduction in the number of 'official' company-sponsored leisure activities, because the company could no longer afford them. The sports days had vanished, and the company actively discouraged financially demanding Japanese traditional practices such as extensive exchanging of seasonal gifts (usually given to neighbours, work colleagues and acquaintances twice a year in mid-summer and mid-winter). Older employees reminisced about such occasions with considerable nostalgia, linking the abundance of such occasions to the 'human' character of C-Life or the 'goodness' of the company. Some middle-aged employees suggested wistfully that, if the economy recovered, the company would once more have the leeway to indulge in such company-sponsored and promoted activities. But my impression from talking to younger employees was that it was unlikely that such practices would ever be revived in the same way as they had been before, even if the economic circumstances permitted. Younger employees saw company-sponsored activities as an obligation and a chore. Whereas the bulk of the social contacts of older employees were within the company itself, younger employees do not have the same expectations that they would be working with their C-Life colleagues for all of their lives, and therefore feel considerably less pressure to cultivate good relations with them. This is ostensibly the primary purpose of company-based leisure activities. Thus, those who enjoy them tend to be the high-fliers and management candidates, who enjoy group activities.

Nevertheless, one institution of Japanese company life is still strongly maintained: after-hours drinking with colleagues. The prevalence of this activity reflects the importance of alcohol in Japan generally. The one situation where employees are relatively relaxed, even in the presence of seniors, and forgiven for slip-ups in their obligations, is when they are drunk. In Japan, in general, almost any kind of behaviour becomes more forgivable on the grounds of drunkenness. Intoxication is frequently seen on all kinds of occasions, in all ranks of people from company president down, and drinking is practically a national pastime. This seems to be connected to the intense competition for status that has been a pervasive theme of this chapter. Drinking is a crucial pressure valve in a society where one can never forget one's place (Van Wolferen 1989). While drinking, a kōhai can complain to a sempai, or make criticisms, and get away with it. A sempai can open up and provide advice of the kind that is not strictly his duty to provide, such as advising a junior to get along better with his fellow employees.

Drinking occasions are frequent throughout the week. In the literature it has been remarked that the Japanese company man spends an inordinate amount of time socialising after work. But this is to overlook the fact that most employees do not make the strict distinction between work and leisure time that is more typical of Westerners. Tsukiai are not social occasions in the Western sense of the word, but rather an indispensable part of work. Many employees use them strategically to improve their contacts in the company and improve their own status; one member of the international section told me that he hardly ever socialised with his dōki as he knew them already and had nothing to gain from socialising with them. This reflects the fact that such events are not participated in simply for pleasure.

In fact, they are often not voluntary at all. If a higher member of the hierarchy asks a junior to go drinking, it is not generally a good idea to refuse. Tsukiai, therefore, can be a serious burden on employees. I asked members of the international section in 1992 what proportion of tsukiai they felt that they were obliged to attend, and their answers ranged from 0 per cent to 50 per cent. In general the older members of the section with responsibility (assistant department head, section head) reported the highest percentage of obligatory drinking sessions (40 to 60 per cent). Older members without office reported few obligatory tsukiai (0 to 30 per cent) because it is these members who have most option in choosing who they want to drink with. The younger members reported that 10 to 50 per cent of their tsukiai were obligatory.

The majority of employees told me that they went out with their dōki either once or twice a week. Overall, the occasions were fairly evenly split between those with sempai, those with dōki, those with kōhai and those with a group, but there were some individual differences. About half the tsukiai were with members of the same section, and half were with members from other sections. The overall picture of C-Life tsukiai, then, is of a large number of social occasions occurring with a variety of company members of different ages and sections.

> H: All kinds of lubricating oils are necessary to help a Japanese company work. People drink. The Japanese company is the same as an army in that you do not know where you will be posted and you do not know who will come into your division. There are just all kinds of people that you don't know at all [wake no wakaranai hito ga] all piled in there together. It is necessary for the company to make those kind of [drinking] occasions available to their employees and for the employees to attend as an obligation [kyōseiteki ni].

Tsukiai, then, play an important role in the running of the company. The need to socialise with different members of the company stems from the need to communicate. In the bureaucratic C-Life where formal communication is slow and inefficient, a thriving informal communication network exists. As we have seen, when important events, such as the restructuring lists, are announced, news is deliberately filtered out slowly by word of mouth to soften the impact. Also, being aware of what is happening inside the company is vital to maximising one's own strategies for success. It is, in one sense, another manifestation of the dual existence of honne–tatemae. The informal gossip network of C-Life is just as important as the formal tatemae channels. When the company partially knows the contents of a certain piece of news a week before the official announcement, it prepares the company as a whole to accept the changes. In other words, it serves as a conflict-avoidance mechanism. Information about the changes is distributed after hours by people walking around to each other's desks to talk, or during tsukiai.

In tsukiai, disappointments are drowned, colleagues are congratulated and speculation about the impact of the changes is discussed. A manager may informally gauge the reaction of his subordinates to an idea, or test the effect of a change he is planning to introduce. In this sense, tsukiai also acts as an informal ringi system. Tsukiai are especially important in the larger company where employees find it difficult to get to know many people on the job. During tsukiai 'they can size one another up, cement informal relationships of trust and respect, learn who cannot be counted on, and establish their own credentials' (Smith 1983: 66).

Tsukiai can also be very much a form of control. Displeasure with an employee can be shown by managers and co-workers refusing to socialise with an employee, and this kind of exclusion can be the worst possible type of punishment (Imai 1981). I discuss ostracism in detail in the next chapter; here I point out that, as achieving a network in the company is essential to success, people who have been ostracised find themselves very much at a disadvantage. This is especially so in a large company with many departments and large numbers of employees. One of the reasons an international section member gave for thinking about quitting but not doing so was: 'Because I didn't want to lose the investment I had made in jinmyaku (literally human pulse) or connections.'

Rohlen reported much the same concerning the social life of employees in the company that he studied. The frequency of social activities comes from the need for 'group maintenance'. A karaoke performer opens himself up to the group, becoming a more closely accepted member of it. Rohlen summarises the differences between the recreation patterns of employees in Japanese and American firms as being overall time, involvement with the work group rather than family or other, and the degree of intimacy achieved.

Women in C-Life participate in tsukiai a lot less than the men do. The respondents whom I spoke to didn't seem to know whether it was directly because they were women, or because of the particular departments they were in.

> O: I wonder how important it is to go drinking... I don't have those kinds of drinking relations with people but I have never felt that it was a disadvantage. I wonder if they are all out drinking. I think that the practice of drinking has got a lot less than before or maybe it is just the people around me. Neither the section chief nor the department head in my department drink. So drinking functions in my department are always planned events where everyone knows about it beforehand and adjusts their schedule accordingly. But I guess people who do it are doing it.

It is important to note that employees are well aware of all these functions of tsukiai. Respondents who felt that they did not go out and socialise enough – whether they did so through personal choice or not – often felt that they were missing out on the benefits tsukiai has to offer.

> O: I go drinking less now because I am older. Younger people are probably still drinking. When I was younger I used to go a couple of times a week on the way home from work. For me to not go is a function of age. Although I might be missing out on company news!

Employees see the danger in tsukiai as well, though.

> P: Sometimes you go out drinking and you start talking about things you shouldn't talk about and when you wake up in the morning you think, 'Oh, my God, what have I said!'

In particular, not only are employees conscious of the functions of tsukiai; they are capable of using drinking sessions carefully to promote their own agendas or gain status. They use them as an arena for strategising. For example, during my follow-up visit to the company, I went drinking with several members of the international section, including the former section head. While I was asking one of the younger members about how his interviews with possible C-Life recruits were going (younger company men are expected to interview possible recruits from the same university as themselves and persuade the more promising ones to join the company), he adroitly used the opportunity to let the section head know that he had spent a great deal of time after hours doing this. All successful employees recognise how to use tsukiai for their advantage, despite the need to take care and judge the situation.

> V: Sometimes you go out drinking and you end up in a quarrel. If you hadn't been drinking, for example, when you went out with your seniors, you would put up with things, or be patient [gaman]. When you work together with your seniors you are careful about what you say or do. So even if you have an opposing opinion to them, you say, 'Don't you think that might be a little bit different?' to question their opinions and use expressions that are prudent or cautious. You make criticisms, but you make them indirectly. But if you go out drinking, you can gradually, gradually let out your honne, your real feelings. It's not always a good thing to talk about work when you're drinking, because both parties can go too far to go back [hikkomi tsukanaku naru] much more than you normally would, if you're not careful. If it goes well, it's OK though.

> P: Yes, although it's much safer to talk about golf or women!

Despite the frequent manipulation and strategising evident in C-Life tsukiai, a lot of the time they are not planned or deliberate occasions. Rather, employees decide to go out, because they have not been out in a while and want to keep up contact, and naturally in the course of the evening they may spot opportunities and orchestrate the conversation in line with a particular strategy.

In this section, then, we have surveyed the set of activities that are not exactly work, but not simply personal leisure time either. We have seen two main points: first, the dominance of company activities over everything else in the lives of many employees, who are essentially on duty 24 hours a day; and, second, the importance of conscious strategising at these events.

Job satisfaction

In this section, I examine how happy, overall, employees are in their jobs, and compare my findings to accounts in earlier literature. The nihonjinron literature on Japanese companies generally assumed that, because the Japanese workforce works long hours, Japanese employees must be satisfied with their working conditions. This is certainly a gross over-simplification of the reality. I found that, in general, younger employees and women in C-Life are probably the least happy. Men whose careers are going well are generally happier. Happiness in general seems to depend very much on the level of insecurity employees have regarding their own positions. When I first entered the company in 1985, it seemed that the prestige of the company reflected greatly on employees. At the time, life insurance was one of the industries that students most desired to enter. But, even at the time, depending on the character of the individual, this may have been negated by the traditional atmosphere and strong hierarchy of C-Life.

In my 1992 survey, I asked the respondents what they thought were the demerits of large Japanese companies. This brought forth a variety of concerns. The answers (in order of frequency) were as follows:

- There is no psychological (seishinteki na) freedom.
- Human relations are irksome.
- Job rotation is decided by the company.
- No freedom.
- Low pay.
- Chances to use one's ability come late.
- It takes too long to make decisions.
- The extent to which working conditions can improve is limited.
- One can't get any time for oneself.
- To be able to express an opinion, one must spend years being patient.
- One can't move the company by oneself.
- One can't see the results of one's labours.
- It is difficult to use special skills one might have.
- Seniority-based promotion dampens the will to work of young people.
- People cease to be competitive.

Interestingly, many of the issues are closely related to those very aspects (job rotation, seniority-based promotion, ringi decision-making, human relations) which were considered in the nihonjinron literature to be responsible for the success of Japanese companies.

There are more factors behind the high level of dissatisfaction. The long hours that we have seen in this chapter can become little more than drudgery. Rohlen found that satisfaction and dissatisfaction in Uedagin centred on the nature of the daily routine ('tedious repetition' and long hours) and the morale of the office group. On the topic of the dynamics of group activity, he states that 'acceptance, participation, resistance, and opposition are the dimensions of the problem' (1974: 119). Later, he describes how incorrect attitudes are regarded as being the source of personal problems in the organisation. According to this outlook, cognitive dissonance and the inevitable stress caused by ambitions incompatible with the system can be reduced. This is Rohlen's treatment of the all-important question that surfaced again and again in my fieldwork and which we eventually made the key topic of the NHK documentary: whether one should mould oneself to fit the organisation or whether one should find an organisation to fit one's personality and personal ambitions.

A constant theme throughout the fieldwork chapters so far has been the lack of clarity over where each individual stands in the company, and how favourably they are being evaluated. This is a very important factor in evaluating the level of job satisfaction in C-Life. The impression I got of C-Life is of a body of people 'afloat', some of whom slowly rise while others sink, but all vaguely heading in one direction or another without any sudden changes. As we saw in Chapter 3, even the personnel department is in constant flux so there is no certain centre or leading body in the company. Van Wolferen (1989: 43–4) describes the Japanese state in the following manner – a comment that could equally be applied to the atmosphere within such a company as C-Life:

> One could label the entire body politic, meaning all and everyone participating in some way in the power process, 'the state'. But this confuses, for the state would become something very nebulous indeed, and we would still have to presuppose accountability, which in turn presupposes a center. How then, is one to label an entity which is not a state, but which does encompass the political life of a country? To me, the word 'system' seems to invite the least confusion. It denotes little more than the existence of a set of relationships, with reasonably predictable effects, between those engaged in socio-political pursuits. The term 'system' is also frequently used to suggest an arrangement of inescapable forces against which the individual is helpless without resort to violence. It hints at something beyond the range of the potentially corrective powers of democratic politics; it is something that cannot be reasoned with – although it may occasionally be duped. As it happens, the Japanese are rarely allowed to forget the existence of socio-political arrangements that are infinitely stronger than any kind of might the individual could ever bring to bear on them and have, at best, only a dim notion that ideally one should have recourse to democratic processes as a means of changing them. (The system)... determines how Japanese life is lived and who obeys whom.

In C-Life, where all the members are in constant transition from one department and one level to another, and where no-one has absolute power to transfer or promote, it is often not a simple matter for a dissatisfied worker to voice a complaint. There may not be any one single person to whom one can voice one's complaints. This, inevitably, produces stress and great insecurity, which, as we saw at the start of this chapter, is a constant feature of life in the Japanese company and something which employees seek to minimise at all times by improving their status. Van Wolferen, from his highly critical perspective of 'Japanese management', says (1989: 49):

> The System is elusive. It eludes the grasp of Westerners who want to deal with it. The Japanese who participate in it cannot get a conceptual grasp on it, much less change it. It exists without most of its participants being consciously aware of it; and it has no shape or form...

Why, given this level of dissatisfaction, do employees work as hard as they do? According to Azumi and McMillan, researchers in Japan have stressed that Japanese workers work hard for the sake of the group – a goal that is in harmony with traditional values. Traditional values are then used to provide an explanation for Japanese working hard; thus, the argument is circular. I suggest instead that employees in C-Life work hard because of the lack of attractive alternatives, the intense competition inside the company for security and status, and the pressure put upon juniors by seniors whose own work relies on the performance of those juniors. These contrast with explanations that some other Japan researchers have put forward (for example, Dore 1973).

In fact, when I entered C-Life in 1985, employees had no attractive alternatives to their current positions once they had reached the age of 26 or so. At this point the best possible course was simply to accept their position and to throw themselves positively into their work to capture the advantages of being in a Japanese company; and, as we have seen in this chapter, the most successful employees do exactly this. As employees pointed out to me, if there is no-one to complain to directly, and to be sure that the power of decision rests in that person's hands, the best one can do in the face of unfulfilled personal desire is to endure. Life in a traditional company involves accepting that what one does in one's career is a matter largely out of one's own hands (see Inagami in Okimoto and Rohlen 1988).

At the age of between 26 to 30, the average employee will get married and begin a family, which is another factor substantially binding the employee to the company because of the way in which housing and home loans are connected to the company. Of the international department respondents, all except one of the members with families answered that they felt they had to work hard for the sake of their families.

Under these circumstances, it may be that a great many employees would leave the company if it were a viable option, and this is indeed what I found. In the survey I conducted in 1992, I found that two thirds of the members of one of the most prestigious sections in the company had entertained thoughts of quitting the company. Reasons given for not quitting included the following:

- The connections that I had made in the company would go to waste.
- I thought of the demerits of quitting.
- I thought it would be losing.

It is also felt that life in a big company like C-Life, whatever its faults, is better than life in a small one – a fact that has often been raised in the literature. One respondent commented emphatically: 'There are no demerits in larger companies compared to those apparent in small companies.'

We saw in Chapter 4 that the employment situation in Japan has become much more fluid in recent years. This is, in part, because large companies like C-Life are no longer regarded as having intrinsically higher status than smaller companies – at least not to the same degree. As long as the perceived status of a large Japanese company was higher than that of a foreign company or a smaller Japanese company, no alternatives were perceived as existing. But in recent years, there has been a great expansion of perception in regard to what makes a company attractive and what work is all about. In the past, C-Life men had a strong perception that an investment had been made in C-Life and to stay would result in recuperating that investment. But now, there are many more transferable skills and industry-wide qualifications that are accepted than there were.

Also, importantly, a belief that it is harder to change jobs than it really is can be said to function as a dissonance-reducing mechanism. People who believe that they have no choice but to remain in the current positions are less likely to blame themselves for miserable working conditions (De Vos 1984; Benedict 1946).

One of the strongest factors in keeping employees working at their jobs, however, is insecurity.

Motivation and choice

In the nihonjinron literature, the typical view of Japanese workers was of a workforce secure in their jobs in the knowledge that they would not be fired. However, even before the bubble, the Japanese workforce was actually characterised by a high degree of insecurity. As Iga (1986: 198) says, 'The compulsive work among many Japanese people is not only a product of their work ethic but it is also a coping mechanism for diffuse insecurity.' Employees of large companies had few chances to change career and were thus very dependent on the company. Moreover, the fact that companies leave the employee to guess how he is really getting along in the company adds to the sense of uncertainty.

'The company' is personified in the personnel department, one of whose main functions is appraising people, but which is in itself a changing group of people in constant flux. As we have seen, nobody knows exactly how practices are carried out in the personnel department and people from this department – especially those higher up – carry something of an aura. Because of the lack of objective, measurable performance evaluations, it is not clear to the average employee how they are progressing in the eyes of the managers or the others in the company. For example, of the international department respondents to my survey, one third answered that they didn't know how the company evaluated them and what kind of role was expected of them in the future, and another third said they had only a partial idea. Iga believes that further insecurity is produced by the strong dependency needs of the individuals. 'Dependent persons are always insecure in a changing society because there is no guarantee that the objects of their dependence will satisfy their needs.' The topic of dependence – or amae – is an important one that I address in Chapter 6.

In this uncertain environment, employees must be optimistic about where they stand, or life would be unbearable. One cannot decide that one detests one's work if one knows that one is going to be doing that work for life. Japanese must justify to themselves the system in which they work. As De Vos (1984: 50) says:

> Japanese would rather distort reality in a direction of experiencing gratification from understanding superiors than distort in the direction of experiencing themselves subject to a malevolent, impersonal, exploitative social system in which they are being used, broken, and cast away as rubbish. Such a view of life for many Japanese would elicit an unmanageable sense of irreparable outrage.

One relieving factor is the knowledge that the section in which they work will be changed every few years or so. Another is the fact that each succeeding year in a

Japanese company is easier, provides the individual with more pay and more status than the year before, and involves more demanding and interesting work. Employees in C-Life who were unhappy with their jobs frequently pointed out to me that the causes of their unhappiness were bound to disappear if they endured for the interim. On the positive side, conditions are constantly improving, but on the negative side, this makes each consecutive year in the company a greater and greater investment, the dividends of which can only be collected through further service.

It might seem, from our discussion in the last two sections, that the only forces keeping employees working hard are negative ones – insecurity and helplessness. However, in discussing the importance of status to most employees, we saw that many people do not simply work hard at their given tasks – they actively strive to rise through the company hierarchy. In the next section, then, I turn to a more positive factor in employee motivation: ambition.

Ambition

At the start of this chapter, we found that many employees are interested in what qualities make someone the ideal employee. When I was conducting my fieldwork, 'leadership candidate' was an expression that frequently came up in conversation. Basically, it meant someone who still had the potential to rise to be a director or even the company president. There are not many of these people in the company. One of my dōki had the following to say about believing he would be a 'leadership candidate' when he entered the company.

A: Did I believe I was a leadership candidate when I joined the company? Well, I was trained as a general worker...

Q: So you thought that you would become a manager from the time you entered the company?

A: Well, everyone thinks that, don't they? All new trainees... When I was a leader in the union [kumiai], I gave out a questionnaire to all the new trainees. One question on the questionnaire was, 'In the future how important or which level do you think you will be able to reach in the company?' The answers were, 'As far as the president', 'As far as director', 'As far as department head', 'As far as section head'. About 30 per cent of the new trainees wrote 'President'. After about ten years that becomes 3 per cent. And after 20 years they say that it becomes zero.

Q: And for you?

A: Of course, I think I will become the president!

Q: So you haven't changed in 14 years.

A: Well, I could get scolded for saying things like this so I will leave it to your imagination!

We have seen that the primary drive for employees is not necessarily to advance at an enormous pace – rather, it is to avoid falling behind one's dōki. When employees considered if they could drop ambition and advancing in the company, the first thing they considered is whether they 'could' drop behind their dōki; whether they could stand the drop in status and social pressure that would result from doing that.

> E: Some people probably don't really want to go up the company ladder. They are just happy collecting their pay and doing whatever they can to live. Those people might want to stay in the company despite the pay-cuts, despite falling behind their dōki.

In fact, among my dōki and those close in age, employees had begun to question what kind of positions they really wanted inside the company, and how far they could still advance in the company.

> E: I don't think that I would be very successful as a sales head. So rather than be the head of a sales office it would be good to be in some kind of staff position inside a branch office. I am part of management now because I am a section head. I became a section head last spring. I was really really happy about that. Well, half-happy and half-insecure about it. It is the start of a new challenge in some ways. Ever since I got into the company I thought that I really want to be promoted... I really want to get ahead. I always said that I want to get ahead. But when I actually got to that age, although I had been thinking that it was a far-off thing I was suddenly there. My dream had come true and I suddenly had to think, so what am I going to do about this?

Employees talk in terms of 'still being on track' for seniority promotion, and analyse their situation in the hope of determining how likely they are to be promoted. Transfers are important in this, because employees can judge if they are still on the right track or not by what position they are moved to.

> Q: When you got into the company did you think that you were a candidate for top management?
>
> J: Um... I don't know... But the company did place me where I wanted to be... into the international department. So I was happy.

As we have seen in this chapter, however, it can be very hard to interpret transfer decisions, and similar decisions may have different implications for different employees. For example, one employee at the time of my fieldwork was a department head in the public relations section – an important section in the head office. But his next move took him to be a branch head in the provinces. For a younger man, this might have been a good promotion. For the department head, it more or less meant that he would be out of the limelight during two crucial years when it would be decided if he would stay in the company or retire. Other employees agreed that such an appointment probably meant that he had reached the highest level he would attain in the company.

Employees who are still on track for leadership have a particularly hard decision when determining whether to leave the company or not. Although in the short term they may be able to get a better position and more chance to learn, in the long term they are giving up the chance – small though it may be – to become the president, director, or member of senior management of a major Japanese corporation.

> J: At the same time that I thought I would quit the company if I wasn't stretching myself, I also had the feeling that I wanted to become company president in the future and that I could really do it. There were other dōki of mine who were trying really hard [gambaru] with the intention of becoming president. I think that they are all fighting really hard with that idea in mind.

Employees agree to a remarkable extent on who is still in the running to be a leadership candidate. The people they cited as being such candidates had good results in the training centre in selling insurance – but not necessarily the best. They were all, without exception, highly individual characters. As we have seen, there needs to be something that makes these employees stand out from their dōki in order to make them leadership candidates. Contrary to what one might expect from the literature, with its emphasis on groupism, leadership candidates need to be very individualistic and have character, to be creative in the sense of creating good ideas, and to be able to take risks and shoulder the responsibility for putting these ideas into action.

When I arrived to film my programmes, one prime candidate had just left for a foreign company. Another, surprisingly, would not let me interview him at all. We learnt why when he quit the company just a few weeks after I finished filming, which caused a great shock-wave through the organisation as he was one of the people thought least likely to be thinking of quitting.

Those who begin with ambition often have their ambitions tempered by their realisation that there are other dōki who are stronger and more suited to leadership than they are themselves. At that point, they can resign themselves to separating work and private life and concentrating on enjoying private life, or they can modify their ambitions to reaching a lower level of management, rather than the very top.

> T: As for whether I had a strong ambition to get ahead… well, even if you have a strong ambition to get ahead, it doesn't necessarily mean that you can do that. I don't know about the people around me, but people lately… I think the people in my year wanted to get ahead as far as possible and that is what they all thought. But I just thought I'd get as far ahead as was possible [watashi wa soko made…]. If I am lucky, I thought that I might be able to get ahead though.

E: I don't really know what you have to do in order to advance in the company. If I am asked if I did anything special to become the first woman in the company to become a section chief, I would just say that I did the work that was given to me to the best of my ability, and even just to do that I battled with people around me and fought and at times I cried. The only thing that I can really say is that I did it with all of my heart [isshōkenmei].

This last comment reflects the typical Japanese emphasis on the importance of effort in success. Indeed, much of what we have seen in this section is reflected in literature on Japan in general. An intense concentration on effort sometimes makes employees seem irrational. But rationality must be defined. Short-term rationality – or rational strategies – should not be confused with a rational approach to life. Maraini, for example, states that 'the Japanese, when defining themselves as rational, do not have in mind the important distinction between rationality as a total way of thinking and confronting the world, and rationality as an instrument of action' (Fodella 1975: 40). Where in the West goals might be tackled with the idea of rationality in mind, the first step being to decide how realistic the goal is, in Japan, we are told, the effort put into it is often seen as the main thing.

These views can be seen in the attitudes of company men for whom work is a war to be won in time. This attitude encourages two things: a long-term perspective in the desire for achievement and an ability to be patient in the present, in the expectation of future rewards (Smith 1983).

On this view, the long-term viewpoint of the Japanese has enabled large-scale success of companies. On the down side, however, taking pleasure in suffering and perseverance can easily turn into masochism in a group situation. Some Japanese explain the behaviour of the Japanese in World War Two in these terms, especially what happened at the end of the war when they battled on in the face of certain defeat. The C-Life employees frequently mentioned parallels that they saw between the behaviour of the C-Life employees and the behaviour of the Japanese in World War Two. They usually did so when reiterating their view that Japanese go on without stopping long after such behaviour has ceased to be rational.

Benedict (1946: 241) describes how Indian Yoga was changed in the context of Japanese society. The techniques of self-hypnotism, concentration and control of the senses were seen as providing ways to perfection. 'In India, Yoga functioned principally as a means of release from the world of illusion (samsara), in Japan it came to be employed as a means of affirmation in the world: it became a self training in perfection, a superior training in efficiency'. One might say that in Japan there is a constant striving for a higher plane of achievement, for success. It could almost be said that, for some Japanese, self-identity is created out of the sum total of what one has achieved.

According to Reischauer (1977: 152), the acquisition of a skill is, for the Japanese, essentially an act of individual will, and the mastery of a skill is viewed as the outcome of the development of the inner self. Smith remarks (1983: 103): 'This is so much the case that I have often been surprised by the revelation of quite unreasonable ambitions and expectations of attainment on the part of my Japanese friends and acquaintances, who appear to feel they can achieve any goal through the application of sheer effort.' It should be easier, with this background, to see how many Japanese can resign themselves to the reality of the organisation and concentrate on striving upwards to achieve the highest place that they can on the hierarchy. Doing so fulfils their sense of identity and satisfies their need to achieve and develop throughout their careers. Job content has thus, traditionally, been less relevant to satisfaction than the place occupied on the hierarchy.

So ambition is an important motivation for many C-Life employees. It is a positive force keeping them at their work, complementing the negative ones discussed in the preceding section, and it reflects some typical aspects of the Japanese mindset in general. We will see how ambition affects interpersonal relations in the next chapter. Here, I go on to consider the effects of ambition and long working hours on employees' families.

Family

One of the principal themes of this chapter has been the remarkably long hours worked by most C-Life employees as they strive to climb the company hierarchy. We have noted that this lifestyle leaves very little time for activities not related to the company. How, then, does this affect employees' family lives?

Among the older generation in C-Life, work almost always takes precedence over home life, and families are mentioned only in tsukiai. The following views, by contrast, are from a middle-aged employee. I tested these on older company employees and although they agreed that family was important, they said they would not visibly mix family and work by having photos on their desk as this respondent had. Many employees do have photos of their families in their wallets, however, and these are taken out and admired during tsukiai.

> S: I'd like to be seen at work as somebody who can not only do their work but as somebody who's a very happy person. I'd like for happiness to come out naturally from me. Of course it's necessary to be smart and to be able to do your work but I'd like to be thought of as somebody for whom family is also important. I have my family's photos sitting on my desk but there are some people who really dislike that. Some of my male bosses say to me, 'Why do you have to bring your family into your workplace?' But I don't think that that should be the case. Or maybe it's because mine is a workplace dominated by women... The women around me sometimes say to me, 'Your family is more important to you than us, aren't they?' If I drew back there and failed to commit to that, I think they would think of me as someone with no firm standpoint, who was neither here nor there. So I always keep my family's photos on my desk. I think that – I'd like the people around me to think that I'm a very happy person and to think that I'm doing insurance sales as my work in order to buy happiness for my family. I think that the employees around me think that I'm a good father. I think that the women salesmen think so. More than thinking that I'm good at my work or that I'm smart, they think that I'm a happy person.

The largest area of conflict between work and family comes, as might be guessed from what we have already seen in this chapter, from the amount of time that is required for the successful employee to advance in the company. In general, C-Life employees sacrifice their families for work when there is a conflict of interest, although there have always been a few exceptions to this rule. I found, though, that employees are increasingly clear-cut about maintaining the formal company hours rather than the unspoken rule of staying at work as long as possible.

> S: So from Monday until Friday I would draw a very clear line and do business but I was able to make a very clear separation at the weekend and that was when we had fun.

> S: I am managing to make it home although it might not look like it. Actually I'm quite a stay-at-home kind of father; I like going home to see my wife's face and my children's faces, but it's usually past ten o'clock when I make it home. I take about an hour to commute. I leave home about seven o'clock in the morning so my children are still asleep and when I get home they're already asleep again so that is a bit lonely. There is no vacation at all for New Year – this year I have to work on 31 December and 1 January both. It can't be helped because I'm in this kind of work.

I found that this posed the biggest problem for newly-married wives without children, especially those with husbands who had been transferred.

> R: S is a really good father. He does come home really late at night. At first (when we transferred from Tōkyō), I was always in tears about that. I'd look at the sky towards the east to Tōkyō – I'd climb on the balcony and look towards Tōkyō and cry. I would say, 'Have a good day!' in the morning to him as he went out the door and at first I would have no-one to talk to all day long until the moment I greeted him when he came back home at night again. He was working from early morning till really late at night so sometimes I thought that it had been better before we got married – at least then we met and talked. But that situation didn't last forever – I had children and so my concentration got focused on the children.

In general, the arrival of children in the C-Life family sharply polarises the roles of husband and wife. The wife becomes fully occupied with the children and is no longer so disturbed if her husband is working long hours.

> R: At the time that he was working at Tōkyō Frontier – the section where four-year-university graduates were hired to work as sales ladies – he always came home with knitted brows and I wondered if he was going to be OK working this hard. It seemed really hard what he was doing. But at the time I was having a really hard time as well. I had three children each a year apart. The youngest child was still a baby so I didn't have time to think about my husband too much. It was three years when both of us were incredibly busy.

R: At home, S is a really good father. I don't know what he's like at work because I've never seen him there. He loves his work, he loves his company, but I think he loves his family more – he's a great father.

S: I wonder if that's really true – well, if she says it, it must be! Well, in my case I was born in 1961 and I entered the company in 1985 so I think that there is some part of me that is part of the old type of traditional society. My loyalty toward the company is really high.

Surprisingly, for some families, the work/family separation alters dramatically when they transfer to the provinces. So, to some degree, the long hours typical of C-Life are dependent on living standards in Tōkyō. Also, employees said there was considerably more pressure to work the same hours as others while they were directly under the department head's eyes in the main office, whereas life was relatively relaxed in the provincial sales offices where they had few seniors. This accords with what we have seen earlier in this chapter, that employees sometimes found transfers to the provinces to be a lot pleasanter than they had anticipated. And that experience helps to highlight what the normal Tōkyō lifestyle is like for C-Life employees.

R: But after we moved to Fukuoka, because it was the provinces and our house was close to the office, and there was no commuter rush and he could go to the office by car, his expression changed completely. In the provinces, the time we could spend together increased dramatically and we could go out every Sunday and it was really fun. It wasn't so much a worry about the children's schools because where there is company housing there are usually a lot of children whose fathers have been transferred so it wasn't that much of a problem. So the population of the children was also changing a lot but my kids were still in the lower grades of school and in kindergarten so they could go into school and be accepted quite easily.

S: It was only in Fukuoka that I was able to get to the hospital to see one of my children being born. Even though she wanted me to go to hospital with her in Tōkyō it didn't work out that way. The hospital was far from the office where I was working in Tōkyō and she doesn't have a driving licence. While we were living in Tōkyō it's not very convenient for transportation. If one of our children got a temperature in the provinces I could just say, 'Well, I'll be home in a minute,' and go straight to the hospital from the office but in Tōkyō once I leave home for work then the two spheres are really separated – it's hard to mix the two. It might not be a good thing to always mix the two but in the provinces I could do it.

R: For example, when my children were born – when my oldest child was born – it was the middle of the night. I hired a woman to be with me at the hospital but my husband was awake all night with me and as soon as my daughter was born he fell asleep. At seven o'clock in the morning he got up and went to the company, rubbing his sleepy eyes. He was there for the second birth as well but not for the third – he didn't make it in time because she was born early. The third child was born much earlier than expected but he came as soon as he could afterwards to the hospital.

S: The doctor took photos of the first and second but because I wasn't there for the third one he took a photo of it in case I thought it was somebody else's – in case I might think we found the kid! So he took a photo of the kid coming out! I thought that I really should be there for the birth of my own kids – although I couldn't bear to stay and watch the umbilical cord being cut – but I was there until then.

R: After we came back to Tōkyō, there aren't a lot of places to go here. Tōkyō is so crowded and everything costs so much money and time goes by so fast. Since we came back we haven't really been anywhere. Before, we used to go really often camping and we kept up relations with different people as well.

S: There are a lot of places for older people to go out to and spend time at, like department stores, but there's not so many places for children to play at in Tōkyō. Well, I guess they could play at parks…

R: They play often at the park just behind our house or the kids go to their friends' houses inside this housing complex. Our lifestyle really changed when we came back from the provinces.

The family/work separation is outlined by the comments of some wives to me that they have no idea at all about the content of their husbands' jobs, or what they are like at work. Where I was able to talk to the wives I quickly realised that husbands and wives have little understanding of what the other does, and surprisingly little interest. Wives don't know exactly what kind of work their husbands do a lot of the time, or whether they are happy at work or not. They do know what status their husbands hold in the company and roughly how many years are likely before they shift to the next post up. Most wives, however, seem to have little interest in the content of their husbands' careers as long as they are drawing steady pay-packets. Some wives told me emphatically that as long as the work was stable, they would prefer that their husbands not advance, as that would take them away from home more. Such lack of mutual understanding about what women and men actually do is behind the frequent recent reports of wives requesting divorce as soon as the husband reaches retirement age.

H: The company employees have the perception that they are working all of the time for the sake of their families. But their families don't really see it in the same way. They think the men are out having fun – well, half-way anyway. There is a big gap between men and women. Men think that because they have been working so hard – well, even though they are drinking half the time they think of that as part of their work – it is an important part of work in order to build human relations inside the company. But women are independent and I think that this is the same as America. So they don't see the drinking of the men in quite the same way.

S: I don't think she can easily imagine what I'm like at work – I think that I'm probably really different – I think that I change completely as soon as I walk into the company. I have to say strict things when I'm in the company to people who are the same age as my mother. I have to say, 'What do you think you're doing! You shouldn't be doing things like that!' If my wife saw a scene like that, she would probably be thinking, 'Should you really be saying things like that to people that are so far senior to you?' So I never say, 'You shouldn't do things like that!' to my wife or scold her in any way.

And also at the company with the customers if I'm in a life or death fight over whether I'm going to succeed or not then it's a very fine line whether my sales pitch is going to make it or not. That is what I'm doing every day. I have that sense of crisis – I don't think my wife has ever seen that in me. The work that I'm actually doing now and what she saw me doing in the training era are completely different regarding the sense of urgency and the seriousness of the work.

Similarly, according to the wives, men are often not aware of what is involved in bringing up children and looking after their everyday needs, and running the household, including the household budget. Even those husbands who see themselves as putting in their best efforts have not much more than a token role in the running of the household. Many are proud of the little that they do manage to do, however.

P: As far as the family goes – in my case, I am quite a family man, aren't I, everyone? I don't think it's difficult to do both. On holidays I look after my family [katei sābisu – do 'family service']. I do spend time with my family and look after them. Everyone does that to the best of their ability, don't they?

Z: What kind of service?

P: Well, I make dinner... or I send my kids off to school in the morning, sometimes. I do that to the best of my ability, yes.

I measure the communication with my family, I guess, basically in terms of how much time we talk together. If I go back early then I have time to talk with them. We go shopping together, as well. That's the kind of thing I do. I really do it properly [kichitto].

As we saw earlier, the model employee S insists that both family and work are important and that the state of each affects the other. But, in practice, this seems hard to achieve. It was evident to me that the company always came first for S in any conflict, even on each and every Saturday, which was theoretically a holiday for the company, and at New Year.

S: If I'm asked which I prefer between being a stay-at-home kind of father and advancing in the company, I think I would probably answer that if your home life isn't going well than your work isn't going to go well either. If my wife isn't happy – if my wife is in a bad mood in the morning – then at the morning meeting in my office I'm likely to show that I'm in a bad mood as well, and to snap about something at the staff. So, if the morning goes well then the whole day goes well. So, in that sense, if the household isn't going well then I don't think you can go well in advancing in the company either. I don't think you can really put all your strength into your work if you sacrifice your family either.

In some senses, for the middle and younger generations, the desire to spend more time with family was an insurance policy in the uncertain environment. The recent media interest in cases of wives taking half of the husband's retirement money and divorcing him as soon as he retires from the company has perhaps encouraged people to communicate more with their families.

> S: However, if you asked me as an individual it is hard to be a normal family man and be happy all of the time – that would be impossible, speaking frankly. The other day I went drinking with six of my colleagues – six of my dōki. All of them were people who had become section heads in the first round – in the first year in which people of my age could become section chiefs. But after five years have passed I might be in the same position as I am now and they may have advanced further than me.
>
> If that were the case – it would be best if both my family is going well and my work is going well. It might be seen as grasping to want so much but that's what I'd like.

For the women employed in the general worker category, family life was considerably different from how it would be for the majority of Japanese women who do not work full-time. In most cases, the pressure to quit the company wins over the desire to stay. Some employees related to me that, having got into C-Life as a general worker, they felt that they had 'proved a point' and were tired after seeing the intensity of company life. Others saw that it would be very difficult to advance in the company despite the company's assurances that they would be treated equally; as we have seen in Chapter 3 and will examine in more depth in Chapter 6, they were never really considered equal to men. When they marry, most women's main concern is whether they will be able to balance family and work. As we have seen above, men generally sacrifice family in favour of work. But in the case of women, there is a very strong societal – and possibly personal – pressure on them to balance the two.

> O: Women often quit because they get married. That is the same for general workers (sōgōshoku). Sometimes it was not because they got married but just because it happened to be an inter-company marriage. Also a lot quit after they get married when they get pregnant. But there are cases that have continued even with kids, even in the countryside, working all the time. There isn't a rule about having to quit if you have an inter-company marriage, but most people do. If they didn't I don't know what would happen. There is one couple where the woman is tantōshoku so

it is possible. I don't think the sōgōshoku in the past were told to quit, but if it was me working in the same company with my husband I wouldn't want to do that. It would be difficult to balance work and private life like that. Although there are people in entirely different sections.

In practice, the C-Life general workers who were women did make considerable sacrifices for their families. One woman whom I saw shortly after New Year said:

E: My father lives by himself in a province some distance from Tōkyō. He came to Tōkyō on 1 January to go to a shrine with my daughter but went back again without seeing me. I had to work because of the Y2K problems.

In Japanese families, the wife often controls the finances, and C-Life families are no exception. Not all employees are in favour of this practice, however.

H: As far as my wife goes, as long as a pay-packet arrives in the bank each month, she doesn't really care about the rest. She is quite traditional. She has nothing to do with my life as a salaryman. Anyway, as far as women are concerned, the bad thing is that the pay-packet goes directly into the bank account. So most wives think that if they go to the bank on the 25th of the month there is automatically money sitting there. That is a problem of the structure in Japan. Whether women have husbands or don't have husbands the pay comes in directly to the bank account. So if the husband wasn't around they would be in trouble, but in practice, even if the husband is away in the countryside or overseas the money still comes into the same bank account, so they just think that's a natural phenomenon, so they don't feel thankful or anything. And in some cases, they think it would be much better if the husband were away and much easier on them if the money is just coming into the bank account. And I think that can be said about a lot of homes. I think that is really strange. In America, the finances are often managed by the guy. I am managing my finances myself. But I hear from various places, the husband just gets 30,000 yen from his wife as pocket money and has to ask his wife earnestly for a 10,000 yen raise. I hear things like that but I think that kind of phenomenon is disappearing lately.

H: Since I came back from America I changed my household so I look after the money now. My wife didn't oppose that. I think my wife understands that my thinking about my work is quite Western. My wife is quite Americanised as well, so she is quite strange in that way. She went and played golf yesterday. She does things like that from her own part-time work. She has her own income. I think my responsibility to my family is to provide a place for them to live, and food to eat and clothes to wear and enough financial help so my children can go to school. I don't do any housework by myself but sometimes I help.

Although the C-Life families are rather neglected, measured in practical terms of how many hours a week is spent on work as opposed to family, the importance of family to the employees is considerable. Families are often the topic at drinking parties, and, as we have seen earlier in this chapter, the ideology of working hard 'for the sake of my family' is important to the C-Life employees. I often felt that this ideology was underpinning their rationalisation of how hard they were working, although in practice it was hard to see how much their families really benefited.

Here, then, we have seen some of the serious consequences of the long working hours endured by most C-Life employees. In the next section, I bring together the themes of this chapter by considering what employees actually think of C-Life. What kind of character do they think it possesses? Do they actually like it, in view of the working conditions we have described in this chapter?

The character of C-Life

The older the employee in C-Life, the more nostalgic they tend to be for the way C-Life 'used to be' and, in general, the greater their affection for the company. This generation did not have to live with the uncertainty of restructuring, and they enjoyed a company with a more extensive welfare system than the present C-Life.

> Z: When I joined the company, Japanese companies were a lot more magnanimous or large-hearted or broad-minded [ōraka na]. So there was a choir in the company and in the choir there were 120 to 130 people and 70 or 80 were women. At the time, all the women were high school graduates and the average age was 20. And I was the conductor. So I have a lot of good memories of the fun times we had after five. I don't know if that was good for this particular company as I don't really know anything about other companies. But my friends went to a variety of companies. There are people among them that say I have worked in this company for 30 years and am really happy and there are people who say I didn't really do anything in the company so I guess I do have comparisons.

> Z: I guess my image of the company is of a family kind of bureaucracy [o-yakunin ikka]. It's a place where we all want to be friendly and get along together. It's a place where everybody wants the company to be better and wants to increase their own pay, and I think that we did that.

> C: I think it is a company that has a great respect for people, to put it simply. They had management policies which stressed a focus on the individual and contribution to society. They really attached importance to individuals and focused on healthy contribution to society.

> C: I think it is really sad that the company has met with such hard times. Well, stocks have recovered a little and the company must be doing a little better. I really want the guys in charge now to do their very best and hope that the company gets back on its feet soon.

Similarly, many middle-aged C-Life employees, once out of the training years and relatively secure in their own positions, settle into company life and see C-Life as a comfortable place in which to work.

A: There are things that I felt were really comfortable about C-Life... that they treat people really well [hito o daiji ni suru]. As I said before, they really treat you very well. In my case, they probably treated me a bit too well!

But opinions about the company were radically different according to the position of the person I was talking to. And as we have seen throughout this chapter, all of the employees I talked to who had quit C-Life were highly vocal about the company's negative points.

S: Working regularly on the weekends when there is no rule about doing so is something that happens in my company – I don't know about other life insurance companies. It's not exactly like a new religion [cult religion] but there are nuances of that – that you have to sacrifice your Saturdays to the company. Well, I'd get scolded if I was heard saying that.

Moreover, the very things that employees mention as favourable about C-Life are also recognised as contributing to its downfall.

E: It is a very kind company and that might be why it is not a good thing. For sales it is probably too kind. For example, in sales, among the sales staff there are those that have switched over to C-Life from N-Life or D-Life or S-Life and they say that after they have quit their companies and come to us C-Life is a really good company. It seems that other companies in the industry are really strict. They are strict about how the results are each month. We look at how results are of course, but we look at things a little bit more optimistically it seems. As if we were all friends in it together [minna nakayoshi de]. If it is a really strict company it seems that there are many cases where you take customers away from other people or have them taken from you, so you compete among the sales staff. To some extent that happens with us as well. But not as much as we hear about with other companies. I think in order to change the company we have to get rid of that kind of easygoing stance. I think that there is something about the company as a whole that is too relaxed. Something reminiscent of a young gentleman with too much money that doesn't need to try hard enough. That might be good in some ways, but for a company that is trying to get profits it becomes [amasa] indulgence: it means that the company loses its edge. The company often is told that the company atmosphere is like that of a 'Keiō Boy' [Keiō University is renowned for wealthy students]. The image of it is that of a young gentleman with money to splash around.

Q: So are the C-Life people all individualistic?

H: No, it is because we are individualistic that we were forced out of the company.

C: The atmosphere of C-Life is very serious. A little too serious so that it lacks versatility and finds it hard to adjust to change [yuzu ga kikanai]. If you say it in a good way it is gentlemanly. There is a real lack of ambition among the people. If you divide it between forward looking and conservative they are conservative. I think they are slow to accept new things or to put in radical changes. For Japanese companies to be restructuring only now is conservative. It is not that they are so many years behind where they should be; it is that the timing of the response is slow.

So, to sum up these comments, some of the positive aspects of C-Life include its comfortable atmosphere, its 'kind' character, its lack of strictness, optimism, and its 'all-in-togetherness'. On the negative side, we have a 'cult' atmosphere, a lack of individualism, lack of ambition, conservative character, a company that is slow to respond to the times. Employees comment that the C-Life men are aware of the need to keep up with the times, and with the competition, but that the overall atmosphere of C-Life prevents them from being able to take any action. Furthermore, the following comment attributes the lack of action to the conservative nature of the C-Life employees themselves.

H: There are people who are aware of this [the need to concentrate on profits] inside the company, but while they are inside the company they just go on going to work every day [nukunukuto], collecting their pay-packet, and if they can get their pay at the very least they think they are getting something, so they don't worry about it [ii ka na to].

Other comments attribute the lack of action to the structure inherent in the company that prevents change. In particular, the fact that different departments in the company and the personnel department are often pulling in different directions was pinpointed.

H: There are often such clashes of interest in the company. For example, the personnel department might bring something up and because they have their work to do and they get evaluated on that work, if they can say they have helped to internationalise the company, they get good points for having done that. That is why they want to do it... But on the other side, the actual department just wants to go on working by themselves (shikoshiko yaritai). Although they just wanted to get by by themselves, the personnel department kept on putting new people into the department. In that sense, because the leadership of a Japanese company is diversified, all the departments are like amoeba. They are doing whatever they like (katte ni). But they are supposed to be working as an organisation and yet things like this happen. They are supposed to be working together in coordination against a common enemy but that is not what happens.

Comments on the character of C-Life, then, are most typically on the following lines: praise for the positive elements of the group atmosphere, followed by criticism of the underside of that same group atmosphere: bullying and ostracism. Additionally, Japanese practices – like ringi – are also mentioned.

> P: There are really a special set of values in the Japanese company that are respected, and part of that is that dōki come in as the lowest rank of the company, developing a sense of joint ownership of the company [kyōyū]. I think that we really have a lot of that. I think that C-Life is a company that sees that kind of thing as very important. In the end, loyalty to the organisation is that same kind of thing. There's a real sense of social solidarity in the company. An image of the organisation as a co-operative [renmei kyōdōtai], even in this time. I think it's a really typical Japanese company. And in that sense there's a kind of exclusion policy [jō i gedatsu] in operation. There are Japanese kinds of practices of creating ideas at the bottom and moving them up to top management, and those practices have not disappeared, they're not crumbling.

Defining the 'group' atmosphere inevitably comes down to common behaviour, common values and conformity. In my own case, when I started to work at C-Life, I was welcomed as a new graduate because, in contrast to other foreigners, I could be formed into a company person.

> P: In Fiona's case, she came into the company straight from university without having worked in the West or in Japan. So in that sense she came as a blank sheet of paper. So I think she just thought that this is the natural way of things, that this is a normal Japanese company. However, she must also have been conscious that there were all kinds of values in the company that were different from what she had known since she was a child. Even in the international department in that sense, the organisation itself was a very important issue for everyone. For example, when we went on a trip for the end of year party, and she was told that she had to sing, then she would sing. She sang something that was pretty over the top as well!

> P: In this age now, if you ask everybody to sing karaoke, there are people lately who say, 'No, I don't want to do that.' Of course that doesn't mean that the organisation is breaking down because of that. But that kind of thing was implicated in everyone having a sense of common ownership and trying hard together [gambaru]. So on things like that, it was decided whether someone was a good guy or not [game]. So they might decide that he wasn't an organisation man [soshiki jin], and be kicked out from the centre to the sidelines [hajiki tobasarechau]. However, in Fiona's case she didn't have any special problems like that. So that was a very good thing for our organisation. So we were able to maintain relations with her without any sense of incompatibility.

Thus, common ownership or being a company man means doing the same as everyone else – in which case one is a 'good guy'. Not doing the same as everyone else invites being 'kicked out'.

Employees constantly describe the atmosphere inside C-Life as murky, unclear, and vague. Both the positive and negative aspects of this are described below. The first comment refers to whether bosses tell juniors clearly when they are being evaluated badly. Clarity is sacrificed in order to maintain good relations.

> I: I don't think there are cases where they don't tell people something deliberately in case they quit the company when they find the personnel department's evaluation is so different to their own. It's not the case that the company will be troubled in case they quit – it's just that it's really hard to tell people.

> I: I think in evaluating people, they have a strange kind of group consciousness [nakamai ishiki] – they want to protect each other in some way. The bosses want to protect their juniors, and the juniors also want to protect their seniors [kabau]. I don't know if 'protect' is really the right word to describe it. Anyway, the issues never become very clear at all. I don't know if that's something which is really bad for the company – well I don't know. That's something which is really hard to say about the relations of humans in the same workplace. I think it's really because, if the bosses make the problems of their juniors clear and open, it might be better for the overall work as a whole, but the individual relations will become bad.

The lack of clarity ensures that open conflict is kept to a minimum. Lack of clarity comes hand in hand with other concepts that are reiterated again and again through these fieldwork chapters: vagueness in pinpointing responsibility, difficulty in evaluating correctly, a certain degree of 'irrationality in behaviour'.

> I: Japanese companies do put a lot of effort into making sure that conflict doesn't occur, but I think it's slowly changing. People's opinions are heard now. It should be decided whether an idea is good or not on the basis of opinions put forward. And I think it will also be the case that responsibility will be pinpointed in the future. Until now, if something was done, people didn't take responsibility for the results… But now banks have gone under, and life insurance companies are going bankrupt; and in that environment, business heads are being asked what their responsibility was for the results that happened. In that manner, that kind of custom is becoming established among Japanese business practice. Well, it might be strange to call that confrontation, but ideologies and opinions are now being discussed among company members. I don't think it's a bad thing for that to happen, for people to gradually say things openly and clearly, and to have the results evaluated properly and clearly. In America and England and Europe, they have that kind of rationality, so that they say their opinions and look at how the results were, and think about the responsibility for those results. Japanese also have to go gradually towards that kind of practice, towards globalisation or internationalisation. They need to achieve these practices or they will fall behind.

C-Life men describe as a lack of 'rationality' behaviour that maintains the social harmony at the expense of what should have been done from a rational business point of view. This conflict between rational business behaviour and social good is a primary theme for the C-Life men, in terms of conflict they face in their everyday work, and in their ideas about how C-Life should change in the future. The comment below, for example, is conclusive in its admission that, in C-Life, rationality is superseded by social or group 'norms' peculiar to the company.

Q: So you are saying that [in C-Life] there was a kind of group consciousness that, even if the methods were unreasonable or absurd, or in other words, irrational, and that you could get fired [hung] at any time, that couldn't be helped?

I: Yes, that was the case.

Q: In that sense C-Life was a group organisation that resigned itself entirely to fate?

I: Yes, it was a group or collective that resigned itself to fate.

We see, then, a variety of opinions about the company, varying dramatically according to the age and position of the employee. Most significantly, there is pessimism about the company's ability to deal with change, and a variety of explanations are put forward for this. These points are expanded on in Chapter 6.

Conclusion

In this chapter, we have learnt what working conditions are like at C-Life, how those conditions affect employees' lives, and their general satisfaction and happiness with the company. We have focused on the centrality of status as a concern of C-Life employees. This is true of different employees to different degrees but, for the most part, the most important goal of any activity in the company is to increase one's status, thereby ensuring greater security in the company. This will become more apparent in the next chapter.

In this chapter, I examine in depth the way people at C-Life interact, their attitudes towards each other, and the general atmosphere of the company. Throughout the chapter, I focus further on the themes that have emerged over the last three chapters: the honne–tatemae distinction; status as the primary goal of most employees; the different levels of ability in gaining status; the different levels of awareness of social rules; and the way in which the times are changing with the harsher economic climate.

6   The company and human relations

Groupism

Groupism is one of the most well-known features of Japanese companies. It is in the context of groupism, and attitudes towards it, that human relations in C-Life must be understood. Here, then, I analyse what groupism means to employees, in both its positive and negative aspects, and examine how it has changed in recent years.

Employees see C-Life's group-oriented character as one of the most fundamental elements of the Japanese company. From it flow other important characteristics of the company such as the training and harsh initiation that we examined in Chapter 4.

> H: In the training dormitory they eat rice that has been cooked in the very same pot as everyone else and they all have a very hard time together going around doing door-by-door sales. There is that army-like character to Japanese companies, especially in life insurance companies, something very Japanese. I think that life insurance is an industry in which the most Japanese characteristics are still remaining.

However, they are divided in their evaluation of groupism, whether it is a good or a bad thing. Sometimes it is described in almost lyrically pastoral terms, sometimes in terms of ostracism:

> H: C-Life is a primitive communistic village society where everyone is important to the same degree. The guys who have ability cover for the guys who do not. There is a lot of mutual sympathy [kyōkan] and emotion-based situations. When inside those kind of societies it is very comfortable. If you get sick then everyone helps you. They help out at funerals. In Japanese companies, if there is a funeral, employees are sent to the funeral to help out as part of their work duties. If a child is born to a company employee they celebrate together. Those events of life are celebrated by the company. There are all kinds of celebrations. The company is a kind of village. The kind of event [gyōji] that were carried out in the co-operative body or community of the village [kyōdōtai] have all been brought into the company environment. If you look at the development of the villages in Japan, after the war in the high development era the people in the villages came out to the city. The people from the villages

wanted those kinds of things so they made the companies into villages: because they were village people... So everyone thinks they should all work really hard together so that they don't get left behind and in times of trouble they should help each other out. In actuality, in former times if you were sick the company would look after you for three entire years.

P: I think the company also thinks about the families; the conditions and circumstances of the families. It is a Japanese company so they would do that, although, some companies might not think about it. They think for instance about how young the kids are, and if the mother is still nursing. Then they would feel sorry for the family and would think twice about laying off the father. For example, it would be pretty rare for someone in their fifties to have an infant as young as that, but there are some cases like that. Or if there are children that are still going to incur big expenses in the future, or if there is an aged parent living with the family. I guess it is a kind of tradition not to do heartless actions.

Thus, on the positive side, groupism involves mutual sympathy, comfort, mutual help, co-operation, and a familiar cultural environment. But it contains negative aspects as well. There is, for example, ostracism for those who do not fit in.

H: In that sense, Japan is really a socialist country, but if you call it a primitive kind of communist village it is the same: everyone is working together but if you don't have the same system... if you are not within the same system, you cannot become a village person so you will always be an outsider.

Groupism is invariably a two-edged sword, as ostracism and bullying are rarely far behind group solidarity. The threat of ostracism and pressure to conform is constantly present in C-Life. We will see this illustrated throughout this chapter.

H: I think there's a kind of group consciousness in C-Life, so that C-Life employees don't talk about the bad condition of the company to outsiders. If they did say things like that they would be ostracised [murahachibu] so they can't. If they did do so, they would be told off inside the company and when they went out drinking they would be bullied by other employees [ijimerareru]. There is also the worry that something even worse could happen – that they could get transferred to a bad section of the company. There are all kinds of things that could happen to them. They could be told to work as a watchman or a porter.

C-Life employees are thus divided over to what degree they prefer a groupist mentality or individualism. We have, for example, seen a very positive view of the groupist mentality. On the other hand, employees almost always praise individualism when talking of a negative aspect of the groupist atmosphere of C-Life. This ambiguity in evaluating groupism and individualism, and the tensions inherent in this dichotomy, were evident all the time when I was conducting my fieldwork. Other writers have found the same thing. Minami Hiroshi (in Fodella 1975: 69) says that this tension 'expresses the tortured rebellion of the individual Japanese soul against the tyranny of the group, and at the same time its instinctive need, and its longing, for the protection of the group'. A person who is dependent on a group for a part of their identity is no longer able to be separate from the group without suffering an 'identity crisis'. This was symbolised in C-Life by the name card: the symbol of an employees' belonging to the company. The C-Life employees associated losing one's name card with losing one's identity.

This does not mean, though, that the individual is completely submerged in the group, or that their personality is lost. Company ideology would argue that the group is used in such a way as to 'grind out the rough edges in the individual's personality, talents, and aspirations to make them compatible with the functioning of the organisation' (Odaka 1986). The exchange between the group and the individual is two-way, in that the individual's 'sense of self is enhanced by being selected to join a group, and the standing of that group is in turn enhanced by its ability to attract individuals of quality and achievement' (Smith 1983).

But as we will see further in the next section, when confronted with the prospect of becoming suddenly detached from C-Life, such as getting fired, the employees do suffer anguish about losing their identity. Employees specifically spoke to me of the problems with having nowhere to belong, with having no identifying name card, and with the resultant loss of self-esteem. This develops the point, introduced in the last chapter, of insecurity. Employees suffer not only from economic insecurity: there is also the risk of an identity crisis – a loss of the all-important good, namely status – if they separate from the company. Later in this chapter, in the section on amae, I analyse some of the reasons behind these fears.

Despite the tension felt by employees between the individual and the group, groupism and individuality needn't always be wholly opposed to each other. Interestingly, some C-Life employees use individuality in a totally different way from what we have seen so far. Rather than contrasting it with company life, they regard the company as a vehicle to allow them to express their identity and their individuality, and develop abilities unique to them.

> Y: My generation? I am in the 'joined with the company' generation for sure. I think that my fate is joined together with that of the company. The company is an arena for expressing individuality, so I would like to be able to express myself here.

It is in the context of the groupist society that the employees interact and pursue their agendas. We shall see this issues emerge again and again. First, however, it is necessary to address the subject of conflict, which complements that of groupism. To what extent is there conflict in the company, and to what extent do employees try to avoid it?

Conflict

Here, I note how conflict sometimes arises in C-Life, and some of the mechanisms that exist to prevent it.

Z: Actually, the company as a whole should be heading in the same direction and not having different objectives for each section. But it can't be helped when that kind of thing happens. There is the annual company overall plan (nendo keikaku) and in determining that there are always departments that can get through things faster. Or it is a matter of power relations or of human relations, or the ability of staff below the department head that influence what happens in that plan.

The level of legally-based control in Japanese companies is quite low. Employees usually told me that they would not think of suing the company if told to quit, or that they would not ever think of taking legal action of any kind. The union was not generally seen as a vehicle by which individual employees could tackle the company. Because, as we have seen, the hiring and firing is done by the personnel section and not the direct departments, there is no clear system to allow a person or group with a minority opinion inside a C-Life department to be formally over-ruled without ongoing human relation problems. Conflict must therefore be settled before it is brought out into the open. It is partly for this reason that 'nemawashi' is extensively used, the practice of making sure that all parties involved in an issue agree on what is to be done before the matter becomes an official decision to be made, thus ensuring quick formal approval. If everyone has agreed to a decision before it is made, the decision is easily implemented, but it can make the decision-making process very slow. The adoption of this system illustrates the fact that there is much conscious effort to avoid conflict in the company.

I: In a Japanese company we try not to have any confrontations. If you sum up the situation, that's the way it is. You don't want to hurt each other. I think that that kind of thing is operating.

Nevertheless, conflict does occur. We have seen, in Chapters 3 and 5, how strictly hierarchical Japanese society can be. Paradoxically, this can be a potential source of conflict, because there are no structures to allow for co-operation between equal groups.

In the rest of this chapter, we shall see these points illustrated many times. First, I discuss another highly prevalent feature of company life: the issue of loyalty.

Loyalty

One of the most important characteristics of working in a Japanese company, as opposed to a Western one, is the high degree of loyalty expressed by the employees towards the company. This loyalty is frequently cited as the reason why they work so hard. In this section, I examine employees' loyalty and the factors underlying it. Where does such loyalty come from?

Employees themselves do not always consciously recognise the factors behind why they work so hard, or why they feel loyal to the company. When I interviewed them, they tended to be very interested in talking about it, because this was the first time that some of them had really analysed how they felt or discussed it at all. This was especially so when I spoke to employees in groups or when we were out drinking. Some didn't really feel they – or their families – understood the reasons behind their loyalty or why they did as much as they did do for the company.

> S: I don't think my wife can understand my loyalty – she brings up the children, she gets their meals, she gives them their milk, takes them to school and back. If the kids get sick she has to go to hospital with them. The weight of those things is different and bigger than the weight of work. I think she wonders why I have to go so far in working for the company.

A very commonly expressed theme, however, is gratitude. Loyalty, for many C-Life employees, is tied up with gratitude toward the company for what it has allowed them to learn or do. This attitude is made concrete in the feeling of obligations towards particular people.

> E: I think that all the sections that I worked at in the company were good. There are many things that I am thankful to the company for. I was able to meet many people and to learn a lot of things from a lot of people. And also in this kind of economic environment, it is hard for women to work for a long time. But even though it is now a very harsh environment, the company looked after me and I am really thankful for that.

I found that my respondents frequently spoke of the need to repay obligations to people in the company. In some cases, this was because the employee had been hired because of a connection and felt indebted. Some employees said that they would feel 'bad' if they did badly in the company, as it would disgrace the person who had helped them to get into the company. One employee, for example, had entered C-Life through his personal connections through a certain company. A decade later, this company went bankrupt, leaving large loans to C-Life. He said that he had not had any repercussions from that from the people around him in C-Life. But people were nevertheless not surprised to hear that he quit the company. Some said that he could hardly stay inside the company in those circumstances.

Interestingly, some of the employees would express feelings for the company as such, whilst others would distinguish between the company and the people in it, and express affection for their dōki and other people in the company. So, even when expressing loyalty to the 'company' is becoming old-fashioned, there is still loyalty to people.

> T: As to whether I have affection for the company? Well, are there any people nowadays who have real affection for the company? Rather than having affection for the company, I think that I was lucky to have been able to work together with really good dōki.

It was therefore necessary to define what exactly we were talking about before asking questions about loyalty. When the company was redefined in terms of the people who compose it, almost all the employees inside the company expressed a very high degree of loyalty. In practice, loyalty to either the company or to other employees was expressed in the same way. One of the principal ways in which employees express their sense of gratitude is by talking in terms of actions such as trying hard for the company, working hard for the company, making personal sacrifices for the company – the kind of attitude we examined in Chapter 5.

> S: I'm really thankful towards my company. You can see in my actions when I go off to the company on weekends that that my loyalty to the company is high.

There is probably also some degree of taking this kind of action first, for other reasons such as peer pressure, and only subsequently rationalising it as gratitude toward the company. Here, then, we see an interesting example of honne and tatemae. The motive reported by the employee may not match his real reasons for behaving in a certain way; yet it may be that he really believes his subsequent rationalising.

As we have already seen, the training period is a vital factor in raising the employees' consciousness of 'belonging' to C-Life. They often connect their feelings of loyalty to this formative time.

> S: So what was the basis of my loyalty for the next ten years? Well, the intake in my year was 50 people. For the first year we all ate rice cooked in the same rice pot. It wasn't like a sports team or anything like that. But there was a great feeling among the dōki that we were going to develop the company altogether, and that tied us together as a group. I think that was probably the strongest factor that raised our loyalty.

For some people, the issue of loyalty to the company was clearly quite emotionally charged. When I conducted an interview with one of my dōki, I found it quite difficult to elicit any responses that really showed his personality and feelings. On camera, he was quite rigid and dry. After really pushing him with a number of increasingly pointed and direct questions about his loyalty to the company, he eventually exploded, saying, 'I love the company! That is all there is to it. I work because I love this company!' His dōki laughed when they were told about this – I told them that we had had great difficulty eliciting his honne – as the employee in question normally didn't show a lot of private emotion, but they knew that he was very loyal and very attached to the company. Such expressions of extreme loyalty and even love for the company are by no means rare.

> E: I felt that they had looked after me in a very warm way [sō iu fū ni attakaku mimamotte kureteiru]... I had been supported by all these people. A lot of them I was incredibly thankful for and to many of them I could never repay my thanks or repay the debt that I owed them, so often, when times were really hard, I would think of that person and think that it is not possible for me to quit. That is really

Japanese thinking. Is it my loyalty to the company? Or to people? Well, companies are made up of people. Among those people there are people that are likeable, attractive… As long as there are people whose personalities I respect, whose personalities I can admire, people who I can never thank enough for what they have done for me… as long as they are still in the company I feel that I want to be there too. I feel that I need to be there to repay my debts. It is probably rather old-fashioned thinking but that is the way that I feel.

While talking of their loyalty, the employees would often end by describing themselves as 'old-fashioned' or by apologising for being so 'Japanese'. Or they would say, 'I know it is silly, but…'

S: I never thought of quitting C-Life. I never thought that I would be able to stretch my abilities more in another company. I think that if I hadn't got into C-Life I would never have been able to get all the experiences that I got in this company. For example, I think there is always drama in great success and I don't believe there is real coincidence in meeting in life. So I think that when I came into C-Life I was meant to have these experiences. If I had gone into another company, I wouldn't have had these experiences. I am happy that I have had the experiences that I have had. There are times that it was really difficult but I am really grateful to this company. I feel that I have to pay back a debt of gratitude to this company. I might be an old-fashioned type of person, and I don't think that the people who got into C-Life in the last ten or twelve years would be able to understand that. I think that my life is really connected with the company.

Even for me, who had worked in this company for two years, it was surprising to hear the depth of emotion from some of the employees. The following comment is from an employee who had just found out that she was on the list to be fired.

E: I really want the company to survive. I don't know what other people are going to feel when they leave C-Life but I really loved C-Life. I am a fool, aren't I? It has already been seventeen whole years since I entered the company. But it is 17 years that I worked for this particular company and I think that it would be tragic if the company that I worked for for 17 years were to disappear. I really want it to survive. I really want to be able to swell my breast with pride and say, 'I used to work for that company!'

The older the employees in the company were, the greater the degree of loyalty and affection for the company they generally expressed. It seemed to me that this was partly because this generation had never had to deal with uncertain economic situations or with the possibility that the company would go under or restructure them. An employee close to retirement said the following:

Z: Where did my love of the company come from? Firstly, when I chose the company I thought that life insurance is a product that is very useful in terms of people's lives and decreasing risks in society. So I felt a sense of mission towards society. That was a big factor. And through doing a variety of different kinds of work the company raised me [sodatete moratta]. I worked for a long time thinking that I wanted to make the company into a better company, so my affection grew in the same way as it would were I raising a child.

Some employees did have a 'drier' attitude. But they also felt that one 'should' have loyalty to one's company, even if one changed companies. Feeling loyalty is the sign of a proper employee.

> Y: I do have loyalty towards the company because they are the ones who gave me the specialist knowledge that I have now. Where does that loyalty come from? Well, if the company doesn't exist then you can't make a living. I think that is the basic start line. I don't say that you have to be 'one heart one body' with the company. I don't mean that you should commit double suicide with the company or anything like that! But if the company wasn't there, if it didn't progress I don't think your own life would go very well either. That would be the same if you moved companies. It would apply wherever you were.

And, as we saw in the last chapter, almost all of the employees whom I spoke to who had quit C-Life were sharply critical of Japanese management in general and C-Life's management in particular. But some of the very same people, on an emotional level, expressed gratitude to the company and were quite nostalgic about it.

> J: I think that the dōki who have quit the company (uradōki) all really like C-Life. I like it too. I feel grateful to C-Life. The reason that I was able to make such a seemingly magnificent (erasōna) job change is also because of C-Life. I am grateful as an individual myself and although the life insurance industry has become really harsh I really hope that the company becomes better.

In general, then, the younger the employee, the drier the attitude in regard to loyalty. Those who had quit of their own accord were also less likely to be emotional about their feelings for the company.

It seems, then, that many employees feel great dependence on the company. I now consider dependence – or amae – in greater depth.

Amae

The concept of amae, as introduced in Doi (1973), is essential to understanding Japanese psychology. 'Amae', according to Doi, represents the feelings that an infant might have for its mother – dependence, or a wish for passive love. It involves a dependence on something and an unwillingness to be separated from that thing. According to Doi, these feelings continue on throughout adulthood in Japan and form one of the most basic underpinnings of the Japanese psychology. Amae can thus provide some explanation for group behaviour. Doi has frequently been lumped together with nihonjinron literature by other commentators; this is rather unfair as he is very careful in his book to emphasise that amae is an emotion felt by all people. However, it is emphasised more strongly in Japanese culture, and also in the Japanese language, where 'amae' is a commonly used word, as is its verb 'amaeru' (to depend upon). 'Amae', taken too far, can have many negative connotations, which I treat in this section.

John Bester says in the foreword to Doi (1973: 9): '...the attempt always to remain warmly wrapped up in one's own environment must to some extent involve a denial of reality, so that the claims of "objectivity" and "logic" are sometimes ignored'. He adds that amae can also foster 'a peculiar passivity of outlook and a reluctance to do anything... that might disrupt the comfortable tenor of life, a reluctance to carry rationalism to the point where it will make the individual too aware of his separateness'. This 'peculiar passivity' of outlook is very relevant to C-Life. Employees who dislike C-Life, or are convinced that the company is going under, are still reluctant to initiate an action for themselves. Many prefer to wait for events to force them to make a stand. Throughout this chapter, we will see, time and again, employees talking directly of the curious passivity, and tardiness of reaction of the company.

Amae is thus related to the groupism we have discussed earlier in this chapter. Doi (1973: 19) suggests that amae is directly related to the development of an individual sense of self, so that someone who has a jibun (sense of self) can control his feelings of amae, limiting their influence, whilst someone who is at the mercy of amae can be said to have no sense of self. We could revise this to say that many Westerners, with their strong sense of individuality, are capable of checking amae, while Japanese with a weaker sense of an individual self are vulnerable to over-dependence. Amae might be said to be a structure that compensates for a weaker individuality and ego, or for a stronger sense of 'role'. Amae is also closely related to the senior–junior relationship, which is at the heart of life in the company. I analyse this relationship, as well as its connection to amae, later in this chapter.

Although amae can, in this way, form a basis for many positive relations, Doi (1973: 120) also concludes:

> The frustrations or conflicts arising from amae bring about all kinds of psychological difficulties. The satisfaction (of being dependent) is temporary and invariably ends in disillusionment. For in a modern age of 'freedom, individuality and self' the sense of solidarity with others that comes from amae is ultimately no more than a mirage.

During my fieldwork, conflict between groupism and amae on the one hand, and individualism on the other, was evident. As we have seen, employees sometimes portray individualism as a negative trait, and standing out from the group, as we shall see later in this chapter, can result in ostracism and bullying. These tensions between amae and individualism within each individual are a major source of conflict with the group. When an individual wants his own way but the group wants something else, the individual is obliged to choose the group over himself.

Other situations can occur 'where the individual develops a sense of having no self as a result of being totally isolated from the group. So strongly, one might say, do people fear such a state of affairs that they will usually put up with anything in order to belong to a group' (Doi 1973: 138). This is illustrated in the oft-expressed intense fear of the C-Life employee, mentioned in the first part of this chapter, that he will become detached from the company and lose the symbols of belonging, such as the company name card along with his identity.

How does amae relate to self-motivation and ambition? In the last chapter, I discussed the ambition felt by many employees, which drives them to work extraordinarily hard to improve their status. We can now relate this to groupism and dependence, because ambition is not simply for the self: it must be understood in the context of others. We saw that many employees say that they work hard for the sake of their families – even when they spend little time with them. Indeed, this attitude may begin in childhood. Rather than disciplining their children outright, mothers in Japan often teach their children that they – the mothers – will be hurt if the children fail to live up to the mother's expectations. Thus, the child's needs are manipulated in order to produce a strong drive for achievement. Smith (1983: p. 71) comments:

> This process of socialisation produces a self that is not independent of the attitudes and expectations of others, making the individual highly sensitive to insult or slight. The pressing need for accomplishment, which by definition will never be great enough, causes the adult individual to invest a high degree of identification with and involvement in whatever role he or she is playing. Japanese achievement motivation which is very high, is based not on training for independence and self-reliance as in the West, but rather on the instilling of affiliative and dependency needs. The experiences of adult life are dealt with in terms of a personality set through early childhood socialisation which, because no other explanation is offered in this paradigm, alone shapes the personality of the adult. It is not a particularly appealing picture.

On this basis, as long as one goes from school to university to a large Japanese company, one may never really need to develop a strong sense of individual identity. Playing one's expected role to perfection is adequate to get by, if not to stand out and succeed to a high degree. There is no need to come to an in-depth understanding of one's own personality traits and map out a career that will maximise the ability to use those personality traits to succeed. Rather, an understanding of one's personality traits is put towards getting along with others. Some C-Life employees certainly find it easy to allow themselves to be led through life in this way. A constant striving upwards toward greater achievement in a clear and set hierarchy is easy in that one doesn't need to consider equally attractive alternatives or to ponder over choices.

However, as we have noted, amae in the company context also has its downside. As Imai (1981: 82) writes, '…just as a child has to suffer parental restrictions if he wishes to depend upon his parents, so have these employees forfeited a number of important freedoms in order to gain protection within the comfortable embrace of life-long employment'. The downside of amae is the lack of emotional independence. By depending on one's superiors or on the company, one loses, to some extent, the ability to be able to think independently. And, as the Japanese company is extremely demanding on the individual, all of one's time and resources come to be spent on the company. In C-Life, men often seem to 'wake up' after the first six or seven hectic years of company life during which they accustom themselves to company life, learn basic work skills and their place in the organisation, and get married, to realise that they have no life left outside the company.

Amae, then, is a very important feature behind the traditional picture of employment at C-Life: it is impossible to understand the group-oriented company without taking it into account. It is by becoming dependent on the company that some employees can succeed without having to express strong personal identity. This is connected to the frequent claims of C-Life men that they have no skills, and no special attributes to make them stand out.

However, the combined effect of the pressures of group life, and the dependence that the individual has on the group, can lead to situations rife with unresolved stress.

Stress

In Chapter 5, we saw that many C-Life employees work very hard, for most of their time, in jobs that they do not necessarily enjoy, and many have a high level of job dissatisfaction. It is little wonder, then, that there is a high level of stress amongst employees. In this section, I focus on less obvious factors behind stress in Japan: the psychological and emotional tensions associated with the phenomena already discussed in this chapter, especially groupism and amae.

Iga (1986: 191), who has written widely on suicide in modern Japan, explains that: 'suicide motivation is considered to occur when a personality perceives a wide discrepancy between ego-ideal and self-conception. The discrepancy is produced by the disparity between goal and available means'. This is particularly a problem in Japan because such high goals are frequently set. Success is constantly presented as a goal by government, the education system and society as a whole. Striving for success, in fact, has become a national obsession. However, despite their aspirations, Iga describes the Japanese as having those very personality traits that prevent them from obtaining their goals: dependence, ambivalence, passivity and resignation, ambiguity of their positions, feelings of despair, a sense of insecurity and inferiority. Stress is the inevitable result.

> Their strong dependency needs and their lack of realistic perception, of future orientation and of strong will power... indicate a 'weak ego'. A weak ego is a natural product of the stifling of individuality by groupism and authoritarian familism and of the tendency towards accommodationism – that is, the tendency to adjust readily to the immediate situation for tension reduction.
>
> (192)

Iga maintains that the desperate competition between companies can apply equally to individuals, and that this is caused by insecurity. Stress is an obvious result of the high-pressure working environment in Japan that we saw in Chapter 5, with its long hours, little leisure time, and endless commuting on hopelessly crowded trains. Iga suggests (39–41) that Japanese show three patterns of behaviour for ego-defence: identification with a group, merging oneself in tradition, or being absorbed in activities. This last pattern of behaviour seems to be the same phenomenon that Doi (1973: 109) describes by the expression 'ki ga sumani':

> The feeling expressed in the words 'ki ga sumanai' (not to be satisfied as in the sentence 'he's never satisfied unless...') is one that arises when things fail to go as one has decided they should. For example... 'I just shan't be happy unless I get this work finished today.'

Doi asserts that the fact that the term for a person suffering from a compulsive neurosis is also an everyday term in frequent usage indicates that the Japanese tend towards compulsive traits. He suggests further that the hard-working qualities of the Japanese could owe something to compulsion (111).

The end result of this – stress – is central to life in a Japanese company. It is a factor not just of the hard-working conditions but also of the psychological submergence of the self into the group, and dependence on the group, typical of Japanese company life.

Here I have explained what can happen when the process of merging the individual will with the group is taken too far, and individuality suppressed. This is not the representative situation of C-Life. Nor is it proof that individuality does not exist. It is more a picture of what happens when the careful balance between individuality and the group is upset; we can see echoes of this in the C-Life employees' comments.

I now turn to the way in which stereotypes function in the company – by looking at attitudes to foreignness among the employees.

Attitudes towards 'foreignness'

The C-Life employees' views of the 'foreign' are very stereotyped. 'Foreign' things – almost always 'Western' things – are set up as an exact opposite of 'Japanese' things. In their interviews, if employees were talking negatively about Japanese management, they would glorify American management. Conversely, if they were praising Japanese management they would denigrate American management as having the opposite characteristics. The following quote is typical of the employee who stereotypes America as the opposite to what he dislikes about Japan.

> H: America accepts everything. No matter what kind of person they are, they say that people like that exist as well and they give them a place to live. Anything goes.

In other words, 'foreignness' is a stereotype. The idea of the foreign and of the Japanese feed off each other: each is defined in terms of the other. By maintaining this simplified idea of what foreignness is, employees maintain their own identity as Japanese. Similarly, foreign culture is often idealised. Employees who express a desire to move to a foreign company often have unrealistic expectations of what it will be like. For example, in the last chapter I analysed the case of T, who was not a success at C-Life and failed to achieve the transfers he wanted. Foreign companies represented to him the elusive goal of becoming a 'specialist' and having less irksome human relations.

> T: I think that going to a foreign company has always been one of the choices. In foreign companies they have Japanese branches (nihon hōjin) with a head in there and not too many people and I think those companies would be very different as far as human relations go. I think that such a foreign company would suit me in the sense of aiming to be a specialist. In a Japanese company you really get sent to various places. And they try to let you learn all kinds of different work in the company. But in foreign companies they try to let you become a specialist. They try to raise such specialists. I think that probably aiming at being a specialist is more suitable to me.

Actually visiting foreign cultures allows employees to gain slightly more rounded views. Spending time in America did make the C-Life employees conscious of deep cultural differences that lie behind different business and educational practices in the two countries. For example, discovering that the concept of equality is quite different in the US and Japan was a revelation for some of the C-Life employees.

> H: The amazing thing about American education is that children are told that they are all different, and that is the basic premise and they try to stretch or pull out the good things about each child and that is their basic position. For example, in middle school there are classes where you can advance ahead in mathematics if you are really good at it. If you are really good at writing you can go to a fast stream English class and stretch your creativity. They don't try to bring people up to all be an equal level, or to bring the bad parts of each person up to an equal standard... The Japanese universities are the worst case of that... Even at university level they make you do mathematics, English, Japanese, ancient Japanese, physics, and science; they make you do all of those subjects. Well, lately it has changed a little bit but in my time you had to study seven subjects and be good at them all round; it was a lot of pressure.

Against the backdrop of the values of a different culture, Japanese cultural values are seen in a new light. The employee quoted below became conscious of the fact that, in Japan, drinking is often a socially acceptable stress-release mechanism.

> H: In America everyone sees psychiatrists, because they're under high pressure. They have to let that pressure off somewhere. In Japan, they go to bars instead.

Another employee discovered that the Americans he met during his overseas stint with C-Life had detailed plans and scenarios laid out for the future. This brought home to him how dependent on the company the C-Life employees are, rather than forging their own way through life according to their own ideas. In the US, this employee started to take the foreign analysts exams that would allow him to switch to a foreign company several years later.

> J: I really felt that Americans had a lot more extensive view of their life's prospects. They were always thinking about the far future. In practice, they would be thinking about a happy retirement – even people in their twenties would be saying that in order to have a happy retirement they were going to take an MBA and invest in themselves… There were a lot of people who had actual detailed plans and were working towards those plans. In an Aesop tale you have the story of the ants who work hard step by step and save up towards the future. The popular image in Japan is that Japanese are like that and that Americans live day by day like the cricket in the fairy tale. But I think it is absolutely opposite. The Americans around me were always thinking of the future and thinking that they had to invest in themselves so they couldn't go out and just drink every day. But because Japanese companies had the life employment system the Japanese employees only had to get by. They don't have a bad lifestyle and they don't have a life of poverty. Although, on the other hand, they cannot hope for a really superb life.

Having one's horizons broadened in this way is not necessarily a pleasant experience. Actually having to work with foreigners abroad raised a lot of new problems of cultural clashes. However 'international' the foreign corps in C-Life considered themselves, they came up against their own Japanese-ness and prejudices when they had to deal with foreigners. The efficiency and superiority of foreign corporations became temporarily forgotten, and the comfort of the Japanese corporation and familiarity of its culture became more important. This is illustrated in the following conversation, concerning an American employee in the New York office who threatened to sue the company.

> H: The employee was told to wait a year but she couldn't wait. She was an Armenian American. She got into C-Life in America, I hired her in America. At that time she was from Ōsaka Foreign Languages University, and she went to Japan on a homestay. She came into the company with the impression that Japanese were quite flitty, but I'm not like that, so I fired her after a while.
>
> W: I don't really know what happened after that, but there was a lawsuit.
>
> H: No, that's not the case. She sent a mean letter to the head of the international department of C-Life in Japan.
>
> Q: So she knew the right way to go about it Japanese-style?
>
> H: That was the scary thing about it. However, she was an acquaintance of T, so T dealt with it.

W: Did it come through a lawyer?

H: No, it just came directly from her. Anyway, the Japanese companies that start up in America are victimised by the Americans who come to work there, because the Japanese don't know those kinds of situations.

Q: So Japanese are naïve?

H: They're optimistic or indulgent [amai – verb form of amae]. They're good people ultimately. Over there, it's a jungle, a dog eat dog world. It's as if you let a domestic animal out into the wild, like a tame deer that goes out into the wild and gets gobbled up.

Q: So did you treat that woman the same as a man?

H: I thought that I treated her fairly. But we couldn't really use her abilities until a year had passed. So I asked her to do boring work for a year. She said OK, but after three months she said she wanted to do a better kind of work.

Q: You didn't ask her to make tea or anything, did you?

H: No, I didn't ask her to do that. That's Japanese culture. If there's no custom of that, then even though you get their understanding at first, they still don't want to wait for a year.

Q: So she didn't think she was being treated the same as a Japanese tea-pouring woman?

H: No, she didn't think that.

Z: It's a cultural thing. After three months, she just wanted to have her ability recognised. That's American society.

H: If it was me I'd have waited three years.

Z: Well, that is you, and you're Japanese –

H: Even though she had no results or past experience [jisseki], she just answered back to people ten years her senior.

Z: Well, she's American.

H: Well, that's unnecessary [sō da to yokei]. If you don't have the ability, then you're just talking off the top of your head.

Z: So if that had been an American company, what do you think would happen?

H: People like that don't get by anywhere they go. There is a range of both Americans and Japanese with different degrees of knowledge, from those who have a little to those who have a lot. But really talented people are modest or humble. She was a graduate of Washington University in International Politics. She had been given responsibility for a lot of work, and had come to the conclusion that the old Japanese guys in the office were evil and manipulative. I didn't really intend to hire her, but she said she'd be OK. She could speak Japanese so I thought that was OK. I told her that she had too much ability, so the work would be boring – it was reception and inputting kind of work. But if she did it for a year, I would advance her to the next step, so I said OK. I had said that, but despite that, after three months she snapped. I thought I had treated her fairly, but she was too short-tempered, because she was an Armenian descendant. If she'd been an Anglo-Saxon she'd have had a longer-term stance. Germans have longer-term stances too. I know Americans of German, French, Italian and Armenian descent. I think it's a nationalistic thing. In London, there are Australians and New Zealanders who are fluent in Japanese. Because they have a long relation with Japan, they have a deep understanding of Japan and are really good. There is one person there called P who was born in Hong Kong. She leans toward having an Asian-type personality. She was discreet and prudent, and didn't let out on the sur-face what she was thinking [zenmen o dasanai], and because that was the case she went well in the company. But in actual fact she was an outlaw among her English acquaintances. She came to work in Japan for a while [six months]. I went out drinking with her once and she was crying. She wanted to go back quickly. The gap was too large for her, in coming to C-Life, and it was hard for her because she couldn't share her feelings.

We can see from the above example that the 'international attitudes' of C-Life employees are a rather bizarre mix of genuine insight into the differences between Japanese and US society, and a collection of prejudices. People are assumed to have the culture of their parents irrespective of which culture they have been brought up in. In this example, non-Japanese behaviour is attributed to being 'Anglo-Saxon' or to being a minority; acceptable personality traits are attributed to being 'Asian'. I talked to the female employee mentioned at the end of this conversation. She is a descendant of Chinese immigrants to Britain, raised and educated solely in Britain. According to her, any 'Asian' traits that they saw in her were a result of her person-ality, and not of an inherited cultural disposition. Largely because of the above prejudices, she had found life in Tōkyō to be extraordinarily difficult.

The conversation quoted above shows that foreigners can have a hard time coping with the Japanese system. Americans who are hired are hired on ability, yet asked to act Japanese in terms of patience and working pace. However, tellingly, when they manipulate the system in truly Japanese style to lodge a com-plaint to the head office, that 'scares' H who would prefer that, in these cases, the employee didn't understand the Japanese system.

One time-worn explanation of the Japanese for why Japan is relatively isolated from knowledge of foreigners or foreign thought was also suggested by the C-Life employees.

J: It might be a little extreme but Japan is an island country where there are not many foreigners. Most Japanese don't know much about foreign cultures or how other people think. I think it is a pity that many Japanese don't have a chance to learn about other places. But I don't think that is going to change any time soon.

There are, I think, considerable differences in attitudes towards foreigners from generation to generation inside C-Life. The younger generation is really much more knowledgeable about foreign things, and much more accepting of foreigners in general. The older generation – and, to a lesser extent, the middle generation – can hardly conceive of foreigners behaving like Japanese or being very fluent in the Japanese language. Their attitudes are particularly stereotyped. One employee, who had been in an important position in investment at the time of the bubble, explained the demise of the Japanese economy as follows:

> Z: Well, I might get scolded by Fiona if I say this, but I think it is an Anglo-Saxon strategy [seisaku] or policy. Japan is a nation of agriculturists but the Anglo-Saxons were a hunting tribe. They didn't have to channel water into their fields and grow and scatter seeds one by one and grow rice plants one by one. They didn't have those customs. For a hunting tribe, if there is prey they go where the prey is and try and kill it there and then. That thinking is still present. I think that that is the main difference between the West and Japan. When the agriculturist Japanese and the hunting Anglo-Saxons fight it out together, I think it comes down to the standards that each society has in place: the social standards.

As we have seen in Chapter 3, the C-Life employees have little tolerance for the 'foreign' when it is let loose among them. We shall see later how people with what are regarded as undesirable character traits may be accused of not being fully Japanese. In particular, the ostracism and bullying of returnee school children – who have lived abroad when their fathers have been stationed abroad for work – on their return to Japan has been well documented. The same kind of phenomenon occurs in C-Life. However, rather than saying that all returnees across the board are ostracised, it would be more accurate to say that those returnees who deviate from the norms in any way are ostracised because they are returnees. Their failure to follow the norms is attributed to their foreign-ness. This is the case even for returnees who returned to Japan as primary school children and who retained no ability in English!

> T: Now I have moved from the international department to the domestic department, it is really different. It was much more comfortable for me in the international department.
>
> H: That's because you were a returnee school child.
>
> Q: So the people in the domestic department saw you as a returnee school child?
>
> T: Yeah, they did.
>
> W: In that sense, there were a lot of returnee school children in the international department. I think it was comfortable for them in the international department.

Those who transferred into the international department mid-career frequently encountered this attitude. The transferees, in retaliation, blamed their ostracism on the 'domestic' and 'backward' attitudes of their C-Life colleagues.

H: The head of the international department evaluated us very highly but when we went to other departments they valued us much lower.

W: They have a complex, maybe. Because the international department disappeared, we had to move somewhere else, but if people like us go into domestic departments the people who are already there... Well, I think I can understand that...

H: If you put things differently, we can speak English; they can't. In their hearts they think that we are above them. And we study too. If you can speak a language you know about history and culture and all sorts of things. We know about things like that and they don't and we know that. We know that they can only understand certain things. They already have an aggressive attitude towards us because we understand things that they don't have. They are not amused by that [omoshiroku-nai]. They don't like the fact that we studied more and know more than them. It gets them riled [kachin to kuru].

My own experiences were illustrative of the typical attitudes towards foreigners of C-Life employees at the time, and how they reacted to having a foreigner in their midst.

Z: We really wanted somebody who could speak Japanese well and someone who could speak Japanese like Fiona was welcomed with open arms. If she hadn't been able to speak Japanese like she did we would have turned her down. Well, I would have turned her down [laughing]. The international work department was interested in hiring foreign workers as well. We didn't have any English-speaking people. So to be able to get someone who could speak Japanese like Fiona and who is also a native English speaker made her doubly powerful. It was a double benefit.

As we have seen, this experiment was not well thought through. I think that, on the surface, my treatment as an employee was equal and even better than others, as was the treatment of the other transferees. The problems that arose were because the structure of C-Life was not set up to cater for differences in category or experience. There were also problems associated with accepting foreigners anywhere in Japan, not limited to C-Life. In fact, the most severe problems that I experienced were associated not with being foreign but with being a woman, as I explain later in this chapter.

Nevertheless, everyone in the company had different stereotypes of how to treat foreigners and I had to deal with those. Some of the transferees had decided that foreign subordinates should be treated strictly – even though I had grown up in Japan and had never worked abroad! Others were adamant that I go through the same tough conditions as others, pushing more work on me than was fair in their zeal to make sure that I was equal. Still others could not reconcile themselves to the fact that I was a general worker, treating me as a visitor, or a secretary. I was lucky in my section chief, however, who treated me fairly and equally with others and in the same way as any other employee, so my day-to-day life inside the international division was without too many problems.

> I: I think that of course Fiona would have been able to advance in the company had she stayed longer than two years. That is even so if she hadn't done the training… In practice she should have gone and trained for one year. She could have got onto that route. And another path would have opened to her. I think there was no wall in the road because she was a foreigner. Even though she is a woman and a foreigner I think she had a chance to get ahead in C-Life. However, on the front of international investment, both C-Life and other insurance companies changed to a negative direction and that might have been a fork in the road. We never hired another foreigner after Fiona.

The following comment is illustrative of my position in C-Life at the time. Some people did think that I was hired to get people used to looking at foreigners! But as other comments showed, by no means all the employees thought that. Within the sphere of my own work – handling a two billion yen portfolio invested in foreign stocks – I was working as other trainees were. The fact that some employees thought that I was there solely to be looked at – while claiming that they themselves had no prejudices towards foreigners – was at the root of the enormous difficulties I faced in being accepted.

> H: I think that the fact that C-Life took Fiona on was a kind of internationalisation. At the time, C-Life was full of people that had never spoken to a foreigner. Because they had made an international department they thought that they had better get used to foreigners. So they thought that if they made her walk up and down here and there they would get people used to foreigners. I think that had a little bit of an effect – just by having a foreigner! So it was enough just to have her walking around to impress among the other employees that this was a normal person too… I don't think that they really expected her to actually do normal work. It was all about having her existing in there. She just had to be there. It was a shock tactic or one type of shock treatment.

So I think that it is true that I had no walls in the road in the company as a foreigner, in a formal sense, but the walls in the road as a foreigner in Japanese society were immense. I cannot imagine that any foreigner, at that time, could have stuck out life in C-Life had they not been through Japanese schools as I had and been thoroughly immersed in Japanese society. We shall see this pattern repeated several times in this chapter: the absence of formal restrictions on a group of people, but the reality being quite different. In my case, the honne and tatemae of the company's treatment of me did not match.

I got along best with the section chief mentioned above, who, to my great relief, treated me strictly and entirely as a normal Japanese employee. As a graduate in Japan, this was what I expected and although it had the same downsides as it had for all the other employees, it was, at the very least, predictable. The most trying experiences for me in the company were battling the indirect prejudices illustrated above. Especially difficult was trying to deal with the behaviour of C-Life employees who had had limited experience abroad and had firm ideas of how foreigners should be treated – some of which were very original indeed.

> P: I didn't have any special attitude about working together with a foreigner when Fiona came into the company 14 years ago. But our company is a very domestic-oriented company. So even if a foreigner was just walking along in the corridor, everyone would turn around to look. And she was also pretty! So, in that sense, I think there was an attitude in the company. There had been experiences in the company before of having foreigners there for a short time, or coming in as trainees, so individually I didn't have any sense of discrepancy [iwakan] or incompatibility. I think she did have a symbolic kind of existence as well though, representing a basically domestic industry that was stating that it was now ready to surge forward [saki ni iku zo]. Yes, a kind of symbol in that sense.

This discussion of foreignness ends the first part of this chapter, in which I have laid down some of the foundations for understanding what follows. Having explained some of the factors underlying the dynamics of interpersonal interaction in C-Life, I now describe that interaction. I begin with a general discussion of the importance of human relations in the company.

Human relations

Many employees – especially older ones – feel human relations to be the best aspect of the Japanese company. I think that many of them, when discussing the positive aspects, were thinking of their training days and the close relations they had with their dōki, and then the close relations they had with other company members which entailed spending a lot of time together.

> C: The things that I would like to see left from Japanese management are the human relations. Such human relations are necessary for the efficient running of the organisation. That shouldn't go so far as to be developed into an ideology in its own right, but still the good points about it could well be kept. This might be strange-looking from the point of view of a foreigner, but the fact is that the relations between the company and the worker don't stop the minute he walks out the door; the company thinks about his family; he drinks together with his co-workers, or socialises with people from work, or does hobbies together with people from work. Even for golf, Japanese company men go with their co-workers. I don't think that that is a bad thing.

Even the employees who had left C-Life or transferred into it told me that the bulk of their social relations were company-based. This reflects what we have seen in Chapter 5, that most employees have few leisure activities that are not connected to the company. The following comment is from an employee who no longer works for C-Life: even though he has left, he hardly knows anyone not at C-Life or his new company.

> H: My network now outside the company that I am working for is the international department from C-Life, who are all now in different companies. So my core human relations have all been built inside the company, including the trading company for which I worked prior to C-Life. Because we were always in the same place at the same time, you develop relations there.

The metaphor of company as family came up frequently in talking with C-Life employees. I think this was primarily because juniors enter C-Life in such a green and inexperienced state: we have seen already that these employees are conceptualised as having only partly-formed individual personalities at this stage. In a sense, their bosses take on the role of 'raising them' to be adults. The seniors share not only their work knowledge but also their life experience with juniors whom they get on well with.

> J: As far as my bosses go in the company it is hard to separate the affection in the relationship and the business relationship. Also, many people say in Japanese society that it really is the case that a company is like a family. Your bosses are the parents and the seniors that are quite close to you are like your older brothers.

> I: There are a lot of customs that have been around for a very long time, and it is a problem of consciousness – people who have eaten rice from the same rice pot become very close – so they don't want to cause waves as they work together. I think that's just a real Japanese thing.

But developing good relations with colleagues is not simply a social matter. On the contrary, employees identify it as one of the keys to success.

> C: If you are like me and have been in C-Life from the beginning, you have people whom you know in all kinds of places inside the company. Human relations, that is. If you just get in you only have work and not human relations. In foreign countries, if you have specialist knowledge it is advantageous, but in Japan success is often determined on human relations.

Some purport to draw strict lines between business and personal relations, although I saw little evidence that they really do this in practice. But employees often suggest that needing to cultivate good human relations, apart from on a purely professional basis, is something that is troublesome.

> A: Communication is when you want to be with somebody and become close to them as a result, isn't it? If you are going to have a hard time doing that, you dislike that person, right? Basically, I don't talk to people who I dislike, unless it is necessary. Communicating on a business level and on a private level are different, aren't

they? Communicating on a business level is work. So it is nothing to do with liking or disliking. You can't afford to say things like that. And I think that it is the same for the other person. So I communicate properly in that respect. It is when you ask for more than that in relations [sore ijo no mono o motomeru kara] you get into trouble.

In Chapters 4 and 5, we have seen the extent to which employees vary in their ability to assess the situation and make best use of it. And the ability to achieve good human relations in C-Life and the consciousness of the need to do so varies vastly according to the employee. This is connected to the fact that some employees like the groupist nature of C-Life, whereas others do not.

A: I didn't have any problems in human relations. It wasn't hard for me to make good relations. I don't understand what it is to have difficulty in making human relations. If you are going to have such a hard time then don't make any!

Advancing in the company is not achieved simply by strategising to cultivate good relations in order to advance. That is, it is not something that can be simulated. Because the atmosphere in C-Life is so close and there are so many dōki who have lived with each other at close quarters during training, the people who do things like organising social events for their dōki are usually genuinely likeable people. It is not really possible to maintain a 'face' at such short distance and for many years. They are seen to be sincere in their attitudes and behaviour. However, they do have to use honne and tatemae extensively in personal relations with other dōki, especially as the gap between those who can and those who can't opens up as they progress through the company. Moreover, these dōki heads have to be very aware socially and politically of what is going at any certain time.

H: In the Japanese case, because people work in the same place for so long, the evaluation according to results is almost nothing. It is only the guys who do things like organising the dōkikai that get ahead. At the moment, among my dōki, there is a guy named Q. He is really good at stuff like that but he is also good at work so now he is the finance department head. He is my dōki. There was another guy who was even better at nemawashi or putting in the ground work as far as human relations go in order to get one's objective at the end … it was P who was really good at that.

Here, again, we see the importance of awareness and consciousness. To succeed in C-Life, it is very important, if not entirely essential, to be aware of what is going on, and able to take advantage of it.

Why is it so important to maintain good human relations in order to advance in the company? For one thing, it is essential if one wants to gain the trust of seniors and thus be entrusted to make one's own decisions and do the work one wants to do.

Y: I am quite satisfied looking back over my life at C-Life. It was relatively easy to say let's do this or let's do that. It was easy to do what I wanted to do inside the company. It was a company that let me do what I wanted. I could propose the ideas that I wanted and when they were accepted I could put those into motion. Is that because I had good relations with my seniors? Well, you have to have good relations with your seniors. If you don't make an effort yourself relations will never become good; you have to put in the work there yourself. In order to keep good relations I think it is important to be aware of each other's position and respect that. You need to think of the consequences of what will happen if I do this, what will happen if I do that... you can't just do things without thinking them through very carefully. In detail... sometimes it is necessary to have closer relations and sometimes it is necessary to leave some distance between you. If you always have the same distance between you relations don't generally improve. You need to be aware of the situation and thinking is this a good time to increase the distance or decrease it? For example, if your boss tells you to do something and you think it is a rather strange order? Well, you have to persuade your boss until he understands the situation. That can take a short time or it can take a long time... at a time like that you have to lay out the logic of the situation rationally... it is like this and this....

Fostering good relationships with one's seniors is also important when it comes to asking advice.

E: If I have problems at work, I usually ask the advice of people who are near to me in line, either above or below and doing the same kind of work. Or if I open up the scope a little wider I would probably ask the advice of a dōki. The kinds of advice I would ask a dōki are probably about how to process information that has come in about the company as a whole. So about ceremonial occasions or such ... I do work within the lines of work. If I think that a junior is the kind of guy who is quite understanding, or a dōki is, I might ask advice of them. Otherwise I would ask a senior who is likely to hear me out properly. I try to make appropriate divisions in what kind of advice I should ask of what kind of people [kuwake].

E: If I have an idea of my own that I want to push past, what kind of process would I take to do that? Well, actually I am quite bad at doing that... really bad at doing it. If there is something that I really wanted to do but I thought that my superiors would totally oppose it and I wanted to get that idea through anyway. Well, I am really bad at doing that. I usually say exactly what I think the moment that I have thought of it. So I often crash against my seniors. Sometimes it is good that that happens and they tell me to slow down. And that it probably wouldn't be a good idea to go straight ahead and do it like that and that maybe it would be a better idea to go round and do it a different way. It would be better if I was able to think things through properly myself and come up with a solid plan first. And then decide which people I should take the plan to and which method I should approach them with. I do put my efforts towards trying to do things that way. But as far as my personality goes, I am not very good at doing things like that, and I often just go ahead and do things impulsively.

In a recent example, there was something that I wanted to put in the plan for next year that was going to the planning department. And I talked about what I wanted to do at a conference. It would have been OK if that had already been laid out on paper. But because I brought it up my seniors at that conference told me it was no good and the plan vanished there and then. Later, other people around me told me that I should have followed the correct order and done this first and then that. I realised that myself and thought I have done it again and regretted it. And got my juniors to put down what I was planning on paper and while getting a different senior to support the plan I took it once more to the department head and explained it and got his understanding on it. My junior wrote up the paper and then as far as order goes, I took it to another section chief and we analysed together why the department head had opposed it. And I was able to make the plan then in such a way as to get an OK on it without incident.

A clever employee, then, will be able to manipulate their seniors to attain their own goals. In practice, a great deal of care is taken in thinking about how best to approach people, particularly seniors. One important skill is presenting arguments in such a way as to persuade one's bosses. Employees told me that they often present the same plans to their bosses three or four times, after supplementing the plans with additional information or ideas that would persuade their bosses. Such manoeuvres take a lot of time, but in the end, the senior is in agreement with the junior, and the junior is happy to carry out the plan, which was his own idea. Everybody is motivated.

Y: In investment, disagreements with bosses came up most often about which stocks to buy and which to sell. Let's buy this one because it is going well or let's sell that one because it is doing badly… but at the same time there are organisational factors involved. We need to change the organisation in such and such a way… Basically I made my own decisions about what to do as far as work and investment decisions went. If there was opposition about something I planned to do I had to be persuasive then and argue the point. Well, everyone was involved in making decisions about different levels of the organisation; the directors, the department heads and the section chiefs. Sometimes there were disagreements depending on the person and their position. In our section we would resolve problems by holding a meeting to air differing points of views, or by circulating a piece of paper with the views expressed on it. Of course there were clashes. The clashes are in many ways the point from which it all starts. If there was disagreement with one of my proposed plans I endeavoured to understand the point of view of the opposing party first of all. I would think about the background to his point of view and think of how I could persuade him of my point of view. Then I would think of a good plan to persuade him. That was my strategy for dealing with opposition.

It is also in an employee's interest if their senior is promoted or does well.

Q: So you can really get ahead on the basis of your human relations in a Japanese company?

W: Well, that is not only in Japan. It is human society. So it is always political and full of factions.

Employees often speak of different factions in C-Life. Generally, they are based around one senior member and include various people under him whom he has worked with and liked. As the senior rises in the company, he tends to pull his juniors up in his wake. Moreover, seniors may form themselves together into alliances. The heads of different departments, for example, are generally grouped this way; and we shall see how difficult it can be for a solitary outsider to cope in such an environment without any allies.

Another group of people whom employees generally try to be on good terms with is their dōki. However, they usually have a different kind of relationship with them than with people who are not their equals. In general, I found that in C-Life employees tend not to consult their dōki very often on work-related problems. They are more likely to discuss these with sympathetic seniors who take on a counselling role. If they are in a dilemma about some issue or another, they rarely seem to talk to dōki about it, except perhaps to one dōki who is especially close. In particular, personal issues relating to the company, such as whether a personnel move was a good one or not, or whether one should quit or not, or how one is being evaluated, are rarely discussed with dōki. This is because dōki are seen, at least in part, as competitors, a fact that I focus on in the next section of this chapter. Employees say that it is difficult to discuss such issues with people of equal rank, primarily because of the desire to maintain 'face'. This is another factor which makes a good relationship with one's seniors an important asset.

A successful employee will recognise that one interacts in a different way with different people. A proven route to success in C-Life is first to prove to be a good dōki through training, and then to be able to make a smooth transition to being a good junior in the first years of company life, and finally become a good senior for the rest of one's career. To be able to be all of these different qualities to different people is an important talent – and the relations that are built up as a result represent as major investment in the company.

J: When I quit the company the largest loss that was involved was losing the human connections [jinmyaku] that were built up inside the company. I had built them up over ten years, those relations, and I also threw away my own reputation. When you go to a new company you have to start building everything from A again. In that sense, I threw away some assets and fear of losing them is one thing that would have kept me behind in C-Life.

How much contact to keep with ex-C-Life people is a difficult issue for C-Life employees, as they are now facing this for the first time. As we saw in Chapter 4, some employees felt so strongly that quitting members had betrayed the company that they refused to speak to them for years afterwards. This stance has generally changed over the years, though, and I didn't meet any people who still had such a harsh attitude.

P: Among the people who quit, some people still have relations (tsukiai) with people in C-Life. I think that some people do but naturally it is toned down a bit. So I
still exchange New Year cards with H or K. That level of relations happens. If I
remember – or when I remember to – I might meet them once now and again. That
happens but people who think that they are rotten bastards for quitting [kettakuso
warui] don't do that, but in a forward-looking way, in spite of the feeling of guilt, quitting needs all kinds of courage. When you go to the next place you still have to try
hard. That is what I think. So, in that sense, I have nothing to say. If they have come
as far as this point, I think if you don't send them off with a good heart or a good
feeling [kimochi yoku] then I would feel sorry about it, and I think that those people
who feel that way are the majority in this company. People are good here. They are
good towards other people too [o-hito yoshi].

At dōkikai, however, it is noticeable that two groups of people form very quickly
– of employees still inside the company and those outside. If the employees still
inside the company are talking about work, the employees who have quit are hesitant to join that circle.

Because of the potentially very long-term nature of employment in Japanese
company, wise employees do their best to keep human relations smooth. Because
of the constantly shifting positions of everyone in the company, employees never
know when a junior they once treated badly might attain a position where he is
well liked by a senior who could do them damage.

I: I think people want to create an atmosphere in the workplace so they can work
together happily [tanoshiku], without creating any waves in the workplace. If they
scold their juniors because they are not as good as they should be, the human relations will be awkward [gikushaku suru], even though the junior accepts what is told to
him at the time. People don't want to create waves in the workplace, and bosses don't
want to be disliked by their juniors; so bosses don't point things out very clearly, and
they don't discuss things clearly either. And juniors also hesitate [enryo shite] from
putting their own opinion forward too much. Everything happens in a [moya moya]
foggy unclear atmosphere. I think everything goes on in that kind of atmosphere. But
that's a really bad thing, isn't it? I don't think that that is the ideal kind of relation
between a boss and a junior. It's just a Japanese kind of custom. It's group consciousness [nakama ishiki]. It's really the way things are done in Japan. And in all kinds of
companies, I think there is the custom of group consciousness [nakama ishiki].

We have seen how vague evaluation by the personnel department can be. In some
ways, the personnel section itself is used as a buffer in human relations. Bosses
who have negative evaluations of their juniors can assign responsibility for it to
the personnel section, and stay detached from the evaluation. This helps to reduce
conflict between seniors and juniors.

I: As a boss, I couldn't say things very easily to my juniors either, even though I felt
that I should be able to. In cases when it really couldn't be helped at all, I would say

things properly; but I really didn't want to be hated, and that desire would come first in most cases. I wonder if this has really changed at all in 14 years? Young people are much more liable to say things clearly and openly [zuke zuke]. These kinds of people who can express their own thoughts have become more common these days, and their seniors have changed as they have begun to accept this. I tried to make efforts towards this as well, but I don't think anything is going to change very fast. I think that a lot of time will be necessary to make changes like that.

The importance of human relations, however, is changing. Some employees regard it as a negative aspect of 'Japanese management'. They point out that, when the interests of human relations and efficiency clash in the company, it is often efficiency that suffers. In their interviews, those most vocal about the negative aspects of Japanese management returned to this point again and again. Those who were less critical regarded this as something that was 'unavoidable' (shōganai). But employees also recognise that, amid the restructuring currently happening at C-Life, human relations tend to be less important.

> X: But when it comes to this age now they look more at work than they do at nemawashi.

Nemawashi, which is associated with the ringi system I have mentioned on pages 22–3, is the practice of gaining co-operation in advance from all people involved in a certain issue.

> X: When it comes to this present age, they are looking at ability in work as well… So now you have to be good at both. Before, if there were 20 people among a year of 20 dōki, they would all have become directors at the end of their careers but now it is no longer that kind of environment.

I now turn to a detailed examination of some of the relationships that make up company life, beginning with the strongest and most important: that between dōki.

Dōki

It is clear that employees have a special relationship with their dōki unlike that with anyone else in the company. As they are neither senior nor junior, they can speak and act as equals. In Chapter 4, we saw the degree to which the foundational experience of the training centre creates a bond between the dōki that lasts for the rest of their careers. Here, the members of the group develop the friendships that are the first dimension of the human relations networks in the company. The training was an unforgettable period for the dōki. I found during my fieldwork that, whatever other topics had to be carefully approached, the topic of training was a winner for everyone. They delighted in telling me about their personal experiences and triumphs, about what other people in the dormitory had done, about who had been caught missing from their room in the middle of the night, about who had gone out drinking and missed the last train.

After their time in the training institute comes to an end, recruits will be assigned to different areas in the company: rarely are more than two recruits assigned to the same section. Thus, each recruit instantly has 50 or so close contacts in virtually every area of the company. Through talking with their dōki about their work, they are able to enhance their knowledge of the whole company. As the recruits get more meaningful and important work, having many close contacts in all areas of the company may enhance their ability to get something done in other sections quickly and efficiently, and can assist in better communications or in the smooth operation of joint projects.

The relationship between dōki in C-Life crosses over into friendship. Because the group is equal in status they need not be constantly on their guard as juniors must be towards seniors. dōki use the same form of language to each other rather than honourary language (keigo). In the international department survey, when asked who their closest friend was in the company, almost all respondents named dōki working in a different section from themselves. The only exceptions to this were the mid-career transferees, who named each other. Indeed, the fact that the mid-career transferees found it very hard to fit in shows how close-knit relationships between the dōki are. Even for those who made an effort to join the dōkikai, it was a miserably sobering experience for them to realise that the absence of that crucial common experience, the year at the training centre, made joining extremely difficult. One mid-career transferee comments:

H: I was invited to my dōkikai as well but I didn't have the experience of doing sales as a trainee in C-Life. I wasn't there when they all did their hardest time so there is no empathy. In the end, even though I went it wasn't fun for me. Everyone just talks about what a hard time they had then. They are just talking about their memories. It wasn't something that I could join in with [shirakeru]. I cannot empathise with the other guys. They don't have the same experience. They talk about what a hard time they had then, so they are like battlefield friends. New employees in a Japanese company are put into a position where they are really on the limits [kyokugen], where they are on the extremes. It is by getting through those extreme conditions together that they become close... It is because I don't have the same memories as they do of having been through that experience, and because we are not in the same position, that they always put distance between us [kyori o oite shimau]. When we go out drinking and they say, 'Oh, we had such a hard time!' then all I can say is, 'Oh, yeah?' So there is no common emotional ground [kyōkan ga dekinai]. They are all buddies. They went as a group and sold insurance together. They went from house-to-house and took insurance. If one guy wasn't able to sell his quota of insurance they would all go ... all turn up at the same house together to support their dōki.

Despite this impression of harmony and closeness between the dōki, however, there are tensions below the surface. In the last chapter, we saw the intense jockeying for status in C-Life. From this point of view, each employees' dōki are also his rivals for status in the company.

As I have suggested earlier in this chapter, the new employees entering C-Life are remarkably uniform in terms of background, education, values, and so on. The fact that the field is so uniform serves to intensify the ever-present dual closeness and competition. It is very difficult to stand out in a field of uniform people without ending up like the proverbial 'nail that gets hammered down'. The person who gets ahead in the company treads a very narrow path between being too successful and thus inviting setbacks, and being diligent but unnoticed.

This is, of course, more easily said than done. There are no absolute standards of achievement in the company, and it is often impossible to tell whether an employee's work is suffering because of personal relations with a sempai, because of problems inherent in the work, or because of the employee's own lack of ability. Indeed, the fact that there are different possible reasons why an employee may be performing poorly is not generally taken into account by the personnel department. In an environment where the standards of achievement and promotion are unclear, employees can never do enough to be completely sure of their good standing. Insecurity is often at the root of the long hours put in by the C-Life workers.

There is thus serious competition between the dōki, and this can lead to great tension under the surface. This can be seen especially as some dōki are promoted over the others, and possibly reaches its height when some are promoted ahead of others to their first management post: section chief. The group of new recruits work for about three years before the first titles are given, and, as a general rule, all of the dōki are promoted together at this stage, unless they have made a very large error of some kind, or displayed a particularly unsuitable attitude. Recently, however, the gap between the first promoted and the last promoted has grown wider. C-Life employees invariably connect that widening gap, and the increasing role of merit in determining job advancement, to a decrease in loyalty.

Rohlen drew attention to these points. Contrary to the stereotypical view of the Japanese company, where dōki are assumed to be promoted at the same time and have equal opportunities, Rohlen reports that the personnel department in his fieldwork had generally summed up their new employees within a few years of entry to the company and identified the outstanding men. What is more, he reports that their subsequent promotion patterns rarely differ from this first estimate.

> S: Has my consciousness about work changed over these 14 years? Well, 50 people have already shrunk to 30. The 50 of us who started off together have already shrunk to 30. On Monday of this week we had a same-year-intake party – dōkikai – with just five of us. It was really fun, though. Even though it's a harsh environment, everyone has a certain degree of belief or trust and is doing what they have to do. It was a really forward-looking party where everyone had the attitude that even though it is a harsh environment they wanted to move once more to rebuild the company, from their own respective positions – to use their own strength.

The fact that dōki are in all kinds of 'respective positions' is very important in creating and maintaining a sense of ownership in the company. And they quickly identify – and learn to trust and follow – the outstanding members of the group: the 'leadership candidates'.

> S: U might be among the most trusted or trustworthy among the senior intake. In the first year we had to pair off to sell. U from the finance department is a real thoroughbred kind of a person inside our company but he does work in a really hands-on kind of a way – even though he's a thoroughbred he has a hungry kind of a spirit. So he doesn't have any show-off kind of tendencies and he is good at relating to other people. So if there's something I don't understand or want to talk about I'd talk to him without hesitation and I ask him how he thinks things are going to turn out. It's not my intention to put a rank on people, but I just happened to have worked alongside him for two years so he's the one I trust more than anyone else.

As we have seen, the dōki generally maintain an impression of being on very good terms with each other. The great ambition and competitiveness is not normally displayed openly. One can never forget that, once one is in the company, one is potentially there for life. As we saw in the last section, this means that it is essential to maintain good relations with as many people as possible. Open conflict is severely frowned upon, as is open competition. An employee who is openly trying to beat his dōki is bound to be hated, and that is a dangerous move in a long-term political game. The best way to be safe is to conform, do what is expected, endure, be patient, and, above all, cultivate good relations with everybody.

The only valid outlet through which to express competitiveness or ambition is as a company member striving for the sake of the company. 'Loyalty', as we saw earlier in this chapter, is a highly prized characteristic, and it is acceptable for employees to boast of their hard work and long hours if they make it clear that they do so out of loyalty to the company rather than out of ambition and competitiveness. The picture is thus one of relative solidarity and harmony on the exterior, but on the interior we find an intense arena of competition and desperate struggle to succeed. There is thus a great difference between the tatemae of good relations and harmony, and the honne of ambition and jockeying for position. Everywhere I looked in C-Life, human relations had a front side and a back side. Negotiating the correct way in between the two at the right times is crucial for success.

Clark (1979) also found this gap between appearance and reality in Marumaru, where people appeared to be on friendly terms but were in fact bitter rivals. Rohlen (1974: 138) confirms this intense rivalry amongst the dōki, noting that the dōki act as the 'standard of comparison for the interpretation of promotions'. The Uedagin employees had an intense interest in such questions as 'At what age do the first of each age set attain each new rank? What percentage of the age set is left behind? After what age is there no hope for promotion to a given rank?' At C-Life, too, the dōki were incredibly interested in gossip about each other and in what I saw in each of them, and what they had said to me. The competition between them was constantly apparent and a key topic of conversation.

I was struck by the considerable discrepancy in C-Life between the accounts of how close the dōki were, and how often they actually met as a group. In practice, there were a number of sub-groups inside the larger dōki group that were 'friends', and that met frequently. The larger group, however, rarely met, despite frequently professing their closeness.

> S: With the dōki, there are only five people who got together the other day, but then everyone is scattered among the provinces so it's difficult to do parties. I think that there are a few parties that go on in Tōkyō. I just got together with a few of the guys the other day because I'd come back to Tōkyō for the first time in a long time. It wasn't an official same-year-intake party – dōkikai. It was just a drinking party that happened for the first time in a while.

Everything involving the dōki eventually led back to this dual theme of co-operation and competition. When I asked my respondents what qualities make someone a good dōki, I was interested to note that ideals of co-operation and competition were both included. The ideal dōki, it seems, has the following qualities:

- someone of whom you could ask advice;
- competitive;
- someone you would want to know privately;
- fair;
- someone you could talk freely with;
- good personality;
- clever;
- capable of being a rival.

The emphasis here is on someone with both ability and talent who provides one with a genuine challenge to beat, and the kind of personality that one would wish for in a friend. The intermingling of these different attitudes towards dōki is shown in the tension between employees' belief that they are very close and the actuality that they are constant sources of comparison, jealousy, spurs to greater success, and rivalry for each other.

> S: No-one really drinks that much – and although they are living nearby they don't actually telephone that much either. We might seem closer than we actually are [shitashii yō de sonna ni shitashikunai kamo]. But our hearts communicate and that's because of that first year. Even though we don't telephone we know that the other guys are doing well from the gossip we hear from people around us. So we don't do that many drinking parties.

> E: I feel that my dōki are my colleagues and my friends [nakama]. In the company we are often told this but my generation in the company was very close. Even though we are this old now when we gather together and hold a party for our dōki, we all return to the same facial expression as when we just got into the company.

Most of them are middle-aged men now but we can go on as friends. I think that we all support each other, but having said that, because it is a corporation inside the company, differences appear at the rate at which we advance and in that sense we are rivals too.

We have seen, in discussing other examples of honne and tatemae, that not all employees feel a discrepancy between honne and tatemae, or between their own views and company ideology. This is equally the case with the relationships between the dōki. The consciousness of rivalry between the dōki varies significantly, particularly in relation to the position of each person inside the company. The following statement is typical of those I heard from employees who had been promoted earlier than their dōki:

E: I crossed the line to become section chief but there are people who crossed the line ahead of me and people who have still not become section chiefs. But we all gather together without any titles [katagaki nashi] and drink and eat together. I feel lucky to be blessed with such friends.

But it was difficult for me to get those who hadn't been promoted early to talk to me, and to turn up at the same places as those who were more successful. I had to put considerable effort into showing that I had no agenda of comparing the dōki, and that they would not be put in uncomfortable positions by placing them in the same (comparable) situations as their dōki in the film. The more unsuccessful dōki were rather easily satisfied with any tatemae kind of explanation that I produced. If I told them I was interested in looking at the good spirit of the dōki, or their closeness, or how human relations are so deep in a Japanese company, they accepted that. This suggested to me that they were less aware of the dual nature of honne–tatemae as it worked among their dōki than their more successful colleagues, and we may conclude that their ability to recognise the duality, and to manipulate it to their own advantage, was one of the key factors behind the success of those colleagues.

Having discussed the relationships between equals, I now examine those between seniors and juniors.

Seniors – sempai

As we saw in the last chapter, the hierarchical structure of C-Life means that, for each employee, virtually everyone else, apart from his own dōki, is either higher or lower than him on the company ladder. The senior–junior relationship is, therefore, one of the most important in the company, and it has been recognised as such by earlier Japan authors, particularly De Vos (1984) and Rohlen (1974).

After their first two years in the company, employees cease to be trainees and are sent to their first real post. Here they are assigned a senior who has been in the section for a number of years. The new recruits are not given any specified job description, but are expected to do whatever their senior requires of them. The relationship between seniors and juniors is thus very much like that of a master and disciple.

In practice, it actually takes the newcomers to C-Life a long time to settle down and resign themselves to their work in a company. Even some of those who turn out to be 'leadership candidates' once they have settled in rebel against the strict company atmosphere in the beginning. An important factor in this is that the middle and older generations who entered C-Life perceived themselves as having no real choice but to submit to the company, since there was little possibility of making a favourable job change. Successful recruits were those who quickly realised what was expected of them and played their passive role the best. By no means all C-Life trainees were willing to submit, nor were they all successful in playing the appropriate role of a new recruit. Some of those who were slow to learn endured a miserably demeaning time until they found their feet.

When an employee has been in the company for two to four years, he becomes the senior of a new employee. So sections in C-Life are hierarchies, where each junior inevitably takes the place of his senior to become a senior himself. There are important implications of this system. These are as follows: first, from the point of view of the senior:

- This is his first direct junior and he thus feels considerable responsibility for him. Obviously, if he is to be entrusted with more juniors in the future, and prove his ability to manage, it is vital that he does a good job at being a senior, which means he must ensure the success of his junior. This involves enabling the junior to produce a reasonable level of work, to be obedient, to conform to company norms and to engage in the expected social behaviour. As the junior's main function is to aid the senior, the senior finds himself very dependent on the junior for his own work results.
- The senior is young enough to understand the problems the junior is encountering in adjusting to work life.

The senior has shifted from being the person on the very bottom rung of the section ladder to his first position of responsibility. He feels considerable pride at being entrusted with a new employee and this breeds a high degree of enthusiasm directed towards managing the new employee well. The situation is rather similar to a second-year fraternity member showing a first-year student the ropes. As De Vos points out, the master often takes the place of parents for the apprentice, and therefore takes on a serious responsibility.

The implications of the system from the junior's point of view are as follows:

- As a new employee he is under considerable pressure, but his direct senior is someone young enough to relate to and to aspire to emulate.
- The junior is conscious that, just a few years before, the senior was in the same position as he currently finds himself in. Equally, he realises that if he does what is expected of him, he will certainly be in the senior's position a few years in the future. This remains the case at every level he reaches in the company.

Nakane (1970: 42–43) comments:

> The essential elements in the relationship are that the kobun (junior) receives benefits or help from his oyabun (senior), such as assistance in securing employment or promotion, and advice on occasions of important decision-making. The kobun (junior), in turn is ready to offer his services whenever the oyabun (senior) requires them.

The relationship between senior and junior is, then, at the heart of successful company life. In C-Life, the entire employment structure, as we saw in Chapter 4, is built around life-time employment. So changing one single aspect of this system simply does not work. For example, as the following comment illustrates, promoting people by ability would have repercussions for the whole workforce. So the sempai-kōhai system maintains the stability of the hierarchy. Having each employee train under a senior and aspire to be at the same level as him in the future is crucial to the maintenance of the whole system.

> V: If the senior is too talented, then the juniors can't keep up with him [oi nukenai] or pursue him. If this was a Western society, he would be quickly promoted, and that wouldn't be a problem, because he himself would gradually advance and leave his juniors behind. He would become a section chief, an assistant department head, and then a department head. However, in the seniority system, he is kept at the level of section chief for a long time. So the people below him are apt to think that there's no way they could do work at the level he does it. And they understand that in their own hearts, and then they might think that they would never be able to do the work of a section chief, because it seems so far above them. The solution is if somebody very talented (like U) goes up in the company [eraku naru], at a faster pace. The posts would open up then. And even if the next person couldn't do things as fast as him, he would already be assistant department head or department head, even at that young age. And the people below him would think, 'Maybe I can be section chief,' and still have some ambition. In the seniority system, it is difficult, but also important, that the people below can attain to the next level. It is also dependent on how good the understanding of the very talented senior, like U, is, as to how his juniors might think of him.

The relationship between senior and junior can be very complex. A comparison of how employees see the ideal senior, and the ideal junior, provides a good insight into the dynamics of this relationship. I asked the members of the international section what they considered the hallmarks of a 'good' sempai. They listed various qualities:

- good people as humans;
- people you can trust;
- they listen to the people below them;
- positive about their juniors' work;

- easy to consult with (sōdan shiyasui);
- they understand other people's position and feelings;
- they have management ability, decision ability and wide knowledge;
- fair;
- they have vision and responsibility;
- they have understanding;
- clever.

This reflects what we saw in the last chapter, and in the present one, about the ideal employee in general. A good senior, it seems, is a good person all round, rather than some sort of superhuman worker. One employee described a particularly good senior in these sorts of terms, as a good, unaffected person:

> S: There are a lot of fake kinds of displays in the workplace. Someone might not get on with someone at all but just because it is their birthday they might give them an expensive handkerchief. But this man never did anything like that – he was completely natural. I spent three years in that workplace alongside him. So I think that I was able to learn something from him.

So honne is appreciated in seniors. I found that C-Life employees generally try very hard to embody the qualities of a good senior. In particular, they give a great deal of thought to how they go about managing their juniors. This is most evident in the comments of sales branch heads, who have a particularly difficult job in managing the large numbers of sales ladies under them. These ladies are recruited by the personnel department, so the branch heads really have no say in the employees whom they are given to manage. As we saw in Chapter 4, selling life insurance is a difficult activity, and suited to a certain type of temperament, so the employee turnover is very high. Unlike normal employees, the sales ladies are employed on a more temporary basis, so they are much freer to leave if they want to. So, in managing these women, branch heads are unable to use force or coercion as they can with juniors, for fear of their quitting. They must learn to motivate by example, and to exhort greater effort by persuasion.

> S: The real job that is demanded of a sales office head is to pull out the abilities of each person under him.

> S: One issue is how much guidance you should give to people... whether you should encourage someone who already likes arithmetic to study some more arithmetic or whether you should show them that there is different ways to do things. I think that it takes a lot of skill to be a sales head; it takes a lot of management skill.

The employee who made this comment, and who is deeply aware of the psychology of his staff and how to motivate them, told me that in the beginning he had nightmares that he would be at work one day, and that none of the women would turn up! He learned slowly that he had to develop the skill of motivating the women. He learns this kind of job-specific skill in a disciple-like fashion from watching his senior handling the sales ladies.

As we saw in Chapter 5, one of the most effective ways of persuading employees to work hard is to work hard oneself and harness their sympathy. I often heard employees say that they couldn't go home because their boss was still working there. Working hard commands the respect of juniors, and also their compassion, so they are motivated to renew their efforts for the sake of their senior. Loyalty to the company, in practice, often comes down to practical demonstrations of loyalty like working hard, and this in turn, often comes down to personal relations: working hard for the sake of a particular person. This relates to what we saw earlier in this chapter: feelings of loyalty to the company are very often connected to feelings of loyalty for particular people – and hard work is acceptable if done out of a sense of loyalty rather than personal ambition.

> O: More important than anything else is to show them [the sales ladies] that you are working really hard and earnestly. If you weren't doing your very best they wouldn't accept you at all [aite ni sarenai]. To show that you are working really hard, when they come to you for advice or with a question, or when they are in trouble with some or another issue, you can't answer lightly. That is the most important of all. And then on my side, when I was in trouble and asked them for help and they gave it I was very sure to recognise that help and thank them for it.

When I interviewed them, employees invariably had examples of mentors from whom they learned how to manage well. In the disciple-like system of learning by example under the guidance of a senior several years older, this kind of learning is extremely important.

> S: I have had one really fantastic senior [mentor] in my career. I don't think the women really wanted or expected him to tell them how to get people to sign up for insurance. They wanted him to help to give them a push, or to motivate them to give them extra energy, or to give them the courage to go out and do the work. I think that was the great thing about him – that he did a lot of different things to help extend the abilities of his juniors. He would say, 'If you want to know more about selling insurance, then ask that person over there!' or 'If you want to know more about making planning reports, then ask that person over there!' and he would assign responsibilities to each person... There are times that it's difficult for me to tell somebody to go and ask somebody else about something that I'm not very clear about. I can't help thinking that it makes me look bad or that it's not very impressive. But that senior had the kind of ability to assign responsibility well. He thought that juniors would be unhappy if he tried to do everything himself. So he would say that it is much better just to leave them to do it themselves. He was very good at using his juniors' ability to its very best... making the best use of people.

In the sales offices, too, the 'human qualities' of seniors are highly regarded. The employees inside C-Life, and the sales ladies whom I talked to, invariably professed a preference for seniors who bring a more personal and emotional relationship into the workplace.

> S: The sales offices are really just collections of normal housewives in a sense. Sometimes their kids are in summer holidays or winter holidays and they can't help but bring their kids along to work. Now say a kid had a cold and had to have the day off school and they brought them to the company – well, if it were me I would say, well, just put him to bed in the corner there, but if it was the branch office head that I learned so much from, he might have bought a wonderful plastic model for the kid to play with, or he might have gone to a candy store and bought something special for the kid.

In the sales offices, money is, of course, a large incentive for the sales ladies. Their income is directly connected to the amount of insurance that they sell, since they are paid commission only. That is the reality. But there is still the feeling that emotional incentives should be present too. The idea that bosses with 'human qualities' are preferable is idealised.

> S: That branch office head would have said that having to put a money incentive on it was because the branch office head didn't have enough authority. Normally, they should have been able to go out and get insurance even without that. In summer he would put ice in a bucket and put cold cans of drink in it. When the sales people came back from their long rounds he would open a can of drink for them and say, 'Well done! You must be hot!' He did this for them himself. And the women would be very thankful and happy... It wasn't anything expensive that he did. It was that he did it himself, from his heart...

The senior in C-Life is, therefore, much more than a boss. His role goes beyond engaging the enthusiasm of his juniors in discharging their duties, important though that is. It is a matter of acting as a mentor in much more than company life – it is acting as a role model of how to live as a 'salary man'. This includes how to interact with others in the company, how to amuse themselves outside the company, how to play golf, how to behave as a businessman who commands respect.

> A: I always had a lot of good seniors. So I often went out drinking with them. They taught me well how to drink [osake no nomikata o yoku osowatte ita]. So they really taught me well.

Seniors, in other words, are supposed to set an example for juniors to follow. Even those employees who do not find a great deal of emotional content in their relationships with their bosses regard the seniors as a model to emulate.

X: In the sales section that I was in we were sales corps. So rather than senior/junior it was a management relationship. You are rivals with the people around you and you have targets so that when you make a mistake, they pull you back. So in that sense you are big rivals and you have big targets in the sense that you look at what your seniors are doing and try to emulate them. And if you see that your senior is progressing [seichō shite iru] you think that you can try hard at your work as well.

A: A good senior is... well, I can't say any individual names, but for example I went to a certain organisation to sell insurance and the guy that I was dealing with inside the company really liked me and he talked to all of the employees there and decided to push C-Life insurance inside his company for me... But because it was an organisation there was a head above him inside the organisation. And we found out that that head had already been approached by a certain life insurance company to take out that company's insurance plan. Because he was at the top, whatever company he chose would become the choice of the company. So the guy that I was dealing with said he would be happy to go with C-Life but I had to do something about approaching the top and finding out what the story was. And I did approach the top guy but he wouldn't really open his heart to me. The way that he talked was a little bit strange and I didn't know what was going on. But at a certain stage the chairman of the company decided to call in the various salesmen from the companies that were trying to sell to them to have a meeting. And I discovered that the other guy that had been trying to sell to the head was none other but my senior from C-Life. So it hadn't been another company at all. It had been another guy inside C-Life! He was in another section to me but he was my senior. And so we were really surprised by what had happened. But I talked to that senior and he had already convinced the top of the company to take out the C-Life insurance. So it was really his doing that the company would choose C-Life insurance. But he said that because I had made a lot of effort at the bottom convincing different people inside the company, that he would give the main work of bringing that policy in to me and that he would just be the sub. Normally, without that senior convincing the head of the company we wouldn't have got the policy. But my senior gave that to me. So I think that that is one mark of a really good senior. And he taught me how he had convinced the head of the company and told me the success story of how he had approached the chairman and I learned how to approach the top members of companies and sell to them.

What kind of qualities are seen in the senior in this anecdote? He has recognised the effort that his junior has put in, sacrificed some of his personal gain to give to that junior as reward, and taught him important knowledge that he needs to advance in his career. This illustrates the role of the senior as educator. A good senior should organise the content of the work and the progress of the employee's career so that they can learn and advance.

S: The work that I'm actually doing is to teach the sales staff how to go out and make the sales but that's not going to work if you're only teaching. You have to make it so that it's easy for them to go and do it. You have to lay open the path for them. I think that that's our work.

In the last chapter, I discussed the importance of tsukiai, and noted that they often act as a forum where seniors and juniors can interact in a different way from normal. Indeed, the emotional content of the relationship with a senior is often centred on drinking. Drinking frees employees from a certain amount of responsibility for what they say, so that they can criticise, complain, and air grudges with less fear of repercussions. Employees say to their boss that they would like to ask 'advice' (sōdan shitai), and if it is a personal matter, they are often invited to go drinking.

> E: My strongest support is a boss I had eight years ago. He taught me a lot. I really liked his way of thinking. In the matter of me losing my job, I didn't exactly consult him, but he listened to what I had to say. Nothing I can say now is going to help. But I wanted to communicate to him how I felt. I wanted him to understand how I felt on being told by the company. So I contacted him and he said, 'Let's go out drinking.' He listened to what I said [kiite moraeta] so I feel satisfied with that. He didn't know for sure so he said, 'Has it come?' and I said yes. He said what are you going to do, and I said 'I've made up my mind to resign.' Well, he listened to what I wanted to say so I felt better after that [sukkiri shita].

A sempai, then, should be hard-working and personable, a trustworthy person with empathy and understanding who can motivate his underlings at a personal level. By contrast, I found that a quite different set of qualities is attributed to the ideal kōhai:

- positive about work;
- hard-working;
- co-operative;
- someone who would do even boring work without complaining;
- fair;
- responsible;
- forward-looking;
- young and enthusiastic;
- capable;
- someone who gets down to work;
- Unquestioning.

Here, the emphasis is very much on work ability, rather than human qualities. The junior is expected to work efficiently and conscientiously, and do whatever is required of him. The most common word I heard to describe an ideal junior was 'shikkari' (solid, reliable).

> E: At the moment among the guys that I am supervising, there is one who is comparatively sound [shikkari]. There is nothing special about him, but in various kinds

of work compared to the other young guys of his age he is seen well by the employees at his workplace, and evaluated highly by his customers, and that is the most important thing.

The sempai and kōhai are thus expected to follow quite different roles in their relationship. As I suggested earlier in this chapter, the most successful employees are those who can effectively play all of the different parts required of them throughout company life; thus, it is important to be able to exhibit the qualities of the ideal kōhai when necessary, and those of the ideal sempai at other times, in order to advance in the company. And that means that these relationships always have political overtones.

The importance of senior-junior relationships in the company is often cited as rooted in the education system and the family. According to De Vos (1984: 53-4), they reflect the 'paternalistic' system, which is deeply rooted in Japanese culture: 'The Japanese... tend toward strong belief in political and social myths about their nation, company, group, or family collectivity.'

Dore (1973) found most Japanese to prefer a paternalistic environment, with all that that entails. He quotes a survey of Japanese national character in which, over 15 years, 82 to 85 per cent of the respondents stated that they preferred a section chief who 'might occasionally make extra work demands even in breach of the rules, but on the other hand would always look after you, even in matters outside of work'. Dore states:

> Those who approved of the paternalist saw him as warm, full of human feeling, flexible, a man with some 'bottom' (literally 'big-bellied'), a boss (oyabun) type, somebody who trusts his subordinates, a man with social sense, a kind human person, a man with leadership powers, a man who thinks of others, considerate, responsible. [The opposite kind of manager]... is seen as cold, lacking in human feeling, inflexible, introverted, self-centred and opportunistic; he thought that everything could be settled by rules, had a slide-rule for a heart, thought of nothing but work, and lacked social sense.

Hamaguchi (1980) asked respondents to choose between pairs of questions, each of which contained a statement emphasising human relationships and one emphasising individualistic orientation. This revealed that 74.7 per cent of the respondents favoured the human relations orientation. When asked to complete the sentence, 'In order to get along with others...' the respondents emphasised the following qualities:

Empathy	28.8 per cent
Mutual understanding	21.6 per cent
Self-control and giving others chances	14.5 per cent
Trust	10.5 per cent
Co-operation	10.2 per cent

Even 20 or 30 years later, these findings of Dore and Hamaguchi still seemed to apply to C-Life. There were, however, differences of opinion between the generations. Even those who complained about the negative aspects of close human relations in the workplace (the requirement to go out drinking with seniors when asked, or the requirement to get involved in the personal lives of seniors, or to help out at funerals and so on) still hoped that the positive elements would remain.

Why do the employees have these preferences? The desire for a 'kind' and 'human' section chief is closely connected to the element of human relations that we have already identified in this chapter as 'amae', or the need to be dependent on others.

As I suggested in the earlier section on amae, life in a paternalistic company is, in some ways, surprisingly easy. As long as one complies with the company norms, one can remain in the embrace of a forgiving environment. It is psychologically easy not to have to make decisions or to take responsibility for one's own life, which is, in a sense, exactly what happens in a Japanese company. If one has no lateral choices – which way to expand one's career, which company to transfer to, whether to change one's line of work – it is easy to concentrate one's entire energies on doing the task at hand as well as one can, and striving in the only direction possible: upwards. Dependence on the company is thus forged and completed, and although the employee may be dissatisfied with the company, the alternatives open to him are often limited. This can result in people enduring remarkably harsh treatment from their seniors.

These points relate to my discussion in the previous section, where I focused on the constant tension between co-operation and competition that marks the dōki relationship. I found that the senior-junior relationship is similarly characterised by a constant tension between strict authority and warm kindness. Rohlen (1974: 124), for example, describes the sempai-kōhai relationship as involving a 'chain of relationships of "good turns"... [which] is not, however, between equals, nor is the exchange balanced... much like a chain letter without the multiple'. He stresses the fact that, because the exchange is between unequals, time is a crucial factor in restoring balance. Rohlen investigates the reasons why a senior might befriend a junior. His informants mentioned 'omoiyari' (feelings of sympathy and compassion), and 'kawaigaru' (the feeling of looking after something smaller and weaker). The relationship always involves emotional content. Rohlen adds (132) that sempai should not be taken as 'pseudo-parents' nor kōhai as 'docile believers in the faith'. Rather 'these two extremes, neither totally contradictory nor totally allied, create between them a fluid context rich in ritual gestures, manoeuvre, and subtle intrigue, and here daily reality is to be found'.

In practice, there are many relations between bosses and juniors that grate very much on both parties. In cases of conflict, the boss generally has the upper hand. Usually, the threat of repercussions from juniors is not so serious as to hamper the boss when exercising his authority.

> E: If someone wants to get ahead he has to have a certain amount of support underneath him. But it doesn't matter that much whether the people under someone like him or not.

Nevertheless, if a junior does not like his senior there are all kinds of surreptitious ways in which he can sabotage his boss's work. Earlier in this chapter, I observed that a clever junior is capable of manipulating his senior to approve the projects he wants. So the importance of maintaining good relations goes two ways. This is especially so given that the bosses do not have the power to fire juniors whom they do not like. This has the tendency to equalise every person's power, regardless of status, more than might be the case in a non-life-time employment situation. Issues in C-Life are, to a considerable degree, decided by majority opinion. As we will see later in this chapter, if there is one boss whose opinion is different from that of the majority of his juniors, or which goes against the C-Life notion of common sense, he will be invariably doomed to lose to that majority opinion. We see in the following comment one way in which juniors can get their own back on seniors they dislike.

> A: Just say that there was a senior called A but he really dislikes me. But A has a senior called B who is above him who likes me. You just have to get B to crack down on A. So if A gets mad at me, he is going to be scolded by B. So in the end he can't get mad at me. You just have to make it like that!
>
> Salarymen suck up [pekopeko suru] to strong people. And at the same time, the people who they suck up to are invariably sucking up to the people above them. I think that that kind of clever method of getting along with other people [umai tsukiai no shikata] is important for Japanese…

At least two of the employees I talked to told me how they had brought about the demotion, and in one case, the firing, of a former boss whom they had disliked intensely and under whom they had suffered for a number of years. In the case of the boss who had been fired, the man concerned had no idea at all why he had been laid off, nor about the behind-the-scenes machinations that were involved in getting him dismissed.

In C-Life, where responsibility is so ambiguous and where it is often impossible to determine who had brought up the original ideas and who should be given the credit, how to take responsibility for work was a serious issue. I discuss this issue in depth later in this chapter. Here, I simply note that employees told me that – as seniors – they wanted juniors who would initiate their own ideas, and also take the responsibility for researching them properly and finding out ways in which to put them into practice themselves. The formal responsibility for any idea rests with seniors, but seniors were most irritated by juniors who brought up ideas but failed to act on them, or who failed to complete tasks that they had initiated.

One leadership candidate recommended clarity of opinion as the best way to resolve disputes, but this was his personal method, and he was strong enough in the company to carry that off. For most employees, this would be a high-reward, high-risk endeavour.

> A: There are always people that you don't get along with [awanai]. If your way of thinking doesn't match with the other person [awanai] then you should tell him the

way that you are thinking. You should say, 'You, as department head, think this, but I think this.' And then if you go ahead and do things your way, and the department head had the correct opinion after all then you should say which was correct. If you say things correctly there should be no problem.

We have mentioned briefly the existence of factions in the company. Senior–junior relations inevitably grow into factions, when a strong senior gathers a number of juniors about him. This is not a prerequisite to advance, but in many cases employees can get ahead by following such a mentor.

E: It is like an army in many ways. Turn left, turn right! It is all-important which battalion you belong to.

However, this depends on the personality of the employee in question. Not all employees manoeuvre themselves through the company by means of such personal relations, although those who don't told me that they may have been hindered in their progress because of it.

E: I wonder if I'd have been in a better position if I'd been in a faction. But I didn't like that kind of world, living looking all the time at the colour of your boss's mood… Such people, even if they think something is black and their boss thinks it is white, change your thinking little by little so things seem to shift to white. If things are black I say they are.

E: In retrospect, when you look at the careers of guys who most people didn't think had a chance any more to make it to the very top, you find that they were often connected to some important guy at the top. Or conversely, someone can be right on track but their sempai doesn't stay in the running for some reason. So it is all-important that you are attached to the right people. There are a lot of timing issues involved. That is the root of all the gossip. 'That guy was OK until then, but he made a mistake around then etc.' For girls it is harder because we don't have the same kinds of relations.

Once again, this central aspect of company life has changed greatly in recent years. I noted at the start of this section that the sempai-kōhai system is closely connected to life-time employment, partly because employees are more likely to endure harsh treatment by their bosses if they do not see that they have any choice; and partly because they are likely to be happy to endure being somebody's junior if they have the assurance that in a few years they will be somebody's senior. But the life-time employment system is now crumbling. There is no longer a guarantee that service to one's seniors will be adequately compensated in the future. In the final analysis, hierarchical management can only be maintained where transfers out of the company are rare, and as long as all the participants agree that the system is fair. There must also be reasonable expectation that the system will continue for the foreseeable future (De Vos 1984). The company must be doing reasonably well and have long-term prospects for these expectations to be appropriate. In other words, the large, stable company is a structure in which such long-term reciprocity can work, but the system breaks down rapidly when the employees lose faith that the system will continue.

We have seen the qualities associated with a good sempai. What of his kōhai?

Juniors – kōhai

In the last section, we saw the ways in which seniors must manage their juniors, passing on both formal knowledge and personal experience and company know-how so that the junior learns how to be a good company man. However, juniors are not supposed to be passive receptacles into which their seniors pour their knowledge. The ideal junior is seen to be someone who has ideas and initiative of his own.

> A: On the other hand, a good junior? I have taught several dozen juniors until now. But a really ideal junior is, as I said before, someone who can say what he wants to do clearly. And somebody who has figured out a way to do the work – someone who can make their own plans or policies and do them. Somebody who can stand up and say things back to me. Somebody who can say, 'I want to do it like this!' So not somebody who wants to leave everything to me. In that case, I would still get them to do the work, but it is better if the person can make their own decisions and do things in their own style. Those kinds of people are the best. I have my own style so they can steal the good things about that style from me. And they should use that and make their own style. Those kinds of guys are doing things well and are talented. If something happens some people say, 'Please help me!' And they are quite endearing [kawaii]. But people who have their own style and have that properly to themselves – they are the kinds of people that you want as a junior.

We have already encountered the importance of ideas being generated at relatively low ranks in the company. Junior employees therefore need creativity and initiative to be able to produce them.

> V: Really talented company employees know what the main issues [kadai] are in the organisation as a whole, and are thinking about what kind of response they should make to the issues. They think through plans by themselves, and tackle their seniors with those plans.

A corollary of this is that juniors shouldn't always adopt an attitude of passive servility towards their seniors.

> V: That is one issue. And another issue is that even if a junior's opinion is different from that of his senior, he debates the point properly [kichin to giron suru] and brings forward all the appropriate arguments, so if he doesn't like it he says he doesn't like it, if he likes it then he says that he likes it. When you give an order, it is on the part of the organisation. Once the order is given then juniors have to

comply with that order, so until it reaches the stage of coming out as a formal order, they need to be able to debate a point properly. Otherwise their seniors cannot make the correct judgement on those issues.

Indeed, it is often the relatively junior members of the department who are the driving force behind it, and this trend is increasing.

Z: I think over the fourteen years the kind of thing that has changed is that the authority of the department heads has lessened at a time when speed is of increased value. Well, it might be the best way for department heads to decide things and carry out things at the top, but the flow of the times at the moment is so fast that they are giving more and more authority to the people below them. And that is the wider trend. If you don't get on that trend then you don't advance speedily. I think that the organisation as a whole is moving towards that trend. That is a large change. Before, it was OK if the department heads assumed a haughty attitude and decided things.

As employees move into management, they increasingly have to make decisions about plans that have already been devised by others. They must act as a control on ongoing processes, rather than as a hands-on mover at the grass-roots level. This becomes more pronounced as they move up the company. Inevitably, the higher the level, the more they become out of touch with change. In such a situation, it is essential for the juniors to maintain their critical faculties.

P: Sometimes the seniors don't understand about the important issues.

V: Bad seniors don't, but there are cases like that.

P: The further up the company they go, the less they understand.

V: So the older the senior is, the more experience they have, and you can say that the possibility that they will be right about their judgement might be higher. But that is only a possibility that it will be higher. For example, if the world is really changing a lot, then if you ask yourself if past experience counts or not, it's not certain that it will count at all. At times like that, it might be the opposite situation, that because you've had a certain experience until now, it might be a disadvantage in your decision-making, or there might be no value in the experiences you've had in applying them to the future. So to determine what's correct, you need to be able to debate the point adequately. Otherwise the senior has cause to worry a lot. If the junior just says, 'Yes sir, yes sir,' in that situation you need to think of the problem yourself, and also think of all the optional answers to that problem. And you need to be able to respond to the issues raised by your bosses, and be able to give good arguments against the questions raised.

The popular view of the Japanese employee has been one of blind obedience to orders but, as we can see, this is not at all the case. Although obedience is normal, it is the ability to step beyond this that is highly regarded and is the key to becoming a leadership candidate.

> V: And another point that you need, is when a decision is made, to actually have the strength and ability to carry out the task. It is often a shortcoming in very bright people that they can criticise issues well, and say, 'If it was me, I'd do it like this,' and you say, 'OK, do it like that!' – but then they can't do it properly. In other words, it's necessary to take on the responsibility for a task.

This section, then, has supplemented the previous one by focusing on the creative and active qualities necessary in a good junior. Juniors are not simply passive disciples of their seniors: they must have initiative and creativity, and they must be ready to take responsibility.

Responsibility

The issue of how to assign responsibility was high in the minds of many employees as I conducted my fieldwork in 1999–2000. It was becoming increasingly clear that serious mistakes had been made in the company, causing problems of every kind as the recession dragged on. How could responsibility be assigned? This issue is complicated by the fact that 'taking responsibility' is a very personal notion in Japan. It involves taking on culpability personally. This is often responsible for business-related suicides in Japan.

   The problems associated with responsibility are connected to the ringi system (see Chapter 3). Because so many people are involved in the process of decision-making in C-Life – from coming up with the idea, to gathering support for it, to pushing it up through the ranks to gain approval from the managers who put their formal stamp on the project – it is hard to determine where the responsibility lies for any matter.

> I: On certain forms, everybody's stamp [signature] would be put on the form. And everyone would come around to agree on the same position, and in the end the decision would be passed up to the president himself.

When the ringi system works, plans are initiated by those closest to the action and by young people in the company who are motivated and ambitious, and know about new technologies and ideas. Thus, as we saw in the last section, junior employees tend to initiate plans. The ideas are tempered by the management experience of their seniors, and, by passing the idea through a number of people, risky elements are thought out and avoided. In this way, senior employees act as a check on the plans. But this system means that, if a plan goes wrong, it may be difficult to pinpoint the responsibility – or, worse, no-one takes responsibility at all.

> A: There are some people who, when the department head tells them to do something and they fail at it, say, 'Well, you told me to do it!' to the department head. But

they actually did the work themselves. So I would say why didn't you oppose the department head at that stage of it? If you did what you were told to do and fail at it, is the department head bad? The department head would say that the junior's way of doing things was bad. Each of them is making it the other's fault.

In practice, responsibility in C-Life is divided between seniors and juniors in an ambiguous way that leaves endless opportunity for interpretation and re-interpretation. Seniors take formal responsibility, although the person who actually made the mistake and holds the 'real' responsibility may be someone else, and they may be known and identified.

One employee told me his own views on how to minimise the uncertainty surrounding responsibility.

> A: In an everyday sense, how are loans divided among seniors and juniors? Well, I can only speak for myself but if people are told what to do... well, I tell my juniors... I give them the whole job to do. But if they fail they can come back to me. I tell them to do it how they like. It is not that I am giving the responsibility away. I like them to fail and I can cover their failure. I can cover their failure and rescue them – then I give it to them to do. But basically the senior person should take the responsibility. So you should assign work within your sphere of authority whether you are a department head or a section head or a director, according to each level. When I was working my seniors were doing roughly the same as what I just said. My boss would tell me to do it however I wanted and that he would 'wipe my bottom' if things went wrong. But because I was mostly given the freedom to do things how I liked, it is actually the opposite. I was able to do it in a free and easy manner [nobi nobi to] and get results. When I reach the same level as that senior I will do things the same way. In fact when I was faced with opposition and got it wrong, my senior did wipe my bottom. Well, my boss and the directors, they all did that. Sometimes, in those cases, they had to make decisions on decisions that I had made on my authority alone. In those cases, they would ask after I had made a mistake... Sometimes when things were not recoverable on my authority alone, they would have to sanction what I had done. They would ask me why I had done what I did and investigate the matter. They would put their stamps on the matter saying that this time it couldn't be helped but that next time they would not do that for me. And I would say that I was very sorry. Sometimes customers were involved in the mistake so the primary issue was that no trouble would be reflected on the customer. Even though it caused trouble inside the company over who would take responsibility.

After discussing the central relationships of dōki, seniors and juniors, I now turn to human relations issues associated with certain groups of people within the company, already singled out in Chapter 3 for special mention. I begin with women. How, in general, are gender distinctions perceived and treated in the company?

Male/female distinctions

> E: Sometimes I wondered in C-Life why it had to be the case that the guys were living all the time looking at the colour of their bosses' mood. I think that women are more honest in some ways. Even if guys hate work they will still turn up and do it. I think that is admirable. Because I can't do it. They say yes to their boss's face and then come back to their desks and do the work, complaining all the while. I think that if they have a complaint they should come out with it up front.

C-Life employees generally agree that men and women have very different characters. The male employees whom I talked to in C-Life thought of women as fundamentally different in character from men. When talking of working with women, before the topic of equality came up at all, the men would tell me their philosophies of what women are like, and why they work the way they do. They did not appear to believe at all that women can work in the same way as men. So, for the C-Life employees, 'equality' means equality of treatment, not of natures. Being kind to women does not mean treating them the same as men; it means understanding women's nature and catering to it. Although the numbers of women general workers that I talked to were limited, from what I saw they wished for equal treatment to men, but also generally believed that women and men have fundamentally different natures.

> S: Our work is based on, and able to exist, because of this society of women [the sales ladies], and I think that we need to be able to understand the special nature and characteristics of women.

Most of the male employees are familiar with working with women. A significant proportion of the sales force are women, much older than the new recruits who must work with them, and with more direct experience in insurance sales.

> S: I think we can say that we are a society where we are only a few men who are standing on top of a society of women. It is not a normal society where there are women inside the society of men.

This is also true in the head office, and for the relations between male bosses and female general workers. I found that the managers give considerable thought to how to cater for women, and try to incorporate this into their management style.

> S: Guys in the workplace don't usually have arguments that much with their seniors compared to women anyway. Women will say even to the sales head, 'I hate you!' And then it is a matter of how you can resolve it and sit down and talk. But women are quite good at doing that. Men tend to procrastinate about doing that. They wonder what they should say. Women are much more open about doing that. They will just come out with, 'Oh, I got an insurance policy, by the way! But, I really hate you and I'm not coming to the company tomorrow'. But then they might

turn up as usual and say, 'Good morning!' as if nothing has happened. And I realise that I have been worried about nothing!

S: Women come to work in part to get away from their homes. So when they come to the office they want to make it a fun atmosphere or make it something that is a little bit different to the everydayness of their lives. It is hard to actually do that in practice but I think about how to achieve that.

For the female general workers, during the period that they had equal status to men, fighting against stereotypes of women was a constant battle. All of the sales ladies and office workers were women. Even though their immediate bosses and co-workers understood the situation, it was still difficult for them to explain to newcomers that some women had equal status to men in the company.

E: The guys around me often said, 'She is a man in the company!' It sounds really strange but they had to say that because there was no other way to say it. If they didn't say that, the person we were dealing with wouldn't be able to understand.

Thus, although they were, in theory, equal to men, this was not really the case in practice. Honne and tatemae did not coincide, just as in my own case as a foreigner. Moreover, the women general workers often found that, even having conquered discrimination in their immediate environment inside C-Life, they had to cope with it in the wider society outside. Customers often assume that all women are office workers, and in order to get good service they need to speak to a man, because he is bound to be more senior than any woman. In fact, in the sales offices, this was almost always true, as all of the sales staff were women and only the assistant head and the head were male.

E: There were times that there were problems just because I was a woman. In social terms… times that I felt that working as a woman wasn't really accepted. For example, sometimes when I went to sell, people would say, 'Bring out a man!' If I was told to bring out a man, I would go and get a man! But I would feel bitter about that. I was the person responsible for the issue. The person who understood what was going on was also me. I would try to explain that, but if the customer wasn't satisfied with that and they were demanding that I bring a guy, I would do that. I thought that it wasn't any use battling at such a time. The most important thing was to have the customer happy. But I felt really bitter about that. Japan as a nation is still really behind.

The C-Life men in the sales offices all mentioned the difficulty of going in as young managers into an environment where the majority of their sales staff was older than they were. However, the fact that they were men mitigated this unevenness to some degree as the women were used to men in authority, no matter how young. The women general workers reported the same problem – being young – as the men, but because they were also women, they were unable to differentiate themselves quite so clearly from their staff; so their position was more delicate, and they had to employ a great deal of tact and care.

> O: Now I am a shusa [junior manager] among the other guy shusas. Most of them are younger than me but they are not directly under my jurisdiction. When I was at the branch office I was doing clerical work so the people below me were all women. And I was also involved in training the women in the branch offices, including older women. In the countryside, I was in quite a feminine workplace for the first time. I had to work with older women who had been working in that region for a very long time for the first time together. I realised that the company could exist because of this army of women working away diligently in the provinces... It is hard to go in as management so young, especially when I was so much younger than they were. But as far as formal position went I was the kakarichō [deputy head]. But they were veterans in the office work, and they knew in actuality far more than I did. So it took a while before they would recognise me as being the deputy head.

However, it was generally accepted that, by going through the training centre, the female general workers had earned the right to be considered different from the office workers. By the time the women general workers re-entered the company environment after those harsh first two years, they had gained enough experience to be acknowledged as a completely different category of worker by the female office workers.

> E: Once I got inside the company, all of the women employees were in uniform. However, I didn't have any opportunity directly to relate or to work with the women office workers. That didn't come until I had been in the company for two years. We did sales training for two years so I was in the organisation with the guys. In my third year, when I went to the branch office as a shunin [trainee manager], and had duties of supervising a number of people for the first time, I was finally working together with the women doing office work. At that time, inside the sales offices, the roles of each person were very clearly divided so the office workers do office work – they are all women – and then there are people like me in the role of trainee manager. Then there are section chiefs and department chiefs and branch chiefs.

> E: After the experience of being in the training centre and coming back, it was almost like being a separate category of person altogether; so in the workplace the lines between the women office workers and myself were very very clearly drawn, and we were able to work comfortably together [kimochi yoku].

My own case illustrated the importance of this factor. The fact that I skipped the training centre meant that I lacked a crucial distinction from the female office workers. Consequently, I found myself working straight away with women office workers who were of inferior status to me – for instance, they had to serve tea when I had meetings with the securities analysts who visited the company – but who had been in the same year as me at Keiō just the year before. This inevitably added tension to the working atmosphere and I had to put great effort into keeping relations smooth.

Going through training, however, was not enough to keep the general workers clearly differentiated from the office workers. They needed to work as hard as the men in order to maintain respect for their positions from the women office workers. If they did this, they found that the office workers were content to be in different categories from the women general workers, because they could see how rigorous that position was.

> E: I think that the difference between the categories of women is not so much the training but the consciousness of each category.

> E: So I was a shunin and I just happened to be a woman. But if you looked from the point of view of the women office workers, even if they had been asked to do so, they wouldn't have wanted to have any part of doing a shunin's work. They used to say to me, 'You have a very hard job,' and draw the line from their side.

The women were extremely tolerant of the situation. Although they had achieved general worker status, they were well aware that only a minority of employees really approved of this whole-heartedly. They tolerated small incidents of discrimination, recognising that in many companies there were still no such positions as women general workers. Annoyance with the backward attitudes was mixed with gratitude to the company for having taken them on in the first place.

> E: C-Life raised me. However, an organisation is made up of people. So if you look at how each and every one of the people inside that organisation is thinking, there are both people with advanced ideas about women working, and there are also people who worry about things like whether general worker women should serve tea to the men or not. I don't think that can really be helped. If there are a hundred people there are bound to be a hundred different types of thinking. That is how an organisation is made up. But it is also a fact that there are some organisations that do not allow any kind of forward-looking thinking at all. There are also companies that wouldn't even open the door when I knocked on the door looking for a job. In that sense, I think that C-Life showed an extraordinary degree of advancement in their thinking.

In the recession, the status of women has become increasingly unclear. In C-Life, women are now once again in a separate category from men, and back in uniform. The general workers expressed regret at this, but also felt that it couldn't be helped.

> E: The organisation is groping in the dark in a sense. Now, in the recession, things have become reversed a little. The fact that women are trying really hard at their work in the organisation is still news because it is something that is still not ordinary. I think that organisations now are grappling with which direction they should go in.

Part of the reason why women accepted the company's reversal on the policy of having women general workers was the fact that they were used to having to battle against discrimination in society at large, not just C-Life itself. The employees recognised that the company's attitudes had to be seen against that wider context.

> E: The opponent that we are fighting against is a culture that has been around for a very long time and that won't be changed in a morning and a night. So when an organisation – that is made up of all kinds of people with all kinds of ideas – tries to define thinking on such an issue; when they have to come up with reasons why they should have to nurture women general workers, then they probably began to think that if they didn't 'bring women up' anymore then it wouldn't be such a bad thing. I imagine that they came to the decision that putting women in the same category as men itself has been a burden from the very beginning.

> E: I think the point is to choose a road as human beings first and within that road then to look last at whether you are a guy or a girl. The problem is with looking at which sex a person is first and foremost. But apparently that problem won't disappear any time soon. But regardless of that, I want to work with an optimistic attitude and with energy. I think that is the secret of making it in a male dominated society.

The women in C-Life often express the same air of resignation that they cannot easily change the situation they are in. Rather, they resolve to do their very best in that situation. I often saw this in C-Life: annoyance at a situation, voicing of frustration to colleagues or bosses, eventual acceptance as they realised they could do nothing to change the situation, and then a resolution either to redouble their efforts at the task at hand, or to opt out of the situation by quitting. This is exactly the pattern we saw in Chapter 5, when considering how employees deal with adverse working conditions and low job satisfaction. Many women accordingly conclude that they cannot get ahead in C-Life, and choose the first opportunity – usually marriage – to bow out. The obstacles they mention in the road of change are, like many of the company's politics and attitudes, subtle and unclear. Thus, they begin to feel daunted by the fact that they are already at a disadvantage in the company by being a woman.

> E: Ever since I joined the company I told people that I wanted to climb up the company ladder and make it... to get ahead. In the beginning I thought without questioning it that if my dōki friends were getting ahead, making natural progress and getting ahead, then I should be able to do that too. I felt quite cocky about that. But when I actually got into the company I realised that compared to how I had been thinking about it when I was a student, there are many and various different kinds of walls inside the company. When I realised that those walls were there and when I felt that I needed to say something about the existence of those walls, I thought that I would have to progress higher up into the company myself before I could say my own thoughts. Even if I said to the company, 'You are drawing lines between men and women here!', there are many people who are unaware of such

things. So in that sense, even people who are quite high up in the company, and who think that they have put women in an environment where they are being brought up properly by the company, somewhere else in their consciousness have a dividing line and are shutting women out. There are many people like this. If you tell those people that they are drawing lines, and making separations between men and women they can't understand that because they are not conscious of that. To make a person who doesn't understand aware, you have to be higher in the company yourself. Otherwise it is not going to work.

E: There probably are guys who are dissatisfied that they have to work under a woman section chief. Well, I don't know if the dissatisfaction comes from the fact that I am a woman. I have the feeling that no-one really looks at me as a woman in the workplace at all! If anyone sees me as a woman, it is probably if something has come up such as me having taken a holiday because I had to go to a parent-teacher association meeting or that kind of thing. At that time they might think, well, she is actually a mother as well.

Most men admitted that there was general discrimination against women. If I asked directly if they were equal in the company, the answer would often be yes. If I delved deeper and asked if there were any cases where women found it difficult, the answer, again, was often yes, and the explanation couched in terms of the different characteristics of men and women. They would agree that women had a hard time in the company (taihen). No-one whom I talked to admitted that they themselves discriminated against women, but most agreed that discrimination existed. When they described concrete examples, they usually focused on the difficulties a woman might face in promotion. The women themselves, however, came up with more specific examples of everyday discrimination – in the way bosses talked to them, in the way they were included or treated. They reported that conversations might stop as they approached, or that they were not invited to some events, usually involving late-night drinking; the third round or so after an official function and the second round. This is quite apart from the unwritten rules, such as that men may smoke at their desks but women may not, and so on. Such rules are discussed at the end of this chapter.

E: If we were just talking about something lightly and someone would come out with, 'You are a woman so you don't understand,' I would hate that. I would just laugh and say, 'You are a man so you should treat me like that!' Well, I can't really remember specific cases, but lately sexual harassment is a big topic. The topic of sex came up just in conversation. Sometimes we were told well, you are a woman so you don't understand. But people say things like that less now.

But I had the feeling that many of the men were completely unaware of these small day-to-day episodes. It is notable, in the quotations which follow, how all the men seem to think of sexual discrimination only in terms of career opportunities.

H: Among Japanese women, there are almost no general workers. They all quit. It doesn't matter how much they try and change things like that if their mind hasn't changed [maindo] then you can't change. The management of C-Life were not able to let them in [ukeirenai].

Q: So why didn't the women's general worker category go well?

H: Because the C-Life management doesn't have the head to let them in [ukeireru atama ga nai]. They think that women are just women; that they are assistants. That concept is strong. But that is the same in all companies. Even in Mazda. They just took women on as managers for the first time so it is the same everywhere in Japan.

W: In America, it is normal for women to become managers, isn't it? In Japanese companies, even if they become managers for the first time Japanese companies are still anachronisms and that is the fact of it. But in so-called excellent Japanese companies or in companies that are called excellent the management knows what the story is, so in Recruit or Sony there are lots of women managers. That is to say that they have the kind of head that understands globalisation. They have knowledge as well. And that is reflected in the company's earnings, as a fact. They are really fluctuating times at the moment so now is a time of great transition.

H: There are hardly any women left in C-Life who graduated from four-year universities. It seems to me that management didn't know how to use those women. They were treated as women and not treated as company employees. When I mean treat them as women, they were just put in sections randomly [tekitō ni]. But there was a glass ceiling. So they couldn't become section chiefs. If you look at Mazda, an American president has come now and made many women management. He probably realised that they hadn't been used properly.

J: If you look at women as general workers, in the end all of them quit. So you can probably say as a policy itself it wasn't successful. It seemed that was the case in all Japanese companies. You hear that, despite the equal opportunity law, women as general workers did not stick in any Japanese company. Another reason for that might be because there were no bosses who really made use of the women general workers. I don't think there was any prejudice amongst my dōki towards the women that came into the company and trained with us. If you just looked at where we graduated from, the women came from better universities – from Hitotsubashi and other national universities. And in training there were some women who had fabulous sales results and also women who had a hard time. The top of our year was a woman. I think one of the problems was that their bosses didn't make very good use of them, even though they were hired as general workers. I don't think anyone was thinking of making them into section chiefs in the future, or into department heads. So the women became aware of that gradually after a while, and realised that even if they continued they weren't likely to become department heads or section chiefs. And I think also that the women wanted to marry and become wives.

> H: In C-Life they tried to put four-year university women in and they did so but they all quit. The management had no intention whatsoever of making them into directors in the future. Other companies had been hiring women and if they didn't follow the fashion it didn't look good so they just did it randomly [tekitō ni]. So they just thought that they would put it to a stop at a reasonable place [tekitō na tokoro de tomete okō to shita]. That was the same for the mid-career transferees. In my case, they made me a section chief but that is as far as I could have got. That was already pre-set [English] that kind of structure, that kind of composition.

To sum up the lengthy comments above, we find a number of factors. C-Life management had no intention of making the women managers, even though they were hired with that promise. The bosses did not 'make use' of the women. That is, employees thought that bosses did not demand challenging work of the women, or set them up in the right places to really achieve in the company. It took a while for the women to realise that that wall was there. When they did, they quit. These comments shed a lot of light on the male employees' underlying attitudes. They think that it is possible for women to be used 'properly', and that it is happening in other advanced companies. They do not think that they themselves are prejudiced against women being equal to men at work. However, somewhat paradoxically, they do not seem to recognise that marriage and work in C-Life could be compatible for a woman.

Women, then, do suffer discrimination at C-Life – not just in their career limitations, but in more subtle, everyday ways too. Another group, who can suffer even more dramatic discrimination, are people who join the company later in life, and I deal with them next.

Amakudari

In Chapter 3, I described the position of those who transfer to C-Life mid-career, and touched upon the difficulties they faced. Here, I examine in depth the fate of one man who, on the face of it, might have been expected to fare better than other transferees. This study will show how powerful some of the factors that we have examined in this and the last chapter can be in the company: groupism, loyalty, and fostering good human relations. In the next section, I apply what we see here to mid-career transferees.

The department head of the international department at the time that I entered the company came from the Bank of Tōkyō. He had worked in the bank until retirement age and then retired. However, he was then re-employed in the private sector, as our department head. This is quite common in Japan amongst employees from élite institutions (such as the Bank of Tōkyō, Ministry of Finance or the Ministry of Trade and Industry), and is known as 'amakudari' or 'descent from heaven'. This kind of arrangement allows élite employees on relatively low wages in the public sector, or working for the top private institutions, to retire early and boost their retirement income by working an additional ten years or so in the private sector.

Everyone involved stands to profit from this arrangement. The employing company gains connections and expertise that they might not have already had. In particular, the new employee is likely to have useful contacts at his former institution, thus providing the company with quick and easy access to the ministries and other institutions that they have to deal with in the course of their business. K, the department head in the international department, was hired from the Bank of Tōkyō, and had senior-level expertise in foreign markets and foreign investments, which was a new area for C-Life. In accordance with what we saw earlier in this chapter about the division of responsibility, the department head did not initiate a great deal of new work himself. Rather, he checked and supervised the work of more junior managers.

As a previous employee of such a prestigious institution as the Bank of Tōkyō, K was given a lot of respect on the surface, but as an outside employee he was never regarded as a 'true' C-Life man. We saw in Chapter 3 how mid-career transferees are often suspected of having problems with loyalty – which is a serious black mark against them. However, K suffered from these problems less than a mid-career transferee would have. The reasons for a retired transferee accepting a position at C-Life are clear and understandable to everyone. The retirement transferee has a valid status of their own: they don't create stress on the system by needing to be accepted not only formally, but informally and socially as members rather than outsiders. They are not expected to act as highly motivated members of C-Life, and would probably be going beyond their prescribed role if they initiated many new things without the prior support of their subordinates. People do not assume that they have changed company because of a lack of loyalty: they understand what the true reasons are.

However, amakudari people in the company have unique problems of their own. A study of what happened to K graphically illustrates some of these problems. I was surprised to discover on my return to the company in 1991 that K had stopped work rather suddenly and unexpectedly. When I asked why, the answer was, after some hesitation, 'Maybe he wasn't very happy at C-Life. After all, he brought his own culture with him.' When I was interviewing employees in 1999, K refused to talk about his experiences at C-Life, which he said he wanted to 'put behind him'. He seemed bitter and frustrated with what had happened there. Because amakudari depend on boosting their retirement income by moving to the private sector, to have left C-Life after only two years was not a good move for K and would have had serious financial repercussions for him. That he chose to leave indicates how unhappy he must have been in C-Life.

The comments of people around him provide an interesting case study of how outsiders fit – or are unable to fit – into C-Life. Although K's status as an amakudari was accepted, some people resented him anyway simply because he, an outsider, had taken the coveted position of international department head. This alone was sufficient to cause a feeling of 'us against him'.

> H: Looking from the view of the people inside, they didn't like the fact that someone had just suddenly appeared from outside and become the department head. So I

think there was quite a feeling of deliberately obstructing him. That's one of the really dirty parts of a Japanese company [iyarashii]. C-Life was a really domestic company so there were a lot of those kind of people in the company – those reject- ing or excluding kinds of people [haitateki]. In other words, they had a very strong group ideology and anyone from outside was regarded as an outsider.

Another problem was that K had, perhaps, not realistically anticipated what it would be like working at C-Life:

P: I don't think he had the feeling that he wanted to come to C-Life and try really hard, there are different forms of people coming into the company by amakudari and I think it was probably the case that he didn't expect to have to work hard.

However, the main reason K encountered problems was that his way of thinking was quite different from that of the people around him. This was partly because C-Life was quite a different environment from the Bank of Tōkyō.

Z: His style was different; the way he did his work was different. He was somebody who had come into C-Life after he had already become important [erai]. I don't think that he thought that everybody below him would just do his work for him, but there was something in that relation that was not clear. His culture was different from ours and communication was really difficult. It was extremely difficult.

P: Banks were far ahead of the medium-size insurer C-Life for international invest- ments and C-Life's internationalisation was behind the times anyway. So even though a department head came in from outside he was just a foreigner [gaijin] and he was the kind of person that hid behind pillars when the work had to be done [hashira no kage ni kakureyō ka to iu hitogara data]. He was Japanese, but it is true that he had the consciousness of a foreigner, that he was an outsider.

J: That was a difficult situation. If you look from the point of view of the person from the Bank of Tōkyō, he would only have thought of coming to C-Life as a variation of amukadari. I think that people in Tōkyō, in an élite institution like the Bank of Tōkyō especially, had an enormous amount of pride. It was a really global bank. And it was a bank that had more activities going on in other countries of the world than it did domestically. For someone from the Bank of Tōkyō to come to an ultra-domestic com- pany like a life insurance company, they would have thought it incredibly domestic. Well, the amukadari department head must have thought that it was a tiny com- pany but from the side that accepted him, the C-Life side, the fact that he had come from the outside was the root of the problem, that is why they could never pull him up and make him a director. So in that case it is not even possible to bring people in to C-Life from outside even at the level of senior management.

The novelty of the new department head's ideas created friction and a kind of automatic opposition to them. The opposition was apparent from several directions.

K couldn't gain the consensus of his fellow department heads, who were competing for resources to bring into their departments. As we have seen, these department heads were already organised into their own alliances, and K was unable to break into this circle of politics since he was by himself. The opposition he encountered from them and others was underhand and unclear: the department head was refused his budget because it was 'dangerous', and he was made to feel ostracised in a social sense, bypassed in the organisation. As a result, his unpopularity in the rest of the company actually impeded the work of his department:

> H: While K was in the international department, and though he was working inside there, he had no real individual relations with other people in the department because he was like an outlying island. From that position I think that he had a really hard time in the company. When he asked someone to give him a budget they wouldn't give it to him – even though he said he wanted to increase the international department budget they wouldn't give him a new budget. Or they wouldn't distribute the budget, saying that it was too risky. At the time there was a domestic loan department and an international loan department but the international loan department wouldn't co-operate with the domestic loan department. There were problems in the way funds were distributed across the whole organisation outside the international department. So, even if they weren't actively involved in tripping us up, there was no backup for our work. For example, even if we told jokes nobody would laugh, or they wouldn't greet us or say hello to us, or they would exclude K from one activity or another. Or they would bypass K and go directly to a C-Life employee at the level above him.

But the problems were apparent not simply in dealing with other departments, but within K's own department, too. He couldn't get the section chief under him to co-operate. The section chief said that it was not a matter of ability, it was a matter of the department head being too far ahead for the C-Life people to catch up with.

> Z: We couldn't get decisions made and we couldn't get things passed and that was the fact. I think that the department head himself had a really hard time. He was at the Bank of Tōkyō and he was leading the new era at that bank and the bank changed accordingly. But in a small company like C-Life, when somebody like that comes in, the gap is too big from the beginning. So putting somebody like that in an international section where there are only four or five people, it was a problem [ōzei ni musei]. At the time, for me as the section chief it was impossible [pei pei].

When the department head comes in from outside, he is hampered by his inability to use the informal communication network in order to convince others of his ideas. He has no dōki among the other department heads, a serious handicap. The others are polite to him but do not openly reveal their feelings. Within his department, he is unable to put his opinions through, causing conflict with his juniors below him.

X: I don't think it was a problem of vertical command. I think it was a problem of the department head clashing with the upper department heads. Among department heads the asset allocation occurs and there were problems with the section that determines that. When it had to be decided how that was going to happen we would make a plan as to how much money was going to be put in overseas investment and a plan as to what we would do over the year and at that time there were a lot of people who would bring out opposing opinions... But at that time the environment as a whole was leaning towards increased international investment so a lot of money did end up being distributed to the international department. But it wasn't because of his strength alone. It was because the whole environment was leaning that way anyway. In a different sense, there was a lot of polite behaviour [enryo] directed towards that department head because we had invited him in from outside. So there was a feeling that nothing could be said against him. From the department head's view, it was a company he had just come to for the first time so he couldn't put ideas through with main force [gōin ni]. Everyone in the international department would say that they wanted to do something but they were not able to do anything. That kind of thing was going on at the time.

The new department head simply didn't fit into the structure of the company, from an informal as well as a formal point of view.

Q: In a Japanese company with that kind of home atmosphere, did the atmosphere change when you suddenly put people in who were from outside?

Z: Well, I think it is a question of the particular people involved. As far as the reception on the company's side goes, we rationalised how we should do that in various ways on the part of the international department. The type of work that we were doing was really large so we always needed the approval from management at the level above the department head. Unfortunately, there was always a line of command that we had to follow. So, if you bring in a department head from outside – a person on that level – and just dump them in the department, it doesn't matter how much the section head is at the level of section head, he is put under water [suimenka ni sarete shimau]. If that happens, then the head has to leave the company and that is how it is resolved.

To get along well in this situation, a great deal of effort would need to be spent in cultivating human relations to appease the sense of suspicion and distrust among the C-Life employees towards an outsider. But it seems that K was not patient enough to do this, or perhaps didn't have the motivation to do it for the sake of a company for which he would work for only a short while.

H: I think it was hard because the department head came from outside – the section chief in the middle was from inside and the people below that again were from the outside (the mid-career investment specialist transferees). The department head – K – who had come from the Bank of Tōkyō would try and do things the same as he'd done them in the Bank of Tōkyō but wouldn't be able to do them so he'd say, 'Well, I'll just shut up then.' I think he was really irritated by the situation.

K was made to feel personally very unwelcome in the company. I particularly remember that whenever he attempted a joke, there was invariably a long, excruciatingly uncomfortable silence during which no-one laughed. As a new employee I was very conscious of this, but I couldn't be the only person to stand out and laugh, out of deference to my seniors and consciousness of my own position; the other juniors were in the same position. So a united front of silence greeted K each time he made a new attempt at pleasant conversation. Of course, he couldn't pinpoint where the resistance was coming from, or do anything about it.

The tiniest difference is enough to make someone stick out of the crowd and be picked on. In the final section of this chapter, we will see that the unspoken rules can be very subtle indeed, with different people aware of them to differing degrees. It is very easy for a newcomer like K to make a mistake, as illustrated in the following example.

> P: For example, if we went out drinking at an drinking party [enkai], we all used to do something called 'ipponjime' which is a kind of a closing ceremony for the party where you clap in a certain way three times, then three times more, then seven times. You always do it at the end but he couldn't do it. People in security companies and life insurance always do that. At the Tōkyō Securities Exchange they also do it. It goes chan, chan, chan, like that! But he did not have that culture and he couldn't do it. At the end it was K as our department head who had to close the ceremony, but when it came to the place for the ipponjime closing he wouldn't know what to do and he would look around nervously and do something lame. His timing was different from everybody else and he had the wrong intervals in the clapping. Things like that happened.

I suggested to my respondents that some of the members inside the company who disliked K had deliberately set him up in situations like this where he would come up against rules that he had not known existed and inevitably fail. This was how it seemed to me when I was at such functions myself, and other members of the company agreed that K had sometimes been set up. Others, however, (including those who might have been at the fore of the setting up) rationalised that the rules existed, and that it was his fault that he had not learned to do it, so it was not a deliberate attempt to foil him at all.

> P: K was the number two (in the finance department) so he had to do his part of the ipponjime ceremony. If K had not been asked to do it and the number three was asked instead, then that would have been audacious of the number three to step in and do it. So that isn't bullying; that was just how it was... It wasn't that the international department was deliberately making him do the ipponjime ceremony because they knew that he couldn't do it. But it was our ceremony and we always do it at the beginning and at the end of everything. In the beginning the master of ceremonies

does a greeting and somebody does a greeting next and does the kampai toast. When that person isn't there the kampai and the greeting are done together by the most senior person, number one. The next person – number two – does the ipponjime. The master of ceremonies is number three. It is usually determined in that way.

Some people did take pity on K:

P: Actually he slowly began to be able to do the ipponjime closing ceremony. I kept him company while he practised and he would ask, 'Is it OK like this?' and I would nod and say, 'Yes, yes, it has got a lot better!'

P, the employee quoted above, was considered a talented leadership candidate. More than anything, he had enormous skill in negotiating his way through the politics of C-Life. He had been head of his dōki for the dōkikai for nearly two decades. Where the other employees in C-Life maintained a stony (and gleeful) silence as the department head attempted to perform the ipponjime ceremony, P took him aside and delicately taught him the ceremony. But he did this surreptitiously, so the other surrounding C-Life people did not see him. In this way he was able to maintain good relations with everybody. As we might expect, P's comments on K's failure at C-Life are particularly acute.

P: As far as work went it might have been because it was him as an individual… because it was his individual fault… but he wasn't very good at making decisions. He was only able to look at things from a very objective manner. If it is your own work, when you come to make various decisions, you put a lot of effort into it and do it, don't you? But he couldn't do that very well. Even though he was right at the top of the Bank of Tōkyō and one of the most important people. The men at the top of the Bank of Tōkyō are more or less like ambassadors and they have ambassador-type qualities so that they attend functions and do things like that, but there were no things like that to do at C-Life and I wondered if that was why he didn't go well. And also I was very frustrated because his decision-making was not clear, and more than anything it was if his opinions were borrowed. It was as if he was a borrowed thing. So he smelt of a lack of loyalty.

We can draw a number of common themes from these comments. The employees generally agreed that K had been a disaster in his role. They put forward various reasons for this. K had come from a large institution into the domestic, insular C-Life and experienced culture shock. He was unable to move in the C-Life hierarchy as he was pushed out on a limb (or, as they put it, started to float) while the real decision-making went on around him. The only way to resolve such a situation is for the floating person to leave the company. It is impossible for one person alone to come in and change the company – even at the level of department head. The only way to avoid such situations would be to bring in a department head and his followers together as a group large enough to be able to implement the decisions they make despite the existing C-Life hierarchy.

Z: If a guy with real power comes in from outside, then what happens? Well, foreign capital companies often do that. But in the Japanese company, it doesn't work if it is a boss just by himself. I think it would be really difficult if the boss didn't... put his own ideas into action. And bring his own staff along with him... and do it large and suddenly [don to]. For example, in foreign capital companies, they have branches as well and if a boss comes by himself and they're all Japanese in the branches, then things don't go ahead very quickly either. You need to bring in the manager and his staff together in one fell swoop [don to]. And if you don't manage things like that, basically it doesn't go well in the case of C-Life as well as in the case of other companies I think it would be the same. Just a boss alone would be no good.

However, employees recognised that this would have to be a very large-scale invasion – and in terms of timing, a surprise attack – as the department head needs to have the power to negotiate resources for his department in competition with other department heads, who, as already noted, are already joined in various alliances. The fact that K 'floated' was a result of this inability to be accepted socially, yet the C-Life employees attribute his inability to be accepted to the fact that he floated, in a vicious circle from which there was no escape.

In the end, the factor that the C-Life employees could not forgive was that K was an outsider, who had come in above them. C-Life had only 'borrowed' him. He didn't belong there – he was an ornament. As we have seen, the C-Life employees suspect anyone in the organisation who doesn't belong there with the ultimate crime: a lack of loyalty. If they haven't been there from the start, it is reasoned, they cannot be 100 per cent committed to the company.

In the next section, I consider in detail what happened to those without K's advantages, who transferred mid-career. Surprisingly, they did not necessarily fare as badly as him, if they were good at cultivating human relations.

Transferees

We have already seen much of the mid-career transferees who were brought into the company to work at the international department. Here I look at how they got on with others at C-Life.

A former personnel manager says:

I: I was the person in charge of headhunting. We got people from foreign banks who were in charge of financial products and from securities companies we got people who were researching foreign investments. I scouted and employed about ten people altogether. Until that time we had never hired anybody from outside. So we had to be sure that the careers of those people that they had had outside of C-Life until then would be adequately evaluated and when they got into C-Life they would start off the same point as the people already in the company that were the same age as them. It was a new experiment so everybody was watching it with interest. And I was able to get everyone's co-operation as to trying to make the new policies work. They mostly were able to mix in with C-Life and work well.

In fact, almost every one of the transferees told me they had had a difficult time fitting in with the ultra-conservative C-Life. Anyone who was different from the 'norm' of a C-Life man suffered some degree of hardship, usually in proportion to how different they were. And it took remarkably little to be regarded as an outsider in C-Life. What small differences there were, were greatly exaggerated. For example, because I was told so many times how different the 'international' members of the company were, I was led to believe that their English ability must be phenomenal. It turned out, however, that none of the 'international' employees spoke the language fluently enough to be interviewed in it for the film. And their attitudes towards foreigners, as we saw earlier in this chapter, were often just as insular and stereotyped as everyone else's.

If the international employees displayed their internationalism in any way, they risked standing out from the crowd and greatly antagonising their colleagues.

> X: When W came out of the international department and came into our present domestic department – the one that sells life insurance to other corporations – he was forbidden from speaking English.

This particular case was mentioned to me several times by different employees involved in it. W was an unusual employee who had spent some time abroad as a student, and then as an employee of another company. He transferred into C-Life in his thirties to do investment-related work. He was a very unaffected, sincere type of person, who might have used English words without even thinking of the effect he could have on the people around him. When the international department ceased to exist, he resolved to stay in C-Life, at least initially – unlike his fellow transferees in the international division – and was transferred to a domestic department dealing in sales of life insurance to corporations. Although he wasn't sufficiently aware to realise that what was acceptable in the international department and what was acceptable in a domestic department would be sharply different, his friends around him were. One man in particular was especially sensitive at interpreting the behaviour of those around him and judging a safe path through the human relations minefield. This was P, who had helped K with the clapping ceremony.

> P: Even though international people have increased there are still very few in this company, so when those guys talk together with one another they would sprinkle English in. I had to take W aside and say, 'You have come to this domestic place now and even though you can speak English you must not use it here, because the people around you don't understand what you are saying. They know 'Yes' and 'No' but if you say anything more difficult than that they are not going to understand you. Then it may become for you as it was for K in the international department.'

Using foreign words, then, would have marked W out and caused him serious problems. This had been another of K's mistakes. Even P was exasperated by K's 'international' topics of conversation:

P: I think that that is the part where the dispositions of domestic people and inter-national people don't match. That was the case; that was a very large part of it. For example, K, when we were talking about whether the Giants or the Chūnichi had won the baseball, would say he was anti-Giants (the most popular team that we all supported). He would say it was more interesting to see the American league. He often talked about the big league (the American league) when we were out having lunch. He just talked and we just listened. All we knew about the big league was Babe Ruth. We didn't know about any of the other players so that sort of talk was very boring for us. It was really intolerable [kamben shite hoshikatta]. We really did-n't want to eat with him. He would talk about the big league and about where in America he had been on driving trips. We would think, 'So what?!'

Even talking about the wrong baseball team, or raising the wrong topic of conver-sation, then, can make a person stand out and become unpopular. The rules governing behaviour in the company can, clearly, be very stringent. Such rules are, of course, unspoken, unconscious rules. They are honne, not tataemae. Yet employees all have some degree of awareness of these rules. Not being conscious of such rules is a recipe for social disaster, as many of the transferees found out promptly. But it is clear that everyone is aware of the rules to differing degrees, varying from a naïve unawareness, like W, to a full awareness, and accompanying ability to navigate them to personal benefit, like P. Here again, then, we see not just the honne–tatemae distinction, but the importance of consciousness of that distinction and ability to manipulate the underlying rules. But this consciousness and ability, although very important, is not alone the be-all and end-all of success. Despite his ineptness with the hidden rules, W was likeable and popular with his colleagues, and as a result was protected by them, and did not fare nearly as badly as he might otherwise have done.

Earlier in this chapter, we saw that the female general employees, when they existed, were theoretically equal to men, but in reality they suffered discrimina-tion and found it much harder to move up the career ladder. The transferees found the same thing. They were promised equal status in C-Life when they were invited to join, and on the surface, I think that they were equal, or even at an advantage compared to others. Most of them were able to work at the overseas offices and to do exciting work in the company. Yet this masked a deeper reality. The tatemae was equality, but the reality was inequality. This is illustrated by the views of one former personnel manager, who had a notably positive view of how the mid-career transferees had settled in to C-Life.

I: There are tricks involved with fitting into C-Life. First of all you have to become a C-Life man. Because all the rest of the men are guys who have been in C-Life all of their lives. They needed to get used to C-Life customs as soon as possible. I think that was the most important thing. To become a C-Life man it is important to understand the C-Life work. So you need to be able to understand the life insur-ance business with the perception that it is your own business. I think the guys coming into C-Life knew that there would be a big gap between them and the guys who had all eaten rice cooked out of the same rice cooker. But I hired them after I had got them to understand that [yoku rikai shita ue de motte nyūsha shite itadaita no de]. So they co-operated in that sense and they made efforts to try and become a C-Life man. And I think they made efforts towards having the same group consciousness [nakama ishiki] in doing their work together with the C-Life guys. W made a lot of effort himself... the other people respected their specialities and looked after them. So there was a mutual getting used to.

But this bears little relation to the reality of what happened. This gap underlines the difference between the formal equality of the outsiders, and the underlying current of ostracism which they had to deal with in practice. The transferees would never be able to make it to the level of director in C-Life or to advance beyond the C-Life employees, and they gradually came to realise this.

J: There is still one transferee inside C-Life, who is extremely talented and has a really global viewpoint. People like that exist inside the company, so I think that the company should just leave all hesitation behind and make those kind of guys into management, but of course that isn't the 'proper' way to do things, because he hasn't been raised from the beginning in C-Life. I don't think they would ever make him a director.

The resistance was all on a social level. It was always there, unseen, and difficult to pinpoint. It was not from one particular person but was in the form of a united resistance. As K, the amakudari department head, found, anyone different encountered strong but subtle opposition, most commonly expressed in lack of co-operation for whatever work it was that they were doing.

H: The hardest thing about doing my work was that I couldn't get 100 per cent co-operation for what I wanted to do. On the contrary, people were involved in tripping each other up or making each other drag their feet.

In response to this, some transferees retreated into a shell inside the international department, as they gave up trying to socialise outside. They rationalised their rejection by seeing the other C-Life employees as domestic, backward and conservative.

H: The people who are superior are evidently the ones who make the money. It was like that ever since I got into the company – there was a lot of friction and discord with the people around me as a matter of course. I don't have any relations with those kind of people [tsukiawanai]. Well, because I was in the international department and that was the sphere of my work in that sense it didn't matter what happened outside – there were some good people inside [the other transferees] and I tried to get on with those people.

We have seen how the male employees discussed discrimination against women exclusively in terms of promotional ability. In a similar way, the managers from that time, when discussing what kind of time the transferees had had in the company, talked of equality only in terms of the transferees' formal position in the hierarchy. In support of their statements that the transferees did not encounter prejudice, they would mention the rate at which they had advanced and that they had been stationed overseas. When pressed, they would admit that it might have been difficult for them in the company, but always with an air of 'it can't be helped' or 'that is the way that it is'.

> C: The people from outside who came into C-Life weren't generally very successful. I really feel there is a lot of difficulty there. In the life-time employment system, almost all of the employees are brought up as 'proper' C-Life employees. So that 'proper' becomes a principle around which the organisation begins to work... If you look at the people who came into the company at the time from outside, if you compared them to the original C-Life people, they didn't have very strong loyalty. When the conditions were right they moved ship which might be an action that is at the vanguard of a new era but I can't help feeling that they didn't have the ability to stick with things and that there was a difference in their loyalty.

This last comment is very revealing. We have seen just how important the issue of loyalty can be, and how it can be connected to the importance of human relations.

> C: The main problem in thinking about transferees is that, if it was me, because I was in C-Life for a long time, I have a very strong affection for the company. So even if someone came along with an offer of better conditions and tried to pull me into another company I wouldn't go because I would want to stay and try to make my own company better. Well, people are all different. But at the very least the guys who shifted into C-Life can't have had a very strong love of the company.

The transferees were also disadvantaged in not having built up a system of contacts within the company.

> C: In foreign countries, if you have specialist knowledge it is advantageous, but in Japan success is often determined on human relations. So it wasn't always good for the people who came from outside. There was definitely no bullying, and no prejudice, and they were treated preferentially as specialists.

Part of the problem was that C-Life simply didn't have the kind of structure that could accommodate new ideas from new people. The company was not set up to recognise outsiders and to incorporate them smoothly into decision-making, because, as we saw in the last chapter when discussing tsukiai, informal personal relations and social occasions form an integral part of the decision-making process.

The C-Life employees generally felt that working hard at human relations was normal and expected. And they expected that transferees would work especially hard at it. Being accepted as a C-Life man is not at all regarded as a right, but as something earned by effort and reluctantly given.

> H: There was a lot of pressure in C-Life to fit into one mould and that pressure was strong – there were people who quit in just one month. One guy came from a bank. He came in as the person responsible for overseas loans but as soon as he arrived he was called in by the section chief and told that from that day on he would be a life insurance man and that he should go away and study life insurance. And with that, he became disillusioned with the company in one fell swoop and resolved to quit.

Thus, management originally intended to keep the new employees isolated from the others in the international department. But of course they did need to co-operate with other departments, and communication broke down when the outsiders had to work together with people from other sections. Because they were missing the crucial dōki links, they had only vertical connections inside the company and were severely at a disadvantage.

> C: I don't think that C-Life was prejudiced against the people who came from outside. Sometimes their promotions were faster than the guys like me that had been there all along. Like W who became the New York office head. I think that in some ways they had advantages. But in the end, how should I explain it... in Japanese society it is hard to judge the movements of a lone wolf. And so, I think that it was also difficult for those guys to do work inside C-Life because they had no horizontal connections.

The transferees did go and find their dōki, that is, the generation who would have been their dōki had they been there from the start, and they met with differing degrees of success. Some were rejected and gave up the effort, retreating into the international division. But others did better.

> Q: W has been really good at making human relations in C-Life.
>
> W: It is because I don't think deeply like he does [pointing at H]. You have to belong to one company or another. I have been doing this kind of work for a long time now. I went and looked for my dōki once I got into C-Life. Even though our work was different we belong to the same generation so our thinking should be the same, right? So I don't have any cause to dislike people.
>
> H: However, there is a problem with that. The other guys don't think like you do. Though there were guys among my dōki who were like you, you just have to realise that they were just those kind of guys.

This last extract is very revealing. Two transferees, W and H, criticise each other's approaches to fitting in socially in C-Life. W was rather hapless when it came to understanding the unwritten rules of the company, but he was likeable and popular with his colleagues. H, by contrast, was more aware of what was going on, but was not particularly able to fit in socially. Thus, despite his low level of consciousness and ability to 'play the game', W was relatively successful, whilst H eventually left C-Life and became very critical of it. Thus, again, we see the overriding importance of good human relations. Consciousness of the rules, and the ability to manipulate them, is a crucial factor in gaining status and becoming a 'leadership candidate' – but it is possible to get on well in the company even without them.

After discussing the discrimination frequently suffered by these groups within the company, I now turn to a more detailed examination of bullying itself. We have seen many examples of how bullying amongst employees works; in this section, I therefore focus on some of the techniques used by management itself to mould its employees into shape.

Bullying

'Bullying' in schools is a popular issue in the Japanese media today. I introduced the topic to one of the English classes held for members of the international section and found the class to be particularly uninspired by it. Eventually, one member suggested that if children were coddled while they were school age they would never survive as adults. 'Bullying in school,' he added, 'is nothing to what they'll come up against in the company.' This points to bullying being a natural consequence of groupism.

In this chapter, we have seen some concrete examples of some of the forms that bullying can take. The most common is social ostracism, in which the victim is excluded from the normal rules of social intercourse. We saw, for example, how K's jokes always met with complete silence. In some senses, however, ostracism in C-Life is a kind of initiation, or even a test. The outsider must discover the way to break through it in order to become accepted by those inside. When they are given purposefully unclear directions, they must work harder to overcome it.

> H: For example, for me joining half-way through into that group-ideology-strong company I found things like – nobody would teach me anything. That's a matter of company time so if they had put some effort into teaching me quickly it would have been better but they were deliberately mean to me [ijiwaru o shite] and wouldn't teach me anything. So they would just say, 'Here it is: do it!' I had to overcome that by progressively going out and getting information for myself. It wasn't such a big deal so I was able to do the work quite quickly anyway. It was really only in the beginning so it wasn't such a big deal.

Once the victim has succeeded in overcoming these hardships, he may, like the employee quoted above, be considered to have proved himself and become accepted by the group. And it seems that even this form of ostracism may be becoming rarer, as mid-career transfers become more common and accepted.

> X: I think that is the same in any kind of company but I think that is less true for companies that are going really well now, such as Sony, or Orix. Companies that are very active internationally wouldn't be able to work if they said those kind of

things so they do things according to ability. Whereas companies that are not going so well have a really strong group ideology so, regardless of ability, they do things the same as they've been doing till now – they go out drinking with their buddies and with their dōki from the school. And Japanese companies put a heavy emphasis on activities like that.

The bullying and ostracism that we have seen so far in this chapter is 'unofficial' bullying. But it was impossible to draw a clear line between this and techniques used by the company itself to prune its employees into acceptable shapes, and to weed out those who cannot be made to fit. We saw in Chapter 2 that the Japanese company is traditionally seen as characterised above all by harmony. But this is often produced by systematically excluding or breaking the spirits of those who do not fit in. When all potential sources of conflict are suppressed, this can result in a kind of harmony. But the techniques involved in producing this uniform body of people can be extreme.

Much of the initiation in companies is designed precisely with the aim of producing docile employees. Backs are often broken through humiliation. A totally unsuitable new employee, who does not respond satisfactorily to this treatment, can be 'encouraged' to leave. I met one Japanese man in Europe who told me that his company (a highly successful newer company) had given him three months' leave. As Japanese companies are not generally known to give three-month holidays, I was curious to know how this had happened. He was a young graduate from one of Japan's élite national universities who had entered this company the previous year. The man seemed to be rather eccentric, though: obviously bright but not able to fit in with the ultra-normal, conformist environment of a Japanese company. This must have been spotted very quickly and a certain chain of events unfolded. One day he would find all the contents of his desk in the rubbish bin; another day he would be missing a chair. Other days, the people sitting around him would mimic his every gesture as he sat at his desk. One can hardly imagine a more cruel way to force a misfit to leave his job. This was especially so given that there would be nothing official, no-one to blame, no reasons stated: just a vague and anonymous build-up of events ending in the man voluntarily leaving. This is the sort of thing – albeit more subtle – encountered by anyone who can't fit in. The following account is from H, the transferee who, unlike W, was unable to fit in socially with his new colleagues.

> H: The kind of bullying that happens is, for example, in work if you're told to do something and you don't know how to do it then no-one tells you how to do it. If you ask someone where to find certain documents for the work they say, 'Well, I don't know!' or just dump a file on your desk without telling you how to do it. The only thing you can do in a situation like that is to solve it yourself by using your own head. If there are people who say bad things about the company they also get bullied or they get harassed. For example they are not asked to the dōkikai, or if they go anyway they are bullied collectively by the rest of their colleagues or they're harassed about why they said things like that about the company. If they are out

drinking they are censured and they could also be demoted [sassen] or reduced in rank [kōkaku], and there are also cases where they are retained in their positions but not given any work. The worst kind of bullying is – well, in my case it was that they wouldn't teach me any of the work at all. I wasn't taught anything.

One day, K admonished us for not working hard enough. Things were different, he said, when he entered the company (shortly before one of the oil shocks). Companies that had hired their normal quota of employees for that year were in a sudden panic about what to do with them all. They increased the pressure on them in an attempt to weed out the weakest and least obedient. In one life insurance company, there were two suicides in the dormitory that year, out of 50 or so new employees. One employee from the same company 'voluntarily' quit. After travelling one and a half hours back to the dormitory after finishing work each night he would be ordered by his boss to be back in the company by midnight to redo the work that he hadn't done well enough in the day.

And it is relatively easy for the rigid structure of the organisation of C-Life to shift towards a more authoritarian stance, once the process has begun for whatever reason; it is as if it has lurched off the rails – it is extremely hard to change it back to normal again. This is exacerbated by the unclear lines of authority, of evaluation, and the inability of juniors to have a say quickly. On one occasion, for example, this intensification of initiation techniques resulted in a large mutiny in the dormitory several years after my dōki were there. Fourteen people quit the company all together, which eventually provoked radical changes in the training and a shortening of the time devoted to it.

E: There was one generation where about ten people altogether rebelled against the training and all quit together. It was the year below me and the last year of the training. There wasn't anything really special in that year. I just think that the training had gone too far. It was a year in which really extreme policies stood out. But the year before that and the year before that as well it was already becoming more and more extreme. There might have already been the desire or the consciousness to put a stop to that when the company decided to abandon the training in its former shape.

O: She is talking about one of the seniors – I won't say which one it is. A lot of the policies became very very strict. And that strictness was a strange strictness... a strictness reminiscent of school. In my time we weren't told anything about what we should wear. We were already society members [shakaijin] and as long as we stayed within the boundaries of suitable clothing for work we wore what we could within the limits of our salaries. And I don't recall ever having been told anything especially about what to wear. But gradually in the years after that they started being told this was good to wear, that was bad to wear. In my year there were five women and 35 men. We had just changed from being students into being members of society. Sometimes just to let off steam we would go together to a swimming pool on our days off... We weren't conscious of doing anything bad so we would just get into our swimwear and go swimming. But in the years after it got really strict so they started to forbid swimwear. So you could go to the pool and guys could swim but women weren't allowed to. In my year we weren't allowed to go the pool at all because our sales were too bad! We weren't allowed to take any vacations at all! It became a strange atmosphere like school. We were members of society but it was like being back at school. I went to a fairly free school and well, it depends on the senior at the time but I was raised fairly freely. I really don't know why it became so strict. And I think it is really strange that they started commenting on clothes. I don't know where the problem started or who caused the problem but they started censoring conversation between men and women as well. So that is one reason that a lot of people quit. Because of those kinds of really stupid things [tsumaranai tokoro].

These phenomena are not restricted to C-Life or even to the life insurance industry. Throughout my filming of C-Life, for example, the reaction of the NHK crew to the different topics we covered was very illuminating. When we began to discuss bullying, the NHK crew regarded it as something absolutely to be taken for granted. The conversation immediately turned to swapping stories of different episodes of bullying they had witnessed inside NHK. They told these with a certain amount of secret glee, as one would expect from survivors talking about those who had failed the grade. One case involved a new employee from Tōkyō University, Japan's most prestigious university. Although he had graduated from this élite institution, inside NHK he had to start at the bottom in disciple-like style in much the same manner as inside C-Life. He was assigned to the historical drama section where his first job was to prod a horse into moving at the correct time for its rider to enter the set. However, he was unable to do this as well as his boss demanded, and he was kept in this position for a full eight months. As a Tōkyō University graduate, he was probably completely unprepared for such mundane work, or to be bad at something so simple, or to be bullied like this. Eventually, he suffered a breakdown. He would come to work, climb up on his desk, and sit on top of it cross-legged and with folded arms, and glare at his boss. This went on day after day until eventually the employee left.

Although this example is relatively direct, most bullying in C-Life is very indirect. No-one knows if they are really being deliberately obstructed in their work or if they are simply facing normal obstacles; neither can they know clearly who is responsible for the obstructing. This creates a perpetual sense of anxiety and stress for those being targeted, as they can't confront anyone in particular, nor can they trust anyone around them as they can't be sure of what anyone's attitude really is.

Paradoxically, the bullying acts as a powerful disincentive to leaving the company:

H: If you know how a Japanese company works you know that if you go somewhere else, you are the one who is going to be bullied, and so if that is an unbearable prospect and you don't have that much courage, you can't move to another place.

Honne and tatemae

C-Life's main office building is situated on a very large, roughly square piece of land in the suburbs of Tōkyō, a little distance from the centre of the city. It is a surprisingly attractive building for a Japanese company, which are usually housed in nondescript modern concrete structures, and it is surrounded by an extensive, beautifully designed Japanese garden. The building is set out on three sides of the land, while the garden surrounding the front of the building takes up the majority of the remaining space. The front entrance and the garden are almost always deserted, and only visitors to C-Life use the official entrance. The official entrance is at the end of a curving driveway that runs through the gardens and deposits visitors at a massive glass-door entrance. On entering the building, visitors find themselves in a large high-ceilinged and marble-floored entrance hall decorated with paintings and statues.

The back entrance, by contrast, which everyone else uses, is squeezed between the back of the building and a narrow suburban street. The street turns into a small, concreted area containing the workmen's rooms, the rubbish removal containers and a back entrance for the C-Life employees. The employees arriving at the company each morning pour through this door in single file.

Conversations that I had with C-Life employees about the front garden, and the two entrances to the building, highlighted the existence of official rules and hidden norms in the company. Employees had different ideas about whether the garden could be used.

Q: About the problem of whether employees can use the official entrance to C-Life…

T: It's a matter of tacit understanding [anmoku no ryōkai]. If you did go there, you wouldn't necessarily get scolded.

Despite T's assurances here, further investigation suggested otherwise.

H: Even though it was raining, a certain guy had his umbrella mistakenly taken home by someone else. So he had to go home by taxi. He was a rich guy. And that incident became the source of lots of gossip. The taxi pulled up at the official entrance of C-Life to get him, and the president of C-Life had just arrived at the entrance in his Mercedes Benz. And after that the taxi came rolling in. The rich guy got severely scolded for doing that.

Employees recognised – but to different degrees – that this incident illustrated a double standard in the company. There was the official rule – the tatemae, or surface reality – and there was the unofficial rule – the honne, or underlying reality. There was no tatemae rule forbidding use of the official entrance. But there was certainly an unseen one.

H: It's the same situation in Y-Life. The employees can't use the official entrance, because it's a double structure in the company.

Q: But there is no clear rule about it?

H: It's a tacit understanding [anmoku no ryōkai]. That's the structure of Japan. There's a surface [shōmen], and there's an underside [ura]. It's a double structure. And that goes across the board for everything.

As this comment suggests, the concept of honne–tatemae is crucial in understanding Japanese behaviour.

E: Japanese like to hide things... I don't think that can be helped... If everyone is all in something together they are more secure.

It is all-pervasive in the company. In delving into topics covered in the interviews, the other side of the story would often come out. One of the most striking examples that we have examined in this chapter is the attitudes of the dōki towards each other. On the surface, they are very close, having 'all eaten out of the same rice pot', as everyone puts it; but, underneath, there is intense rivalry, and they do not, in practice, meet together nearly as often as they usually suggest they do.

S: Although the dōki seem to be quite close we might not be as close as we seem. A lot of us have a lone-wolf mentality – we're all very individual. We all hate being told to do this or do that by people; everyone has their own colour, everyone wants to protect their own castle.

S: There's also dōki of mine in my company housing complex but I don't really talk a lot to them.

Through honne–tatemae, Japanese seem to hold two conflicting realities at once without feeling any discrepancy between the two; the two realities belong to different spheres. So, for example, harmony in the office is often the tatemae while perpetual conflict just below the surface may be the reality.

Rohlen found that bank leaders can express a determination to develop more individuals in the bank yet criticise any actual independent action. He concludes: 'Context makes a big difference for such expression, and it is best to understand management as inherently ambivalent on such issues' (1974: 69). It was not exactly a case of ambivalence, though. It was just that it was accepted that opinions might be different in different contexts. Honne–tatemae, then, acts in one way as a dissonance-reducing mechanism, and as an alternative to a conflict-resolving mechanism, allowing employees to have a publicly conformist opinion while holding their own equally valid beliefs.

How do employees themselves think of honne–tatemae? I found plenty of opinions on the matter. C-Life employees were generally open and interested to talk about honne–tatemae in the company as a normal part of life. This is behind most gossip, and the act of collectively working out what is real and what is face is almost a company-wide pastime; certainly for those heavily involved in office politics – which includes almost everyone. They were always appreciative when they saw I understood the tatemae of a situation, and found it interesting to hear what I thought was the real issue behind situations they had been pondering.

First, a negative side to the distinction is recognised. For example, employees accept that in many cases the company ideology is more form than substance.

> P: There is a management ideology that says that knowing company customs and culture comes in useful. So that at least you should know those things by heart. Well, it's a useless kind of idea. I don't know all the customs by heart! But in form [katachi to shite] I think there is a big proposition that if you've been in the company for a long time then you should know all kinds of things like that. I think that is the case.

And in many cases, talk of tatemae is very negative, such as when criticising someone for having a false opinion.

> H: In Japan there is a double structure: words and practice are different. When we [the mid-career transferees] went into the company we were told that we wouldn't be discriminated against but in actuality we were discriminated against; in promotion and those kind of things. Stupid guys would get to be section chiefs ahead of us. I was the last to be promoted. On the surface, it might have been such and such, but in reality it wasn't the case, so it was double-tongued. It's a shrewd kind of arrangement.

> H: The fact that the Japanese are often said to be untrustworthy stems from the fact that there is a surface and an underside and a double structure.

Mostly, however, honne–tatemae is seen as a natural and inevitable part of company life.

> E: Japanese are used to honne–tatemae all their lives... probably since they go to school anyway. But then again... even in the house there is some degree of tatemae as well. I think they learn it mainly at school. I guess it works to eliminate [haijo] individuality. It is difficult to accept individuality in Japan. There is one category and within that there is a certain amount of freedom but if you stick out beyond that box...

Indeed, employees regard being able to use honne and tatemae well as a skill. The employee below spoke with some pride of learning to 'hold back a bit', as a talent learned in the process of becoming a company employee.

> E: I'm bad at using tatemae and honne. I always mess it up. I always get told 'Think before you speak!' By both sempai and dōki... They say, 'You can't go around saying things like that!' I've learned to hold back a bit.

> E: Well, there are people who can get away with saying what they want [hone]. There are also those who, well, it's not exactly flattery, but those who jump left

when their boss says left and right when he says right, people who do the right thing when the situation calls for it. Some people go a really long way just on tatemae, they are just really good at it, their bosses like them. Everyone says, I wonder why that guy got so far. Maybe 80 per cent of the people who become directors are those who everyone understands why they did, but 20 per cent of them, people look at them and say I wonder how he did it. They say well, he managed to pull it off [umaku yatta na].

E: People who go well inside the company are people who can use them both well, who know thoroughly when to use which at what time.

The skill is a very important one to acquire. We have seen, throughout these field-work chapters, the lack of clarity which characterises many processes in C-Life, such as evaluation or planning. Employees accordingly described C-Life as a murky world where everyone was feeling their way along. Indeed, during the NHK filming, the NHK staff found it hugely amusing to see me struggling to translate a string of words peculiar to this opaque world. The vocabulary of opaqueness – none of which I can translate terribly well – included such words as moya moya (unclear), zuru zuru (to drag on), nanto naku (somehow). When to use tatemae and when to use honne was an important tool in feeling one's way in the murky politics of C-Life.

E: There are times when I don't say things that I think because I don't want to cause waves in the workplace. Well, it might be strange to call them waves. I want to do my own work without discomfort and I think that other people do as well. There are times when I say what I really feel. It depends how other people take that...you would have to ask them.

C: Characteristics of C-Life? There is ura/omote, back and front sides to issues, the formal face and the reality behind the face. There is an intensity of emotion [jō ni atsui] and a disinterest in personal gain [ri ni satoi].

As we have seen throughout this chapter, it is sometimes possible for someone to transgress the hidden rules without realising it.

H: People who used the official entrance without realising what they had done got talked about behind the scenes [kage de]. That's the really dirty part about Japan; that people talk behind the scenes, not openly on the surface. The person concerned is the only one, in the end, who doesn't know that everyone's talking about them.

In this comment, a further element of honne–tatemae becomes clear. Those who transgress the hidden rules are not told about it. It is for them to find out what the hidden rules are. Those who do not know the hidden rules 'float'. But those who transgress them and are ostracised do not necessarily know why they are being ostracised or how to remedy the situation. In fact, they might not realise that they are being ostracised at all.

Conclusion

This chapter has built on the themes raised in the earlier fieldwork chapters to examine in depth the atmosphere of the company, focusing on human relations and the different kinds of relationships found in the company. Throughout it, I have concentrated on issues of honne–tatemae. In Chapter 7 I explore these issues further and present my conclusions.

7 Ideology, groupism and individualism

In this chapter, I consider the issue of the individual and the group in Japan, on the basis of what we have seen at C-Life in the body of this book.

Individualism and individuality

What do we mean by individualism and individuality? Individualism is a particular concept of the self, which sees it as in some sense autonomous and not bound by external constraints. Those who emphasise this point have generally associated with it ideas of morality, privacy, and rationality. Individuality, on the other hand, is a universal quality, part of human nature. It represents the fact that the individual has agency. It may be said, moreover, that the mere fact that any two people are not exactly alike, and do not share the same body or spatio-temporal location, means that their experiences cannot fail to be different. They have different perspectives on the world. Thus, individuality is a universal condition, whilst individualism is a concept, one which is most typical of Western societies. As I have noted already, 'the West' and 'Western' can be problematic concepts (they are often ill-defined or ambiguous) but I follow the authors cited in using them here. Failure to separate individuality from individualism has greatly confused the debate under discussion here. Obviously, the fact that a society rejects the notion of individualism does not mean that its members lack individuality. But some writers seem to make an implicit assumption otherwise. This has great relevance for this book as I discuss a similar confusion in the Japan literature between 'groupism' as an ideology and a lack of individuality.

Individualism in Japan

Before discussing the concept of individualism in Japan, we need to take a moment to notice how the concepts of individualism (a specific concept about how the individual should be) and individuality (the existence of an inviolable individual self) have been confused in the literature. Indeed, some anthropologists argue that the notion of individualism itself is a concept special to 'Western culture'. In this view, to prioritise the individual over society is to attempt to analyse other cultures in terms of 'Western constructs'. Dumont (1986) suggests that the

West's emphasis on the individual is a result of the influence of Christianity. Similar points are raised by Asad (1983). Indeed, individualism, according to Durkheim, is a product of society like religion or morality. Similarly Mauss (1985), writing of individualism as a cultural idea about selfhood, also assumed that individualism is a social construct of Western society. These writers thus explain individualism by reference to social phenomena. Some also conclude that *individuality* is a construct of Western society. This is reflected in the Japan literature, as we will see below, by some writers who seem to argue that the self doesn't exist in Japan at all.

To be an individual in C-Life was firmly connected, in the dominant ideology, with the idea of becoming a member of society (shakaijin). In this context, to become truly adult, to become a person in one's own right, was associated with adopting a role inside the social group, and growing as a human within the context of that role. Like Dumont in India, I found that any individual inside C-Life who had a Western idea of individualism was sharply at odds with the Japanese ideology in C-Life. However, the C-Life employees were influenced in their ideas of individuality by the ideologies in Japan concerning the individual. But each of them had their own core values as individuals, and retained the possibility of accepting or rejecting the current ideology about how an individual should be.

Individualism, as a particular concept, may indeed be more common to the West than to Japan. However, individuality, as a real phenomenon, is clearly not. The points I have made above, together with those illustrated throughout the fieldwork chapters, indicate the reality of individuality in Japan. Moreover, the concept of individualism is not alien to Japanese thinking. No society is fixed in its traits, and even in the West Christianity itself only evolved into the thinking that the individual transcends society hundreds of years after Christ.

The fact that the C-Life employees accepted the ideology that the individual should grow by conforming to the group and growing within its precincts is important. As I have already pointed out, individualism is concerned with particular historico-cultural concepts of the self. One description of individualism includes such concepts as moral and intellectual autonomy, rationality, self-knowledge, spirituality, right to privacy, self-sovereignty, self-development, voluntariness of participation in society, market and polity (Lukes 1973). Japanese concepts of how humans should ideally be include quite different ideas. Individualism, as I have stressed above, cannot be confused with having an individual self; the Japanese are clearly individual with the universal quality of agency, interacting with others from their own individually distinct perspectives on the world. Bearing this point in mind, we may ask what the Japanese concept of the individual is.

In my view, individualism, as Durkheim maintained, is a product of society like religion or morality. In C-Life the employees' idea and consciousness of themselves as individuals was evident. But the ideology of what an individual should be and how one attains the status of an individual is sharply different from that of many Western countries. Indeed, in Japan, 'Western-style' individualism can be equated with selfishness and lack of appropriate respect for the group. As De Vos (1984: 15) says:

In Japan the 'individual' will is defined as part of selfish immaturity. The true individual finds his maturity in willing to be at one with social purposes of a family group. A woman loses herself in her family roles; the man's occupation takes him out of his family but he also finds familial-like social bonds and a sense of loyalty and dedication directed toward his occupational group.

De Vos argues that, whereas in the West people begin to create their own identity or are expected to do so in their teenage years, development of this kind of individuality comes much later in Japan – if it comes at all. Company recruits are still expected to be relatively passive and lacking in personality. In this view, one's role in the group, rather than an individual personality, is more emphasised. Roles are clear and pre-scribed: one only needs to conform to the role and act as one is expected to. This is confusing expression of individuality with having an individual will.

The Japanese attitude, just like the Western attitude, may be seen as a positive or negative element of the culture, depending on one's own cultural viewpoint. Smith (1983: 134) says:

It must ... seem to us that in their concern to maintain social order, the Japanese have too thoroughly discouraged the open expression of individual-ity, in which we are likely to see the ultimate strength of any social system. The Japanese, with equal certainty, are likely to feel that the Americans have so inflated the importance of the private self that we run the risk of dissolving the bonds that must exist in order to hold any human society together.

What is more, the ideology of what an individual should be, and what their rela-tions with other people and with company and society should be like, was in continual transition, even in the short period during which I observed the com-pany. The idea of what an individual is and should be, and how an individual should relate to the company and to society, changed considerably, moving away from a traditional model that recommended submerging one's individuality in the social sphere. In some ways – but only some – it changed toward what we might term 'Western' ideas: of finding work that matched one's 'individuality', for example, while in other ways it remained distinctly foreign to Western concepts. For example, I found a clear conservatism of new university graduates and a wish to be 'life-time employed', sharply counter to common assumptions. Examples such as these warn us not to take recent trends in Japan as a one-way clear-cut transition towards Western culture.

In sum, I think that in C-Life we can see that individuals had a firm sense of their individual selves. These ideas were influenced, but not wholly determined, by dominant ideas of how the individual should be in Japan.

The individual in the Japan literature

What has been said about the individual in the Japan literature? Much has been made of Japanese groupism, which, according to the nihonjinron literature, was one of the traits in which Japanese were said to differ from the 'West'. The Western identity of the Western self lies in the autonomous self. Again, Lebra (1976) claims that the individual in Japan is simply a fraction of the whole, not a self-sufficient individual.

William Caudill notes that Japanese mothers generally believe that children are born asocial and must be socialised. American mothers, by contrast, believe that dependent children must learn independence as they mature. Rohlen stresses the standardisation of shudan seikatsu. In every stage of life the same emphasis on social lessons is repeated.

I argue in this book that, just as some anthropology on Western countries has confused individualism with individuality, the literature on Japan has confused the ideology of 'groupism' with an actual lack of an individual self.

There are a number of authors who have written on self and other, honne–tatemae, soto–uchi (see p. 9) including Bachnik and Quinn (1994), Doi (1973, 1985), Kondo 1990, Bachnik 1992, and the contributors to Rosenberger (1992). These have largely talked of the Japanese self as embedded in society, even those who are looking at alienation in Japan. Smith (1983) sees the Japanese as having no fixed centre from which the individual has a non-contingent existence. All is relational: the self is created in relations. Japanese gain from associating themselves with roles, situating themselves to others. The successful Japanese has mastered his anti-social instincts (although Smith adds that they pay a price, with an underlying psychological malaise from stress due to conformity). Plath (1983) sees the relational side of the Japanese as being people-related. The mind is occupied by a life-long struggle to carry out one's responsibilities to others.

Doi (1973) suggests that mutual dependence in relationships removes individuals' need to find independent identity. Freedom is achieved by maintaining harmonious relations with others. Thus, the self being acculturated (influenced by the prevailing ideology) to be conscious of self in relation to others. This is very important for a discussion of ideology and practice in Japan, as the ability to separate ideology from practice or front-side from back-side is an important criterion in the attainment of social maturity or 'individuality' (hitorimae – a person in one's own right).

Some of these writers emphasise the importance of a good knowledge or consciousness about how to use honne and tatemae properly in Japan. That is, an ability to regard the self and other in a culturally appropriate manner is essential. Tobin (1992: 24), for example, says:

> To have a proper, two-tiered Japanese sense of self one must learn to make… fluid and subtle distinctions, learn to step back and forth across the gap dividing omote from ura in the course of a single conversation, or indeed, even in the midst of a single phrase, as a slight wink of an eye or a change in the level of politeness of a verb ending suddenly signals a slight but crucial warming up or cooling down of relations.

Learning this skill is, indeed, crucial to success. Japanese regard the inability to distinguish between honne and tatemae as extremely naïve and immature. This is a key reason why Westerners, who are stereotypically unable to distinguish between honne–tatemae, often seem simple and childish to the Japanese, and black and white, or transparent, in their motives. A consideration of the stereotypes of Westerners in the popular imagination and on television confirms this.

As we saw in Chapter 6, it is through the acceptance of a role, in finding a place in society, that an individual is thought to develop. Schools stress that children become co-operative and social. As a teenager in Japanese schools, I learned at an early stage that I had to suppress my real thoughts and learn to play a role, and that the better I played the role the more I was rewarded.

The key constructs soto–uchi, honne–tatemae, and omote–ura are therefore concerned with the distance that separates one from others. There are several facets to this. For one thing, using honne–tatemae, and playing an appropriate role, is a learnt skill. Tobin *et al.* (1989) look at how preschool children lack the skills of differentiating formal and informal. So to distinguish between honne and tatemae is a taught social value – a socio-cultural construct of Japanese society and ideology.

Moreover, roles vary. There is a multiple self that is different with each relationship. Even Benedict (1946) saw Japanese as having a number of different circles – obligation, or human feeling – within which their actions are determined. Different contexts may involve different circles. Lebra (1976), similarly, suggests that contradictions in behaviour are caused by shifts in context; this is social situationalism. He sees Japanese as careful and observant social actors. Taking situation and context into consideration sheds light on the plural quality of human life. It explains how we have different perspectives at different times and situations. Lebra emphasises that the multiple self also contains an 'inner self' that is a focus of self-identity. Thus, he treats self and society as an interactive process. Self is the centre of a nexus of shifting relationships. This is in sharp contrast to the West, where we typically assume opposition of self and society. Ohnuki-Tierney 1987 argues that the Japanese are fundamentally reflexive. I suggest that the same may be said of all societies. In all societies, we learn a difference between self and society, and learn to understand the particular rules for expressing tatemae. This – the variation in rules between societies – is where the cultural differences lie, not in the fact that honne and tatemae are learned at all.

So it is wrong to suppose, as some commentators have done, that there is no such thing as individuality in Japan. As I have stressed in this chapter, we have to be careful not to confuse having a self at all with how the self is culturally defined. Japanese socio-cultural constructs emphasise the relational nature of the self. This is a heavy part of the school education and home education too. But it does not mean that there is no self at all. In fact, my fieldwork shows that, regardless of Japanese constructs that emphasise the self's embeddedness in relations with others, there clearly is an individual self. Moreover, the degree to which people conform to the ideology of the embedded self differs according to the individual. Thus, one retired man from my fieldwork was still in close and constant relation to the company, where they still called him by the last title he had had in the company, while another had no relation whatsoever with the company, disliking groupism, and didn't ever tell new acquaintances where he had worked.

Plath (1992) begins to question whether the Japanese are proceeding to a view of themselves as individualistic, because of the consumption-oriented society. This view is based on an association of the Western notion of the self with self-interest, an association shared by Dumont (1986). This is particularly interesting in our discussion of C-Life. My feeling is that individualism and self-interest are not necessarily associated. Rather, capitalism by definition invites a certain type of self-interest. The individualism of the West is something that was in place long before the capitalist market system as we now know it (Macfarlane 1994). I do not think that C-Life employees became any more self-interested as the economy began to change. Rather, my fieldwork presented in this book suggests that they were all self-interested, and following individual strategies for individual gain, even against the greater good of their colleagues or of C-Life. But the possibility of whether or not they were able to follow their strategies towards self-interest within a group model changed as a result of the economy. As the system of life-time employment began to crumble, and the ability to change companies in search of a better job became more available, it was no longer the case that employees would necessarily maximise their own self-interest through the ideology of loyalty to the company. This being the case, they were forced to reconsider their options, and as a result many changed route from being company-oriented to career-oriented.

Honne, tatemae and the individual

With these points in place, we can move to a more detailed analysis of how honne and tatemae work. This issue has great relevance for whether we see the individual in Japan as immersed in the group or not. My stance is that all people, Japanese or Western, have what Goffman terms 'front regions' and 'back regions', or honne and tatemae as we can translate it in this case. There is thus a conceptual line between the two 'regions'.

The point I wish to stress here is twofold. First, this line is not fixed. Second, it varies according to the situation: thus, the same individual may draw it at different points when talking to different people, or even at different times when talking to the same person. The following table indicates some of the different levels at which the line may be drawn. At each of these levels, there may be an ideal to strive for, or to present to those outside the group. But underlying that is the practice, which may be different.

I suggest that the line that is drawn between 'front' and 'back' regions, between soto and uchi, honne and tatemae, and shifts between these different levels, reflecting the level of the group with which the individual associates himself. Any two people will, at some level, be members of the same group, and, at lower levels, members of different groups. Inasmuch as they share a group, they may discuss it in terms of what the members of the group actually believe about it, or their personal meaning (honne); inasmuch as they are members of different groups, they may present the ideal picture of their own group (tatemae). Two people from different nations share only the most general groups (for example, the group of humanity); two people from the same family share very small groups (from the group of humanity, through the group of that nation, down to the group of people from the same town and from the same family). Consider again the chart: the more groups two people share, the more they are likely to share honne and the lower the line between honne and tatemae will be.

To illustrate what I mean, consider the following hypothetical example. Think of a Japanese C-Life employee discussing Japan with a foreigner who has just arrived in the country. The C-Life employee may put the 'inside' at the level of the Japanese nation, and consider everyone else 'outside' this group. He is aware that there is an ideal image of Japan, which differs from his individual meaning, what he believes to be the actual case. Since he is talking to someone who falls outside the group in question, he presents the ideal picture to them, aware that it is not reality. It is tatemae, not honne.

If, however, the same employee is speaking to an employee from another Japanese company, the situation will be quite different. As far as Japan is concerned, they are both members of the same group, and discuss Japan in terms of honne, their individual interpretations of the situation. But the conversation then turns to C-Life and its impending bankruptcy. In this context, the two are no longer members of the same group. The C-Life man is now talking 'as' a member of C-Life, to someone from outside that group. He may now have an agenda: he may wish to present a good image of his company to those outside it. He will therefore describe the company in terms of the ideal, although he is aware, again, that this does not match his individual meaning. The line between honne and tatemae is therefore set at the level of the company, which is the highest level at which the two individuals are separated. Everything higher than this level is discussed as honne, everything below as tatemae.

We can keep extending the situation to ever-smaller groups. The employee may talk with a fellow C-Life employee. Now the line is lower, and they discuss C-Life in terms of honne. But if the conversation turns to their families, it may be that the employee wishes to present an ideal view of his family: his fellow employee is, at this level, outside the group. He therefore presents a honne view of everything higher than his family, but only a tatemae view of his family. And so on, down the table.

I argue – tentatively, as my fieldwork extends only to Japan and not to any Western nation – that the line drawn between honne and tatemae also shifts in the West. But it shifts less often and less clearly than in Japan. The line is most frequently set between the individual and everyone else, or perhaps between a married couple and everyone else. Because the concept of group is stressed very much less than in Japan, there is much less likelihood of a Westerner drawing the honne–tatemae line between, say, England and the 'foreign', although of course this does sometimes happen. The honne–tatemae line may be drawn in

Honne	Nation
Where the line is drawn varies according to context.	
	Group
Shifting line -----------------------------	Family
	Marriage partners
Tatemae	Individual

Figure 7.1 The shifting nature of honne and tatemae

other cases too, of course, such as between those who went to public school and those who didn't. And there may be marks to denote those who know what the line is.

Westerners frequently have enormous trouble in dealing with the concept of honne and tatemae. They wonder why the Japanese say different things at different times. Why do they say things that are clearly untrue? How do they hold two beliefs that are clearly inconsistent? Is it a conspiracy to confuse the Westerner? If we accept that the honne–tatemae line is situational according to the varying divide between inside and outside, then we can see how it is possible to answer all of the above. Incidentally, we can see the terrible difficulty with obtaining information if one is not an 'insider', thus meriting a tatemae opinion and not honne.

If we look once again at a hypothetical example, for many Japanese who are sent abroad, to say 'my country' may be prestigious and a sign that one is still on the ladder in the company hierarchy. But say that it is not a prestigious destination but a clear sign that one has been shunted aside and is losing one's rung on the ladder. Although my informants may have been open to me on other topics, if going to my country was seen as a step downwards would they have talked in derogatory terms of my country to me? I imagine that the honne–tatemae line – not on every topic but on that particular topic – would be drawn between Japan and my country. The employees might talk of their resentment at being sent to a god-forsaken place among themselves but not in front of me. So tatemae is a situational stance that is dependent on where the line between inside and outside is drawn.

Postscript

C-Life went under a few months after my fieldwork ended, in what was, at the time, the largest bankruptcy in Japan since the war – until 11 days later, when Kyōei Life followed suit. Although the possibility of C-Life's impending doom was certainly high in the minds of my respondents during my final phase of fieldwork, I have not discussed the period of the bankruptcy itself in this book, as it had not yet become actuality. My focus here has been on the inner workings of the Japanese company and employees' perceptions, so although the company ceased to exist not long after my final period of fieldwork, I have generally spoken of it in the present tense in these chapters.

References

Abegglen, J. (1958) *The Japanese Factory* Glenco: Free Press

Alletzhauser, A. (1990) *The House of Nomura* London: Bloomsbury Publishing

Allison, A. (1994) *Nightwork: Sexuality, Pleasure, and Corporate Masculinity in a Tokyo Hostess Club* Chicago: University of Chicago Press

Alvesson, M. (1993) *Cultural Perspectives on Organizations* Cambridge: Cambridge University Press

Asad, T. (1983) 'Anthropological conception of religion: reflections on Geertz' in *Man* 18, 2

Austin, L. ed. (1976) *Japan: The Paradox of Progress* New Haven; London: Yale University Press

Azumi and McMillan (1976) in L. Austin ed. *Japan: The Paradox of Progress* New Haven; London: Yale University Press

Bachnik, J. (1992) 'Two "faces" of self and society in Japan' in *Ethos* 20, 1

Bachnik, J. and Quinn, C. eds (1994) *Situated Meaning: Inside and Outside in Japanese Self, Society, and Language* Princeton: Princeton University Press

Beck J.C. and Beck, M. (1994) *The Change of a Lifetime: Employment Patterns among Japan's Management Élite* Honolulu: University of Hawaii Press

Ben-Ari, E., Moeran, B., and Valentine, J., eds (1990) *Unwrapping Japan: Society and Culture in Anthropological Perspective* Manchester: Manchester University Press

Benedict, R. (1946) *The Chrysanthemum and the Sword: Patterns of Japanese Culture* Cleveland and New York: Meridian Books

Brinton, M. (1989) 'Gender stratification in contemporary Japan' in *American Sociological Review* 54

Brinton, M. (1993) *Women and the Economic Miracle: Gender and Work in Postwar Japan* Berkeley: University of California Press

Carrithers, M., Collins, S. and Lukes, S. eds (1985) *The Category of the Person* Cambridge: Cambridge University Press

Chalmers, N. (1989) *Industrial Relations in Japan: The Peripheral Workforce* London: Routledge

Christopher, R. (1983) *The Japanese Mind: The Goliath Explained* New York: Linden Press

Clammer, J. (1997) *Contemporary Urban Japan: A Sociology of Consumption* Oxford: Blackwell Publishers

Clark, G. (1979) *The Japanese Company* Cambridge MA: Yale University Press

Cohen, A. (1985) *The Symbolic Construction of Community* London: Routledge

Cole, R. (1971) *Japanese Blue Collar: The Changing Tradition* Berkeley: University of California Press

Creighton, M. (1992) '"The Departo": merchandising the west while selling Japaneseness' in Tobin (1992)

Curtis, G. (1969) *Election Campaigning, Japanese Style* New York: Columbia University Press

Dale, P. (1986) *The Myth of Japanese Uniqueness* London; Sydney: Croom Helm

De Vos, G. (1984) *The Incredibility of Western Prophets* Amsterdam: University of Amsterdam

Doi, T. (1973) *The Anatomy of Dependence* Tokyo: Kodansha International

Doi, T. (1985) *The Anatomy of Self* Tokyo: Kodansha International

Dore, R. (1973) *British Factory, Japanese Factory* Berkeley: University of California Press

Dumont, L. (1986) *Essays on Individualism* Chicago: University of Chicago Press

Eisenstadt, S. N. (1990) *Japanese Models of Conflict Resolution* London: Kegan Paul International

Embree, John (1939) *Suye Mura: A Japanese Village* Chicago: University of Chicago Press

Emmott, Bill (1989) *The Sun also Sets: Why Japan will not be Number One* London: Simon and Schuster

Fodella, G. ed. (1975) *Social Structures and Economic Dynamics in Japan up to 1980* Milan: University of Bocconi

Fukutake, Tadashi (1981) *Japanese Society Today* Tokyo: University of Tokyo Press

Fuse, T. ed. (1975) *Modernization and Stress in Japan* London and New York: EJ Brill

Gibney, Frank, (1998) *Unlocking the Bureaucrat's Kingdom: Deregulation and the Japanese Economy* Brookings Institution Press

Graham, F. (1992) University of Oxford, M Phil thesis

Hendry, J. and Webber, J. eds (1998) *Interpreting Japanese Society: Anthropological Approaches* 2nd ed. London: Routledge

Hunter, Janet (1993) *Japanese Women Working* London: Routledge

Iga, M. (1986) *The Thorn in the Chrysanthemum* Berkeley; London: University of California Press

Imae, M. (1981) *Sixteen Ways to Avoid Saying No* Tokyo: Nihon Keizai Shimbun

Inoue, S. (1997) 'Changing employment in Japan' in *Japan Forum* 9 (2)

Ishida, Hiroshi (1993) *Social Mobility in Contemporary Japan: Educational Credentials, Class and the Labour Market in a Cross-National Perspective* London: MacMillan

Ishihara, S. (1991) *The Japan That Can Say No* New York: Simon and Schuster

Iwao, Sumiko, (1993) *The Japanese Woman: Traditional Image and Changing Reality* New York; Toronto; Oxford: Free Press; Maxwell Macmillan Canada; Maxwell Macmillan International

Kahn, J. (1995) *Culture, Multiculture, Postculture* London: Sage

Kamata, T. (1982) *Japan in the Passing Lane: An Insider's Account of Life in a Japanese Auto Factory* New York: Pantheon Books

Kaneko, S. (1997) 'Diversification of employment types and changes in the employment system' in *Japan Forum* 9 (2)

Kelly, William W., (1991) 'Directions in the anthropology of contemporary Japan' in *Annual Review of Anthropology* 20

Kondō, Dorinne (1990) *Crafting Selves: Power, Gender, and Discourses of Identity in a Japanese Workplace* Chicago: University of Chicago Press

Kosaka, K. ed. (1994) *Social Stratification in Contemporary Japan* London: Kegan Paul International

Krauss, E., Rohlen T. and Steinhoff, P. eds (1984) *Conflict in Japan* Honolulu: University of Hawaii Press

Lam, A. (1992a) *The Japanese Equal Employment Opportunity Law: Its Effects on Personnel Management Policies and Women's Attitudes* Suntory Toyota International Centre for Economics and Related Disciplines, London School of Economics and Political Science

Lam, A. (1992b) *Women and Equal Employment Opportunities in Japan* Oxford: Nissan Institute of Japanese Studies

Lebra, T. (1976) *Japanese Patterns of Behaviour* Honolulu: University of Hawaii

Lebra, T. (1984) *Japanese Women: Constraint and Fulfilment* Honolulu: University of Hawaii Press

Lise, S. and Moeran, B., eds (1995) *Women, Media and Consumption in Japan* Richmond: Curzon

Lo, J. (1990) *Office Ladies, Factory Women: Life and Work at a Japanese Company* Armonk, NY: M.E. Sharpe

Lukes, S. (1973) *Individualism* Oxford: Blackwell

Macfarlane, A. (1994) *On Individualism* Lancaster: Centre for the Study of Cultural Values

Maraini (1975) in G. Fodella (1975) *Social Structures and Economic Dynamics in Japan up to 1980* Milan: University of Bocconi

Mathews, G. (1996) *What Makes Life Worth Living: How Japanese and Americans Make Sense of Their Worlds* Berkeley: University of California Press

Matsunaga, L. (2000) *The Changing Face of Japanese Retail: Working in a Chain Store* London: Routledge

Mauss, M. (1985) 'A category of the human mind: the notion of person, the notion of self' in M. Carrithers, S. Collins and S. Lukes *The Category of the Person* Cambridge: Cambridge University Press

McCormack, G. (1996) *The Emptiness of Japanese Affluence* Armonk, N.Y.: M.E.Sharpe

McLendon, J. (1983) *Office: Way Station or Blind Alley?* Albany, NY: SUNY Press

Miwa, Y. (1996) *Firms and Industrial Organisation in Japan* Basingstoke: Macmillan

Moeran, B. (1984) 'Individual, group and seishin: Japan's internal cultural debate' in *Man* 19, 2

Moeran, B. (1986) *A Japanese Advertising Agency: An Anthropology of Media and Markets* Richmond: Curzon Press

Moeran, B. (1990) 'Making an exhibition of oneself and the anthropologist as potter' in E. Ben-Ari, B. Moeran and J. Valentine eds *Unwrapping Japan: Society and Culture in Anthropological Perspective* Manchester: Manchester University Press

Moeran, B. (1995) 'Reading Japan in Katei Gaho: the art of being an upper-class woman' in S. Lise and B. Moeran *Women, Media and Consumption in Japan* Richmond: Curzon

Moeran, B. (1996) *A Japanese Advertising Agency: An Anthropology of Media and Markets* Richmond: Curzon

Moeran, B. (1998) 'One over the seven: sake drinking in a Japanese pottery community' in Hendry and Webber (1998)

Morris-Suzuki, T. (1998) *Re-inventing Japan: Time, Space, Nation* Armonk, NY: M.E. Sharpe

Mouer, R. and Sugimoto, Y. (1981) *Japanese Society: Stereotypes and Realities* Monash, Melbourne: Japanese Studies Centre

Mouer, R. and Sugimoto, Y. (1986) *Images of Japanese Society* London: Kegan Paul International

Nakane, C. (1970) *Japanese Society* Berkeley: University of California Press

Odaka, K. (1986) *Japanese Management: A Forward-Looking Analysis* Tokyo: Asian Productivity Organization

Ogasawara, Y. (1998) *Office Ladies and Salaried Men: Power, Gender, and Work in Japanese Companies* Berkeley: University of California Press

Ohnuki-Tierney, E. (1987) *The Monkey as Mirror: Symbolic Transformations in Japanese History and Ritual* Princeton: Princeton University Press

Okimoto, D. and Rohlen, T. eds (1988) *Inside the Japanese System: Readings on Contemporary Society and Political Economy* Stanford CA: Stanford University Press

Osawa, M. (1993) *Feminization of Employment in Japan* Tokyo: University of Tokyo

Ouchi, W. (1981) *Theory Z: How American Business can Meet the Japanese Challenge* Reading, MA: Addison-Wesley

Patrick, H. and Rohlen, T. (1987) 'Small-scale family enterprises' in K. Yamamura and Y. Yasuba *The Political Economy of Japan, Volume 1, The Domestic Transformation* Stanford, CA: Stanford University Press

Pharr, S. (1984) 'The tea-pourers' rebellion' in Krauss *et al.* (1984)

Plath, D. ed (1983) *Work and Life Course in Japan* New York: State University of New York Press

Plath, D. (1992) *What's an Anthropologist Doing in Japan?* (video recording) Richmond IN: Earlham College

Prestowitz, C. (1988) *Trading Places: How we Allowed Japan to Take the Lead* New York: Basic Books

Reischauer, E. (1977) *The Japanese* Cambridge MA: Belknap Press of Harvard University Press

Roberson, J. (1998) *Japanese Working Class Lives: An Ethnographic Study of Factory Workers* London: Routledge

Roberts, G. (1994) *Staying on the Line: Blue-collar Women in Contemporary Japan* University of Hawaii Press

Rohlen, T. (1974) *For Harmony and Strength: Japanese White-collar Organization in Anthropological Perspective* Berkeley: University of California Press

Rohlen, T. (1989) 'Order in Japanese society: attachment, authority and routine' in *Journal of Japan Studies* 15, 1

Rosenberger N. (1992) *The Japanese Sense of Self* Cambridge: Cambridge University Press

Sakakibara, E. (1993) *Beyond Capitalism: The Japanese Model of Market Economics* Lanham, Md; London: University Press of America

Sako, M. (1997) *Japanese Labour and Management in Transition: Diversity, Flexibility and Participation* London: Routledge

Saso, M. (1990) *Women in the Japanese Workplace* London: Shipman

Sethi, S., Namiki, N., Swanson, C. (1984) *The False Promise of the Japanese Miracle* New York: Pitman Publishing

Shirae, T. ed. (1983) *Contemporary Industrial Relations in Japan* Wisconsin: University of Wisconsin Press

Smith, R. (1983) *Japanese Society: Tradition, Self, and the Social Order* Cambridge: Cambridge University Press

Smith, R. (1987) 'Gender inequality in contemporary Japan' in *Journal of Japanese Studies* 13 (1)

Steven, R. (1983) *Classes in Contemporary Japan* Cambridge: Cambridge University Press

Sugimoto, Y. (1997) *An Introduction to Japanese Society* Cambridge: Cambridge University Press

Takamiya, S., (1970) *Modern Japanese Management* London: British Institute of Management

Tobin, J. (1992) 'Japanese pre-schools and the pedagogy of selfhood' in Rosenberger (1992)

Tobin, J., Davidson, D., and Wu, D. (1989) *Preschool in Three Cultures: Japan, China, and the United States* New Haven; London: Yale University Press

Turner, C. (1995) *Japanese Workers in Protest: An Ethnography of Consciousness and Experience* Berkeley: University of California Press

Van Wolferen, K. (1989) *The Enigma of Japanese Power* New York: Alfred A. Knopf

Vogel, E. (1979) *Japan as Number One* Cambridge, MA: Harvard University Press

Whittaker, D. H. (1997) *Small Firms in the Japanese Economy* Cambridge: Cambridge University Press

Wolf, M. (1983) *The Japanese Conspiracy* New York: Empire Books

Woronoff, J. (1980) *Japan: The Coming Social Crisis* Tokyo: Lotus Press

Woronoff, J. (1986) *The Japan Syndrome: Symptoms, Ailments, and Remedies* New Brunswick: Transaction Books

Woronoff, J. (1991) *Japan as-anything-but-number one* Basingstoke: Macmillan

Yahata, S. (1997) 'Structural change and employment adjustment in the post-bubble recession' in *Japan Forum* 9 (2)

Yamamura K. and Yasuba Y. eds (1987) *The Political Economy of Japan, Volume 1: The Domestic Transformation* Stanford, CA: Stanford University Press

Yoshino, K. (1992) *Cultural Nationalism in Contemporary Japan: A Sociological Enquiry* London: Routledge

Index